American Indian Lives

ALMA HOGAN SNELL

Grandmother's Grandchild

My Crow Indian Life

EDITED BY
BECKY MATTHEWS

University of Nebraska Press
Lincoln and London

(∞)

First Bison Books printing: 2001
Library of Congress Cataloging-in-Publi-
cation Data. Snell, Alma Hogan.
Grandmother's grandchild: my Crow
Indian life / Alma Hogan Snell; edited by
Becky Matthews.   p.   cm.—(American
Indian lives) Includes
bibliographical references (p.   )
and index. ISBN 0-8032-4277-8 (cl: alk.
paper) ISBN 0-8032-9291-0 (pa: alk. paper)
1. Snell, Alma Hogan.   2. Crow
Indians Biography.   3. Pretty-shield (Crow
Indian)   4. Crow women biography.
I. Matthews, Becky.   II. Title.
III. Series. E99.C92S656   2000
978.6′0049752′0092—dc21 [B]
99-39032 CIP

For Bill Snell Sr.
and my second daughter, Pearl Jean,
worthy of the name Pretty Shield
because of her strength, keen insight,
and wisdom.

In memory of
Frank Matthews

My grandmother told me, "Words are holy. Treat them with respect. There's power there."

Alma Hogan Snell

Contents

PHOTOGRAPHS

MAPS

Foreword

PETER NABOKOV

On a stormy winter's evening about ten years ago a bunch of us converged at a Fort Smith trading post at the foot of the Montana Big Horns. Glowing from a spotlight that diffused under snowdrift, the place looked like some fairytale haven turned out by a Walt Disney workshop. From the freezing porch we were led somewhere to a large, extra warm kitchen and eating room where the window panes ran with condensation. A woman of uncertain age, wearing an apron, beamed in our direction before bending toward an oven as a cluster of steaming pots rocked on the gas burners above. She must have been a raving beauty, I remember thinking. But when the woman stood up to level that inviting, almost flirtatious smile at us, and her amused, intent eyes caught the light, and I noticed her unearthly smooth skin shining from the heat, my heart gave a quarter-twist. Then I also sensed the protective presence of the white-haired, craggily handsome man sitting off to the side, seemingly shy and still as a rock but clearly not missing a beat.

The love story of this couple, Alma and Bill Snell, is the throbbing heart of this book, the only American Indian autobiography I know about that tackles the twists and turns of an enduring grand amour – the sort of true-life, hard-times, rural romance the best country-western songs describe. As yet another entry in the life-history corpus of the Crow Indians of south-central Montana, Alma's story – together with Marina Brown's forthcoming autobiography of Susie Yellowtail – makes that tribe the major Native American donor to this ever growing literary genre.

But Alma and Bill's tangled journey to family happiness, with its classic theme of love lost and regained, is actually a memoir of Alma's three great passions. For the lady bending over that stove was raised by her adored, highly traditional Crow Indian grandmother, the wise, confident subject of Frank Linderman's 1932 classic of Crow life as seen through a woman's eyes, *Pretty-shield*. Later, Alma would tell me of her girlhood nights snuggling on the wooden floor of her grandmother's cabin, wrapped up with the old woman in smoked buffalo robes, as if absorbing her essence. In these pages we discover how this particular Plains Indian culture imprinted the profound bond between these two remarkable women so that it matured as light as an eagle feather and as strong as shrunk rawhide. And finally there remained Alma's abiding faith in Jesus and the devotion to charity and justice that stemmed from her joyous ecumenical spirit. These were only deepened by the sufferings and witness-bearing described in this deeply personal chronicle. And so in this declaration of one feisty woman's life, the carnal, the domestic, the spiritual, and the multicultural are closely and fearlessly interwoven. Any writer will tell you that is a feat.

It was during my research into Crow uses of tobacco in the late 1980s that I kept hearing about this Crow "herbalist," Alma Snell, and her husband Bill, who lived in the last mobile home as you climbed toward the Pretty Eagle fasting site and the other Big Horn recreation area overlooks. Then some hunters who had contracted for Alma to prepare one of her "natural food" feasts backed out; luckily, I was on the grapevine when the call went out for guests. The exact menu that cold night escapes me, but I do recall buffalo ribs and stew and floured venison strips, gravies thickened with ground turnip, fried bread and cornmeal muffins, side dishes of unfamiliar cooked plants, followed by unusual wild berry puddings and pies. Everything in the spread was sumptuous – none of the stringy, gritty, bitter results I remembered from other repasts "off the land."

Then, over pots of black coffee, came the real treat. I forget what started Alma off, but soon our chairs were tipped back around her, and the pretty lady began to cook with words. I am a listener to how people use language, and Becky Matthews has done a superb job of capturing Alma's original, almost antiquated, sweet-voiced, poetical speech with a suggestion of southern lilt. Someone's heart "develops a flutteration"; a scrap between school kids "got into a high crescendo"; of Crow male and female relations, she says, "we held the men like glass in our hands"; her perturbed husband gets "his mind in a kind of web"; during hard times with the white man, among Indians "laughing was a kind of bridge"; what the violence-prone Indian militants of the 1970s spoke was "error riding on the back of truth"; and her grandmother prayed "every morning of the world."

Spicing her string of stories with such spontaneous words and phrases and delicious details, moving intuitively through her personal experiences without any apparent agenda but following inspired transitions of the moment, Alma made us "see" the scenes and settings – many fleshed out in this book – of Crow and Assiniboine backcountry in the 1930s and 1940s. And although life was tough, rations were meager, racism in Big Horn County was rampant, and Indians were the forgotten minority, she made us laugh and laugh, or held us in suspense, or made us shiver with the undercurrents of youthful desire, or had us shaking our heads with dismay at what those Crow families and their women endured back then. Her rendition of grandmother Pretty Shield prescribing a sun dance to cure her granddaughter's lovesickness for Bill, then backing out when she questioned the unfamiliar form of sun-dancing imported from the Shoshones in 1940, was racier in my recollection than in the book. One could visualize this frisky, impossible-to-handle young teenager in love, could fear for her yet be aroused by her life-seeking energy. Alma held us in that room until 2:00 A.M.; none of us wanted these ripples of delight to end. The feeling of community that cold winter night, the widening sense of a whole melodrama in its historical setting that she conjured in our imagination – I've never experienced a storytelling like it. And the silent, white-haired man sitting in the corner, listening along with us, knew that for this evening we had all fallen in love with his wife.

But this book also offers intimacies that would have been inappropriate and confusing that evening. Alma does not wear her feminism on her sleeve; these pages are drenched in it. So instead of getting polemics about women's powers and roles, instead of that insistent, straining tone that often belies the depth of the solidarity being extolled, we get specific pictures and real-life pain and endurance. We go through her first period, feel the pangs of love, are reassured by the protective huddle of supportive age-mates and horrified by the treachery of others, soften to a grandmother's words, worry whether there's enough food in the cupboard, shudder at the omnipresence of male predation yet remain compassionate to those awkward men who just want some company. Alma stumbles, suffers, fears, dreams, struggles, and yet manages to develop maturity and idealism without losing her sense of humor or wonder.

An academic might say that this narrative illustrates prevalent thinking about the creative ways that people selectively blend traditions without losing cultural control, and that from her not wearing braids to her ardent Christianity to her talking to plants and receiving vision-songs out of the blue, Alma epitomizes the successful *bricoleuse* – "she who mixes and matches." And she or he would be right. But I prefer to think of Alma's book as a giver of gifts – of tasty feasts and phrases, to be sure, but also of something more urgent, of stories that offer encouragement for lovers of the natural world and inspiration (and cautionary tale) for the spirited of heart.

Acknowledgments

BECKY MATTHEWS

One of the blessings of working on this project has been the opportunity to make new friendships and strengthen old ones. A multitude of people from one corner of the United States to another generously assisted us in countless ways.

To begin at the beginning, we owe a special debt to Charlene James-Duguid, under whose auspices, as director of Smithsonian Institution Research Expeditions, Alma and I met. Charlene encouraged our work from day one to the finished product. So did Fay McCoy, who actually arranged the event that brought us together. As postmaster of Fort Smith, Montana, Fay served as our chief communications network in the days before Alma had a telephone. As a friend, she has been unflagging in her faith in this book.

Peter Nabokov of the University of California at Los Angeles told Alma in 1995 that he was a "friend of her project," and he certainly has been. He read this work in its early stages, believed in its potential, and made a number of valuable recommendations for its improvement. The same is true of Tim McCleary of Little Big Horn College in Crow Agency, Montana. In addition to offering perceptive suggestions, he patiently helped us with translations of the Crow language and in the production of maps.

Other people on the Crow Reservation provided significant assistance. Eloise Pease shared her bountiful knowledge of Crow history and culture. Magdalene Moccasin of the Little Big Horn College Archives was an ever smiling, always knowledgeable source of information. Dora Old Elk helped us verify names and dates. Julia Williamson, Sarah Shane, and Winona Yellowtail Plenty Hoops supplied information about traditional cooking and plants. Laura Lee, now in Arizona but originally from Crow

Agency, shared documents and memories associated with her mother, the late Minnie Williams, a founder and longtime president of the Crow Women's Club.

Lillian Bull Shows Hogan, the widow of Alma's father, gave us marvelous stories about that gentleman, as did Mary Elizabeth Hogan Wallace, Lillian's daughter.

Alma's sisters, Pearl Hogan and Cerise Stewart, along with Cerise's husband, Francis, spent hours helping us compile and clarify data. Bill Boyes of Maryland gave us useful information about Alma's grandfather Goes Ahead.

National Park Service personnel Darrell and Sandi Cook, Theo Huggs, Myrna Little Owl, and Steve Clark assisted with logistics as well as words of encouragement.

Georgia folks who have boosted the project are Fran Prescott, traveling companion extraordinaire; Rose Tully, peerless proofreader; and Edie Whitaker, counselor in crisis after crisis. Without the computer expertise and steadfast friendship of Jan Ferguson of Columbus Technical Institute, I would have thrown in the technology towel rather quickly.

Bob and Sally Hatfield (Sally is Frank Bird Linderman's granddaughter) have been more than generous with their memories, photographs, and home. Myrtle Bentley Hubley, daughter of Chester and Laura Bentley (who served as Baptist ministers at Crow Agency for decades), has been most gracious in giving us valuable time in her home and allowing us to enjoy the benefits of her mother's talent as a photographer. Laura Bentley took many of the historical pictures in this volume.

Alma wants to say special thanks to Robin Klein of Montana State University for her insights on ethnobotany. I want to express appreciation to John Lupold of Columbus State University for introducing me to the wonders of oral history, and to Ruth Crocker of Auburn University for helping me discover questions to ask about women and history.

Our sons and daughters and their wives and husbands have been wonderful throughout this whole endeavor. They all believed in our venture, and each in his or her own way sacrificed time and resources in support of it. We want to tell the Snell siblings and their spouses (Pearl Jean and James Buchanan, Faith and Jim Chosa, Bill and Karen Snell, and Ted Hogan) *and* the Matthews clan (Gayle and Bob Radford, Nancy and

Mark Willis) that they and their children and their children's children are among the reasons we persevered.

Finally, through it all, the strength and affection of Bill Snell Sr. sustained us, as did my memories of those same qualities in my late husband, Frank Matthews.

Grandmother's
Grandchild

Introduction

BECKY MATTHEWS

By the rivers of Babylon, there we sat down, yea, we wept, when we
remembered Zion.
We hanged our harps upon the willows in the midst thereof.
For there they that carried us away captive required of us a song; and they
that wasted us required of us mirth, saying, Sing us one of the songs of Zion.
How shall we sing the Lord's song in a strange land?

Psalm 137:1–4

On a snowy Montana morning in April 1995, Alma Hogan Snell, a
seventy-two-year-old Crow elder, stood in the well-equipped kitchen of
her comfortable modular home, extended one arm westward toward the
pine-topped ridges that rim Bighorn Canyon, stretched the other toward
the eastern hills that once were home to buffalo herds, and said, "I feel
like I'm pulled in two directions. I live in this modern world of high
technology, but I desperately want to hold on to the past." With that
thought, work on this book began.

Both the contemporary world and the past were close to Alma in the
spring of 1995. Since 1988 she and Bill, her husband of almost forty-eight
years, had lived on reservation acreage known as Windblowing Place.
(Its original owner was a woman named Windblowing.) Other residents
included a docile gray and white cat, an exuberant golden retriever, and
a ferret named Meezu, to whom Alma sang Crow lullabies. A Macintosh
400 Performa computer, a VCR and satellite television system, a microwave
oven, and a top-of-the-line food processor were among the furnishings of
the Snell household.

In the yard were a hot tub, a riding lawnmower, two storage sheds,
a weathered American flag, and a rose bed and vegetable garden both

carefully tended by Bill. Warm springs bubbled into nearby Lime Kiln Creek and supplied water for the yard, the hot tub, and the gardens. (In the summer of 1876 a band of Lakotas, fleeing the scene of their victory over George Armstrong Custer at the Little Bighorn, stopped briefly at those springs so that warriors could soak their wounds in the healing mud.) Next to the vegetable garden Bill had constructed a wooden trellis as a "shade" beneath which Alma cooked and served traditional Crow meals to visitors from near and far. Beside the shade stood a canvas tipi in which Alma had placed articles representing the Crow past and symbolizing her dedication to the preservation of Crow culture. Ruts of the Fort Smith Wood Road crossed the lawn behind the tipi and ran northward, into neighbor John Bullinsight's pasture. To the south loomed War Man Mountain, which had received its name when fur traders explored the area in the early nineteenth century.[1]

Alma and I had met in the summer of 1994. As a research assistant for the Smithsonian Institution, I enjoyed one of Alma's meals and listened eagerly as she explained how her ancestors had derived sustenance and medicine from the land. Then Alma began to speak of Pretty Shield, her grandmother, who had reared her and helped her to understand and value Crow traditions. "Grandma," the subject of a 1932 biography by Frank Bird Linderman, devoted the last years of her life to bringing up Alma and her brothers and sisters. She did so with humor, courage, and infinite love. Because she was thrifty and old-fashioned, she outfitted Alma in high-topped shoes and long dresses while other girls wore slippers and shorter styles. As Alma recalled her life with Pretty Shield, I wept silently. I was thinking of my own grandmother, a tough little Southern Baptist who had a profound influence on my life. Like Pretty Shield, she loved her grandchildren deeply, and she pinched pennies by dressing them in out-of-style, oversized, but serviceable clothes that would assure more than one year of wear.

Drawn together by memories of grandmothers from different backgrounds but with similar hearts, Alma and I discussed the possibility of my editing her autobiography. Several months later we made a commitment to each other. At its center has been the idea that Alma is the author of her life story. I am her editor. The words belong to Alma. Her voice is clear, and her unique manner of speaking combines the Crow past with more than seven decades of twentieth-century living.

Alma is truly a product of the transition to reservation life that the Crow and other Plains people made at the end of the nineteenth century. Her mother was among the first generation of Crow women to be born on the reservation; her grandmother was among the last who could recall the buffalo days. When Linderman asked about Crow life after the buffalo were gone, Pretty Shield answered, "There is nothing to tell, because we did nothing."[2] Her words echo those of Plenty Coups, a Crow chief, who also told his life story to Linderman. Plenty Coups said, "When the buffalo went away, the hearts of my people fell to the ground, and they could not lift them up again. After this nothing happened. There was little singing anywhere."[3] Alma believes that a great deal happened after the buffalo disappeared. This is the message of her life and her book. She witnessed, experienced, and exemplifies the resilience of her people. For her, their songs continue.

A LONG FAMILIARITY WITH CHANGE

By the time of Alma's birth in 1923, the Crow people had a long familiarity with change. They had once belonged to a group of Siouan-speaking villagers who lived as semisedentary horticulturalists in the Missouri River valley. At some undetermined point (estimates range from as long as five centuries ago to as recently as 1676) the Crows separated from their farming relatives and became hunters, ranging across an area that extended from the Missouri River in the north to the Wind River Mountains in the south, and from present Yellowstone Park in the west to the Powder River in the east.[4] The landscape is compelling, powerful as the life-giving rivers that flow from its rugged mountains, peaceful as a meandering stream shaded by a grove of cottonwoods. Here and there, buttes, rock outcroppings, canyons, and cliffs appear amid the rolling grasslands that dominate the terrain. Above everything arcs a never ending, ever changing sky that, according to the mood and time of the day, shares its colors with the grass, cliffs, canyons, rocks, buttes, and mountains.

As nomadic hunters, the Crows viewed their homeland as a place of abundance, but they also understood that drought and other natural disasters could create hardships. The buffalo herds that fattened on the lush short-grass prairie were the key to their survival, for these animals provided food, clothing, shelter, tools, and other implements. Early buffalo hunts were held by groups on foot who would surround a herd and drive the animals over steep cliffs that have come to be known as "buffalo jumps." In the mid-eighteenth century the Crows, along with other peoples of the Great Plains, acquired the horse from southern neighbors who had contact with the Spanish. Crow men began hunting on horseback, and horses became a reason for and a means of persistent warfare with nearby tribes such as the Lakotas, Cheyennes, Arapahos, and Piegans.[5]

The transition from horticulture to hunting and the acquisition of the horse profoundly shaped Crow culture. Their explanations of their origins, their tobacco ceremony (their most enduring ritual), their mythology and folklore, and, in essence, their sense of being Crow reveal an abiding concern with regeneration, a concern rooted in the fact that they once were farmers who recreated themselves as hunters.[6]

Crow history and culture offer vivid reminders of the problems associated with viewing natives of the area through a single lens. Diversity is a key to Plains life. Images abound of feathered warriors constantly at war with white intruders and of Native women who were either compliant maidens or overburdened wretches, and these views contain elements of truth. The reality of life on the plains, however, is far more complex *and* more instructive of the human condition than popular literature and Hollywood indicate. Not all the men were noble combatants; indeed, vicious brutality, including mutilation of corpses, marked some of the intertribal battles that occurred before contact with whites. And although a handful of tribes did make war on whites, most sought some form of accommodation with the newcomers to the plains.[7]

Women had significant and varied roles in tribal life. Among the Crows they exhibited considerable power, spiritual and temporal; they exerted extensive economic influence and assumed essential places in family life, the unifying force in the tribe's society. They participated in major religious rituals, experienced visions, and received and used exceptional spiritual powers known as "medicine." According to Crow mythology, women made crucial decisions about the creation of the world.[8]

Traditionally, the Crows lived in loosely organized bands that traveled independently but came together for special events, such as large buffalo hunts. A council of warriors governed each band in a democratic fashion so that all members had opportunities to voice their opinions. Politically, women became skilled in circuitous uses of power. Artist Rudolph Kurz reported that he observed Crow women speaking in council meetings in the 1850s, but this may have been an unusual occurrence, or he may have misunderstood what he saw.[9] Alma Snell suggests that women tended to exercise indirect political power by exerting influence on their husbands. She says, "They *talked* to their men, and the men listened. If a woman wanted her views put before the council, she approached the gathering. She would say, 'I wish to speak to' – a certain man, maybe her father or her husband or her clan uncle. The man would say, 'I will speak to her privately,' or, 'Say on.' If he said, 'Say on,' she would be speaking to the man, but the council would hear her words. In that way she made her views known to the council."[10]

Historically, Crow gender relationships illustrate a point made by recent studies of American Indian societies. In many instances the roles and status of men and women appear as complementary rather than hierarchical. The Pascua-Yaqui scholar Rebecca Tsosie argues persuasively that Euro-Americans invented and then imposed upon Indian cultures the idea that female tasks such as food gathering and child rearing were inferior to the hunting, political, and military activities of men: "Importantly, a primary distinction between the definition of women by Europeans and that by Indians was the Indian emphasis on individuality. While Europeans defined women in relation to male figures, American Indians generally perceived women and men as individuals with specific talents, abilities, and clan-sanctioned roles." Her ideas reinforce a cogent reminder from Patricia Albers that even as Native American cultures were far from static, "the conditions of women are not seen as invariant but rather varied and changing."[11]

For the Crows the pace of cultural change accelerated in the early nineteenth century when they encountered whites. In 1807, American fur-trading companies began to build outposts in Crow country along the Missouri, Yellowstone, and Bighorn Rivers. The fur trade brought new technology, such as guns and iron implements, as well as new problems to the northern plains. Infectious diseases inflicted serious population losses, and competition for trade and territory stimulated intertribal conflict. Pressures became so great that by midcentury the trader-turned-chronicler Edward Denig was predicting the imminent extinction of the Crow people.[12]

On the heels of fur traders came American government officials and soldiers, determined to secure the western frontier. In 1825, Crow leaders signed a treaty of friendship with the United States, and this peace agreement, surprisingly, held up. Despite the vicissitudes of nineteenth-century life on the plains, the Crows never waged war against the United States; their chiefs decided to remain connected with American strength in the hope of surviving hostilities with Indian enemies who surrounded and outnumbered them. In the 1851 Treaty of Fort Laramie the Crows and six other Plains tribes agreed to cease hostilities, to accept designated territorial boundaries, and to allow the United States to build roads and forts through tribal lands. The government promised to pay $50,000 in annuities to each tribe for a period of fifty years. An amendment to the treaty passed by Congress (though rejected by the Crows) reduced the fifty years to ten.[13]

Increased white demand for tribal lands led to another Fort Laramie Treaty in 1868. This document established the reservation system. The Crows promised to reside permanently in a specified area of about eight million acres; the United States pledged, "No persons except those herein authorized [government employees] may enter the reservation." Further, to ensure the "civilization" of the tribe, the Crows would "compel their children, male and female, between the ages of six and sixteen years to attend school." Each head of household was to receive seeds, tools, instructions in agriculture, and 320 acres of land to farm. The seeds of assimilation planted by the Treaty of 1868 produced an unexpected harvest. The Crows remained on their reservation but tried to live by hunting the rapidly diminishing supply of game; as a result, hundreds died. Crow population, estimated at 3,500 in 1865, had dropped to 2,456 by 1887 and to 1,740 by 1910.[14]

With conditions among other Indian signatories of the 1868 treaty mirroring those of the Crows, white reformers began to push for change. In 1887 the General Allotment Act, familiarly known as the Dawes Act, divided reservations into individual allotments with some land to be held communally. The goal of the act was rapid Americanization of Indians, but for a variety of reasons – most important, white land hunger – it failed to achieve its purpose. The decades between its passage and 1920 were a period of relentless attempts by the government to open reservations to white settlement.[15]

By the time of the Dawes Act, change had become an important element in Crow life. The Crow people derived strength from the knowledge that their ancestors had survived the transition from village farming to plains hunting. The hunter-ancestors had learned how to regenerate themselves under difficult circumstances, as had the Crows who first encountered whites. Reservation Crows clearly understood that their future was inextricably connected with their ability to maintain and adapt legacies from the past.

Crow leaders tenaciously resisted white encroachment on their land. In 1916, Chief Plenty Coups told the Senate Committee on Indian Affairs,

"This makes the sixth trip I have made here [to Washington]. I came here, absolutely without any fear, knowing that in any event I have friends who will give me a square deal. I come with my heart open." After considerable testimony and debate, the committee postponed a decision on what an Indian Rights Association pamphlet called "a threatened raid" on Crow lands.[16]

When Plenty Coups led a Crow delegation to Washington in 1917, he brought more than an open heart; Crow luggage contained medicine bundles and war regalia to provide spiritual assistance in the battle with U.S. senators. The evening before the Crows were to present their final arguments against opening the reservation, the tribesmen went to a zoo and collected buffalo chips. They returned to their room in the National Hotel, spread the symbols of their war power before them, made a fire of buffalo chips, sweet grass, and Nez Perce root, and listened to Plenty Coups, who reminded them, "This is not a sham of medicine. Right now we are preparing to fight a different kind of fight. We must fight to protect our women and children." The group ritually recounted stories of their origins and of past battle glory, then selected Robert Yellowtail, a twenty-eight-year-old product of Riverside Indian School in California, to speak for them on the following day. Yellowtail, who would become the preeminent Crow politician of his era, persuaded committee members once again to postpone their verdict on Crow lands.[17]

The Crow visit to Washington in 1917 is significant for several reasons. The reservation remained closed to white expansion; Crow leaders gained political sophistication in negotiating with the United States; and the selection of Yellowtail as spokesman marked the passage of power from the older generation to educated young men – described by Plenty Coups as the "short-haired boys."[18] Finally, the hotel ceremony signaled that despite growing diplomatic acumen and generational transitions, Crows were determined to retain traditional values. As Crow warriors had done for centuries, Plenty Coups and his group drew strength from their heritage. In 1917, in the capital of a powerful industrial nation, a war party prepared to protect homes and families through rites that were timeless to them.

The battle over reservation land culminated in 1920, when Congress passed the so-called Crow Act. The law provided a formula for dividing reservation acreage, except the Big Horn and Pryor Mountains, among all tribal members. Each allottee received title to approximately 1,000 acres.[19] But the Crows, in winning a major victory, may have lost the war.

Whites made huge inroads on the reservation by purchasing lands from individual owners or, more commonly, by leasing allotments. That system provided cash for the lessor but discouraged him from working his own land. By the mid-1930s, Crows were working 158,148 acres, or 7 percent, of their land; whites, 1,965,700 acres, or 92 percent. In the words of tribal historian Joseph Medicine Crow, the reservation had "become a paradise for white men."[20]

Reservation life presented many challenges to the Crow people. In the area of housing, Medicine Crow recalls that although the government constructed cabins and houses, "it was not unusual to find a new house filled with tools, saddles, harnesses, and chickens while the family [by choice] lived in a tipi or a tent." He believes that houses caused many diseases and deaths. Tipis had better ventilation, and the idea of maintaining sanitary premises was foreign to people accustomed to moving from place to place. The government's "Report on Hygienic Conditions of Indian Homes" (1923) certainly presented a bleak picture: only one-quarter of the homes had toilet facilities; half of the households took drinking water from streams or irrigation ditches; and families of two or more generations typically crowded into houses with no more than three rooms.[21]

Despite these hardships the Crows were able to create, according to anthropologist Fred Voget, a thriving "reservation culture that preserved core beliefs . . . while conforming to the formal demands of dress, schooling, church, and legalisms of the local American culture." Matrilineal, exogamous clans helped to hold society together through a process of reciprocity. Certain clan members had definite obligations to others. A young man, for example, always gave the first animal that he killed to his clan aunt, who in turn offered prayers for his future success. Voget argues that respect for the duties and behaviors associated with clan membership helped many Crow people resist external pressures that threatened to divide them.[22]

The Crow population, which was dispersed across six reservation districts, increased from its 1920 nadir of 1,740 to 1,963 in 1930. Settlement patterns tended to follow those that clan and band connections had established during the early years of reservation life. At least one village existed in each district, but the towns of Lodge Grass in the "Valley of the Chiefs" and Crow Agency, the center of government administration, were the largest. Households consisting of several generations were typical, so that kinship proximity and the influence of family elders promoted continuity in Crow customs, language, and social relationships.[23]

Change, however, continued to be a strong influence on Crow life. According to historian Frederick Hoxie, "Crows in the 1920s and 1930s lived at the intersection of culture and circumstance; within that zone they defined their identity in the modern era. In it, the Crows believed themselves to be a part of a continuous community even though they were products of a new reservation social system and participants in new religious patterns; they followed new leaders and lived their lives within the constraints of new economic realities."[24]

New religious patterns had begun to emerge when Christian missionaries came into Crow country. Before Christians arrived on the plains, Crows believed in a world in which humans, plants, spiritual phenomena, and the earth itself formed an inseparable whole. Thus, mundane events possessed sacred significance, and tribal gatherings became reminders of the unity of life.[25] In the words of Joe Medicine Crow, "The world in which the Crow tribesman wandered palpitated with life." Life had begun when a duck dived into the water that covered everything and brought a clump of mud to First Maker, who used it to create land, rivers, rocks, plants, and animals. First Maker gave some of his power to all that he created; then he created the Crow people. He gave them clans, the sweat lodge, the sun dance, and sacred tobacco seeds, and he taught them how to use these gifts to gain power from both animate and inanimate elements in the world.[26]

Although prescribed behaviors governed each religious ritual, individual Crows chose among different methods to align themselves with supernatural powers. Some sought adoption into a Tobacco Society in order to plant the seeds that represented regeneration and assured tribal and personal prosperity. Some sought visions in which a medicine father, usually in the form of an animal, plant, or celestial object, would adopt and empower them; others used the sun dance to gain power to retaliate against an enemy, and still others sought assistance from medicine men and women who had special powers and authority. Many Crows combined religious practices into individualized forms that served their own particular needs.[27]

When Protestant and Catholic missionaries brought Christianity to the reservation in the late nineteenth century, Crows responded in a variety of ways: some rejected it completely; others embraced its doctrines wholeheartedly; still others blended traditional beliefs with Christian tenets. In 1910 some Crows began to participate in the peyote ceremonies of the Native American Church, and again there were those who merged its teachings with other beliefs so that an individual might consider him- or herself both a Christian and a peyotist.[28]

Unitarians, who built the Montana Industrial School near the confluence of the Bighorn and Yellowstone Rivers in 1886, were the first Christian group to establish a missionary presence on the reservation. Catholic priests of the Jesuit order had made periodic visits from about 1880, but it was 1887 before they opened their first school and mission at St. Xavier. A year later they established St. Charles Mission in Pryor. In 1896 James Burgess, a Congregationalist missionary, came to Crow Agency. Baptists, who set up a school and church at Lodge Grass in 1903, took over the Crow Agency Mission in 1921. By that time, because of their strong influence in eastern districts of the reservation, they had become its predominant Protestant group. They sometimes found themselves in contention with Catholics, who were most numerous in the centrally located Bighorn District surrounding St. Xavier.[29]

From their earliest days among the Crows, missionaries were concerned with education. Crow leaders in the Lodge Grass District originally invited Baptists to their community to start a day school, not a church. Crows believed that the best way to teach their children was to give them vivid examples of desired behavior and abundant encouragement. During the buffalo days, children had constantly been with adults, watching, listening, learning. Thus, Crow parents wanted day schools as an option to sending their children to off-reservation boarding schools or to any of the three boarding schools on the reservation. Euro-American reformers, however, believed that the only way to promote the assimilation of Indian children into "American" culture was to remove them from family influences. In 1884, prior to the Unitarian and Jesuit efforts, the U.S. government had built a boarding school at Crow Agency. In 1895 the community acquired a federally funded "public" day school, but it was originally open to white students only.[30]

In 1920 the federal government agreed to pay the state of Montana a fee for each Crow student enrolled in a state-supported school. By 1922 there were 236 Crows in twelve public schools on the reservation, and 68 Indian students in three parochial day schools. Some parents of white students who attended public schools on the reservation and other white Montanans strongly resented the Crow students because Indian families did not pay state property taxes.[31]

Not only did the Crow people want their children nearby; they wanted to continue their historical tradition of frequent family, clan, and tribal gatherings. Their fondness for social activities caused great concern among reservation officials, who repeatedly expressed ideas similar to those of agent S. G. Reynolds: "The frequent dance took the Indian from his home, and his garden and his grain were neglected. The dance was always associated with horse racing, gambling, gift-giving and adoption ceremonies." To keep the Crows on their farms during summer months, Reynolds promoted the idea of an October fair, "as nearly like the old-time eastern country fairs as possible," with awards for excellence in agricultural and homemaking skills. Crow leaders agreed to participate in the weeklong festival if they could camp together, dress in "old-time" regalia, race their horses, and perform traditional dances. The first Crow Fair occurred in 1905.[32]

While agents wrote glowing reports about the success of these annual agricultural exhibits, the Crows – having learned from their compromise with Reynolds that they could gain bureaucratic approval for cultural events if they hid them beneath a layer of "civilized" behavior – came to view the fair as an opportunity to celebrate themselves. In her autobiography, Agnes Deernose, cousin of Alma Snell, describes how the Crows used "American and Christian holidays" for their own purposes. The year began with a New Year's dance; people put on their finest traditional clothes and "showed off." In February a Washington's Birthday celebration featured a parade of warriors and a war dance. Large family picnics marked Easter activities. For several days around the July 4, clans camped together along Lodge Grass Creek and celebrated Independence Day with a parade of their best horses and a mock battle so that men could "count coup" (win battle honors). Fireworks and concession stands that sold hamburgers, candy, and soda pop added modernity to the occasion. Agnes says that Armistice Day was "another White man's celebration we took over." Calling the observance "Soldier Boy's Day," the tribe held a two-day feast in 1918 to honor Crows who had fought in the First World War. In Agnes's words: "When they celebrated with a 'glad dance,' they sang a song, 'Iron Hats, we got the best of you!' When they sang this song, the women jumped up and down." The annual round of celebrations ended with Christmas, which "we observed in Christian services, but we also had our own dances."[33]

Although substantial numbers of whites were living on the reservation by the decade of the 1920s, they kept themselves separate from the

Crows. They might come to observe dances or other celebrations, but there was little interaction between the two groups. One white official from St. Xavier reported in 1926, "The only whites that mix with Indians can be safely traced to the missionaries and that is because they have to. . . . There is no race friction but there are times when race prejudice is very noticeable."[34] Alma Snell recalls that during her girlhood Crows and whites attended the same church (the mission at Crow Agency) but maintained separate seating arrangements. She says, "Both the whites and Indians wanted it that way."

REMEMBERING A CROW LIFE

This was the milieu in which Alma Snell spent her formative years. Her parents were George and Little Woman (Helen) Hogan. George Hogan, a graduate of Carlisle Indian School in Pennsylvania, was one of the short-haired boys described by Plenty Coups. He served for more than twenty years (without pay) as secretary of the Crow tribe and was a member of several Crow delegations that traveled to Washington to negotiate with the federal government. Little Woman, the daughter of Pretty Shield and Goes Ahead (who had been a scout for Custer at the Battle of the Little Bighorn), died before Alma's second birthday. Pretty Shield, by that time a widow, assumed the responsibility of caring for the Hogan children.

Perhaps because she was the youngest member of the family, Alma became, in the Crow way, a "grandmother's grandchild," which means that the strongest individual influence in her life was Pretty Shield. For the Crow people, grandparents were and are important in the nurturing and education of all grandchildren, but as the term implies, a grandmother's grandchild experienced unique opportunities and obligations. Such a child developed exceptionally close ties to his or her grandmother, relying on her for security and receiving from her lessons in everyday living and in tribal traditions. Grandmothers taught by example, and a child had the twofold responsibility of learning by observation and of providing assistance with daily chores that might be difficult for an elderly woman. Alma's narrative reveals the enduring power of her relationship with her grandmother. Pretty Shield taught her to pick berries, dig roots, tan and sew hides, play hand games, sing traditional songs, remember the old stories, and respect nature. In sum, she demonstrated the value of using the past as a means of living in the present.

Such knowledge became increasingly important to Alma as she matured and faced physical but not spiritual separation from "Grandma."

As an adolescent she attended boarding schools in South Dakota; during World War II she struggled through several personal crises, including the death of Pretty Shield in 1944; and after the war she married Bill Snell, an Assiniboine man who had been her high school sweetheart. She spent most of her adult life away from the Crow Reservation, either among the Assiniboines in northern Montana or on other reservations while Bill worked as a law officer for the Bureau of Indian Affairs. Alma became a food service supervisor for the Indian Health Service. Upon retirement, she and Bill returned to Crow country, where they live exceptionally active lives. Some of their activity centers on their family, but much of it is associated with Alma's work as a cultural preservationist. In this endeavor and countless others she continues her life with Pretty Shield.

Building on a legacy received from generations of Crow and Assiniboine women, Alma is determined to conserve and interpret the wisdom that has been passed down to her. She began in a modest way as a guest lecturer for reservation schools, and she now gives presentations at universities, museums, national parks, and learning centers throughout the West. She has participated in several programs for educational television. In the mid-1990s, she served on the advisory council for the design of the projected National Museum of the American Indian, to be established in Washington DC. Her teaching focuses on foods and medicines that were important in the past, and like her life, her lessons skillfully blend the essence of yesterday with the realities of today.

An important reality in Alma's life is her commitment to Christianity, which she views as an integral part of her heritage. The first three names in the baptismal records of the Congregational church established at Crow Agency in 1896 are Goes Ahead, Mrs. Goes Ahead (Pretty Shield), and Helen Goes Ahead (Little Woman). George Hogan too was active throughout his life in the affairs of that church and in the Baptist church that followed it. Despite criticism from some traditional Crows who condemn Christianity for its effects on Crow culture and from certain fundamentalist Christians who reject all Crow traditions, Alma is comfortable with her faith and confident that she can retain a sense of being Indian while adhering to Christian teachings. In her words, "There was power, and power met power, and they blended. It's a life. It involves the *soul*. The soul is something that goes on."[35]

Alma's reflections on the pull that she feels between past and present are similar to sentiments expressed by other Indian women who have related their life stories. In *American Indian Women Telling Their Lives,*

Gretchen Bataille and Kathleen Sands observe that the tension created by acculturation is a common theme in many personal narratives but that the narrator's choices in response to those pressures – her individual experiences and personality, and the ways in which she perceives and tells her life – make each story distinctive.[36]

This is true in Alma's case. Her story, along with a growing number of works by other Native American women, refutes long-held Euro-American myths about Indian womanhood. Cherokee scholar Rayna Green, who characterizes such myths as "the Pocahontas Perplex," argues that from the earliest days of contact, Europeans created images of the Indian woman to fit specifically European needs: she was most often either a "princess" such as Pocahontas, who helped heroically superior white men conquer the Americas, or a degraded "squaw" who was essentially subhuman and therefore inconsequential. Thus, "the Indian woman is between a rock and a hard place. Like that of her male counterpart, her image is freighted with such ambivalence that she has little room to move. . . . They are both tied by definition to relationships with white men, but she is especially burdened by the narrowness of that definition." Further, claims by many white Americans that they are descendants of a "distant Indian princess . . . make it impossible for the Indian woman to be seen as real."[37]

Alma Snell's life and the way she tells it make it impossible for one to see her as anything *but* real. Her narrative is filled with joy, poignancy, passion, compassion, suffering, and survival, but its most persistent theme is love. The remarkable love that Alma shares with Bill, her husband, equals the power of her devotion to her grandmother. And although many Indian women recall the impact of grandmothers on their lives, her memories of Pretty Shield generate new understanding of just how real "Grandma" was. Linderman's work with Pretty Shield provides a rare opportunity for the examination of life histories that span generations. Produced under radically different circumstances, the autobiographies of Alma and her grandmother combine to provide a richly textured view of Crow women over an extended period.

PRETTY SHIELD AND SIGN TALKER

The collaboration between Pretty Shield and Linderman in 1931 was unprecedented. It was the first time that a Euro-American man and a Plains Indian woman had worked together to present her life story. Ethnographers had found women useful as informants, and Linderman himself had relied on them as interpreters, but no one had attempted a book-length autobiography. In Linderman's words:

> Throughout forty-six years in Montana I have had much to do with its several Indian tribes, and yet have never, until now, talked for ten consecutive minutes directly to an old Indian woman. I have found Indian women diffident, and so self-effacing that acquaintance with them is next to impossible. . . . I had nearly given up the idea of ever writing the life of an old Indian woman when Pretty-shield delighted me by consenting to tell me her story.
>
> Of all the old Indian women I know Pretty-shield would have been my choice, since in her the three essential qualifications for such story telling are in happy combination, age that permits her to have known the natural life of her people on the plains, keen mentality, and, above all, the willingness to talk to me without restraint.[38]

Pretty Shield's qualifications proved to be highly compatible with those of Linderman. Indeed, the two partners exhibited some strikingly similar character traits. Each had a strong sense of adventure, an abiding passion for nature, a desire to construct an authentic record of the past, and a spirit of persistence in the face of hardships. They both enjoyed laughter (sometimes at their own expense), could tell a good story, and displayed a kind of integrity that enabled them to respect the humanity of others.

As a boy in the Midwest, Linderman could only dream of the sort of adventures that Pretty Shield experienced on the plains. He constantly studied United States maps, looking for a wild place, and he "felt glad when the Flathead Lake country in northwestern Montana territory seemed yet to be the farthest removed from contaminating civilization. I'd go as straight as I could to Flathead Lake."[39] In 1885, with seventy-five dollars and two traveling companions, he left his home in Chicago for the "far removed" place he had selected. Neither his money nor his comrades lasted long; soon Linderman was alone in a leaky wilderness cabin with a dwindling supply of food, an ancient gun, and an axe – with which he had wounded his foot. He was sixteen years old. At this point in his adventure he encountered his first Indian. A Flathead warrior named Red Horn, who "had taken more scalps than any other living member of his tribe," happened upon Linderman's camp. The two became such friends that "for many years after our meeting, I knew my first Indian intimately."[40]

During his early years in Montana, Linderman worked as a trapper, frequently with Indians as partners, and as a guide for white hunters. When he married in 1893, however, he realized he needed a more settled way of earning a living and thereafter became a mining assayer, owned a furniture store and a newspaper, was elected to the Montana legislature, and moved his family to Helena, where he served as assistant secretary of state. Later, he achieved success in the insurance business. All the while he continued to create bonds of affection and trust with native people. According to his daughter, Norma Waller, "The years the Crees and Chippewas [who were exiles from Canada] camped on the outskirts of Helena, he carried on a one man crusade to feed and clothe these homeless Indians. It was a common sight in Helena to see a line of Indians led by Chief Little Bear standing across the street . . . looking up at my father's office windows and waiting for the sign from him that they could come up. He was their friend and he did all in his power to help these people who had lost their all to progress."[41] He campaigned effectively to help the landless Crees and Chippewas secure a reservation in northern Montana and continued to voice concern for their rights after they had gained a land base. So appreciative were they that Day Child, a Cree, wrote to him, "If my father came back and stood on one hill and I saw Frank Linderman on another hill I would not go to my father. I would go to Frank Linderman. You know I do not lie. This is the truth."[42]

The more time Linderman spent with the Indians of Montana, the more he became convinced of the urgent need to preserve the memories of their traditional lives before those who could remember passed away. He published his first book, *Indian Why Stories*, in 1915. In 1917, after saving enough money to provide for his family, he built a comfortable log home for them at Goose Bay on Flathead Lake and moved there to write full time. He extended his contacts with native people, and ultimately three tribes adopted him. The Crees named him Man Who Looks through Glass; to the Blackfeet he was Iron Tooth; and the Crows called him Great Sign Talker.[43]

Among the Crows, John Frost was a particularly insightful friend. In a 1926 letter to Linderman, written after the two men had spent some time together in the Pryor Mountains, he said, "I do hope that we will meet again some time at the water of many tongues. What I mean by that is what you heard in the Creek while lying awake. . . . I thought we Indians were the only one[s] that understood the language of the waters and the sighs of the pines. When I am sad I go into the Mountains and listen to the many songs of the Creeks and the soothing words of the pines. You could not of surprised [me] any more by saying what you heard in that Creek than if you had taken a gun shot at me. I would not open up my heart to anyone else but you, for they would say I was crazy but you understand."[44] Frost, who helped Linderman collect data for *American*, the life story of Plenty Coups, wrote a letter after its publication in which he praised that book and discussed the possibility of a similar project based on the life of a Crow woman. In less than a year, Linderman was working with Pretty Shield.[45]

In March 1931, after returning from ten intensely productive days with Pretty Shield at Crow Agency, Linderman wrote to a family friend, "I've had a fine visit with old Pretty-shield, a medicine-woman of the Crows. I'll write her life story from 40,000 words of notes I took from her. I've never seen such a memory as the old girl has, and she's 74. I'm fond of her, and shall never forget her."[46] A short time later, Linderman reported to his daughters:

Pretty-shield is a wonderful old soul. I like her very much. She did the best she could, and never once hesitated for a name or a date, or a location. I never saw such a memory – and above all, she loves fun – is funny herself. . . . "I will hide nothing from you, Sign-talker," she said. "Ask me whatever you will, and I will answer you truthfully." And she did, bless her old heart. We worked ten hours a day for ten days, and she was always on hand at the appointed time, too. How I did wish that I could speak her language. The old agency records show that she is 74, and yet her mind is as bright as a new dollar. Speaking of her troubles, which I myself broached, she said; "Yes, I've had trouble. I've raised my own children and two families of grandchildren, and these new times made me trouble – but I've tried to keep it out of my eyes."

But you'll read the book. I'll do it – have already started it.[47]

Published in 1932, Pretty Shield's story, originally titled *Red Mother*, was a critical success but a commercial failure. Linderman's friend, the author Frederic Van de Water, wrote, "I've read your *Red Mother*. It stands alongside *American* and deserves its station. It's beautifully, sympathetically, *simply* done. Me, I envy you. Somehow you've learned to put words – and just a few of them – exactly where they belong."[48] The *Christian Science Monitor* commented approvingly that *Red Mother* "was needed to complete the picture of the Crows. It should help to dispel the misconception of the Indian woman as a wretched drudge, and it should add to our understanding of the universal kinship of mankind."[49] But Linderman's publisher, Richard Walsh of the John Day Company, was less encouraging: "About *Red Mother*, there isn't too much to say. It is getting some fine reviews. It is not getting much sale, but then nothing is, except a few spectacular books."[50] Depression years were a bad time to try to sell books.

In the mid-1930s, although Linderman had become extremely disheartened by the sales record of his work, his friend and fellow writer Hermann Hagedorn predicted, "Your books are going to live. *American* and *Red Mother* are both much more sure of a future a hundred years hence than anything of mine that has brought in coin of the realm."[51] Six decades later, Hagedorn's words ring true: the life stories of Plenty Coups and Pretty Shield have become classics. General readers enjoy their character portrayals, drama, and vivid descriptions of bygone times. Scholars find in them a wealth of historical and ethnographical data. Both works are standard references in all studies of Crow life, and *Pretty-shield* is a valuable source of information on native women of the Plains. Some instructors at Little Big Horn College on the Crow Reservation include it as required reading in their courses on native history and culture. Excerpts appear in anthologies ranging from *The Last Best Place*, an elegant collection of Montana literature, to *Second to None: A Documentary History of American Women*, a text for courses in women's history.

"I HAVE MET THE PAST"

American and *Red Mother* were the first Crow life stories to be published. In 1923, Two Leggings had told William Wildschut, a field researcher for the Museum of the American Indian in New York City, of his life as a rather ordinary warrior who sought but never attained the full glory associated with warfare. His narrative remained unpublished, however, until Peter Nabokov edited Wildschut's original manuscript in the early 1960s. Told from a masculine viewpoint, *Two Leggings: The Making of a Crow Warrior* provides clear images of everyday Crow life at the end of the buffalo days, though like Plenty Coups and Pretty Shield, Two Leggings refused to discuss what happened when his people began to live on their reservation.[52]

Various perceptions of reservation life, however, are present in recent Crow autobiographies of members of Alma Snell's extended family. During the 1990s three descendants of George Hogan's mixed-blood half-sister Elizabeth "Lizzie" Chien (or Shane) and her Crow husband, Hawk with the Yellow Tail, published their memoirs. In *From the Heart of Crow Country*, Alma's cousin Joe Medicine Crow weaves a partial narrative of his own life into a volume on Crow history, humor, and outstanding individuals. Lizzie's daughter Amy was Joe's mother; his father was the son of Medicine Crow, a renowned chief, visionary, and political leader during the period when Crows were making the transformation from hunters to reservation residents. Joe Medicine Crow, the historian, highlights the life and achievements of Chief Medicine Crow and other Crow warriors. He also pays tribute to his mother's brother Thomas Yellowtail, who became an important sun-dance leader and healer in the latter years of this century.

Interestingly, in *his* autobiography, Tom Yellowtail explains that when he was about six years old, he received the name Medicine Rock Chief from the then elderly Chief Medicine Crow. Yellowtail, who was born in 1903 and died in 1993, drew on what he titled "Exposure to Traditional Life" in the first half of his book; the second half emphasizes his understanding of and involvement in the sun-dance religion.[53]

Traditional life and religion appear as themes also in *They Call Me Agnes: A Crow Narrative Based on the Life of Agnes Yellowtail Deernose*. In this work, Fred Voget combines the experiences of Tom Yellowtail's sister Agnes (born in 1910) with those of her husband, Donnie Deernose, and other informants to depict "some of the hardships faced within the reservation system as the Crow struggled to overcome the restrictive weight of limited resources and tried to achieve a secure, independent, and personally satisfying economic existence."[54] Voget suggests that Agnes and Donnie Deernose, along with many other Crows, learned to synthesize traditional roles with Christian beliefs. The two were active members of the Lodge Grass Baptist Church, where even Tom, the sun-dance chief, held membership and supported the energetic participation of his wife, Susie, in church affairs.

Agnes Deernose, who is still alive at this writing, was the first Crow woman since Pretty Shield to recall, for publication, issues associated with Crow womanhood. Her descriptions of birthing and child-care practices, family relationships, educational opportunities, courtship and marriage customs, and the annual round of Crow celebrations are illuminating. But because Voget decided to construct a composite story based on discussions with a number of Crows, *They Call Me Agnes* has an impersonal quality that makes it difficult to know Agnes Deernose as an individual. Like other Crow women, she appears reticent about revealing much of herself. Alma, in contrast, is thoughtfully, even courageously, outspoken. Of all the Crows who have produced life stories, she is unique in her range of experiences away from the reservation, in her willingness to discuss crucial events with unreserved emotional intensity, and in her ability to connect herself and her generation with memories of a grandmother.

Despite its exceptional characteristics, Alma's story contains a number of ideas that recur both in traditional autobiographies and in recent literature by Indian women. According to Rebecca Tsosie, these themes include the importance of "place," not only the native woman's connection to the land and its resources but also her "place within the changing social relationships of her tribe, her perceptions of herself as a 'traditional' Indian woman or one influenced by nontraditional concepts and values, and finally, her honest appraisal of her hopes, dreams, and ever-changing, often painful reality." Tsosie's comparative analysis of the autobiographical genre and contemporary literature of all types emphasizes the importance of remembering: "Indian women writers, in particular, are all too aware of the modern tendency to 'forget' what should not be forgotten; the older traditions, the recent (painful) history, the harsh realism of the modern world. The older Indian people recognized the need to keep memory alive as they perfected the art of oral history. Today, the modern written works of many Indian women fulfill a similar function."[55]

Separately or in tandem, the autobiographies of Pretty Shield and Alma Snell help to keep Crow memory, thus culture, alive. Moreover, they have a place within current scholarly discourse on diversity. Feminist scholars emphasize the interplay of gender, race, and class in historical developments. Proponents of the "new western history" insist that the western story, which continued well past the 1890s of Frederick Jackson Turner, involves people of both genders and a variety of cultures. Multiculturalists advocate inclusiveness as they introduce the voices and explore the agency of marginalized people. Specialists interested in American Indian women address their empowerment and their roles as agents of both continuity and change. Recent investigations of the development in various tribes of distinctive women's cultures suggest that such bonds grew from mutual participation in countless life experiences, such as work, play, birthing, child rearing, healing, and religious activities. The life stories of Pretty Shield and Alma resonate with these themes. Both works offer opportunities for analysis, although each seeks to tell a straightforward story.[56]

Alma is a consummate storyteller. She speaks with conviction, with candor, and with the awareness that although her narrative is intensely personal, it is also culturally and historically important. She and I worked on her book over a three-year period, mainly during summer months. The process began with a long series of taped interviews, most of which took place at Alma's kitchen table. At first, she was wary of recording procedures. She said, "The tape recorder has no spirit," meaning that she was reluctant to try to communicate with a machine. We decided that I would be present for all taping sessions, would also take notes, and would help prod her memory with questions. I had to ask few questions. During the summers of 1995 and 1996 we spent about three hours a day working together. Since we had no agenda to guide our discussions, Alma spoke of topics as she thought of them. Consequently, the tapes have continuity in terms of her thought processes, but they lack chronological sequencing.

Spontaneity enlivened the time I spent with Alma. I quickly learned to be ready to take notes anywhere, at any time – frequently while we dashed about the countryside in Alma's Chevy Lumina, which I named the Red Pony because of the way she drives it. Places brought up memories, as did contact with a wide range of people.

A moving event occurred on June 24, 1995: for the first time in history, the National Park Service held ceremonies at the Little Bighorn Battlefield National Monument to commemorate the involvement of American Indians in the history of that place. Alma, her sisters, and many other descendants of Goes Ahead – including Alma's grandson Jade Snell in a full-dress U.S. Marine uniform – joined other Indian people in a ceremony of remembrance and reconciliation. The day began with a silent parade in which Crows and Arikiras whose ancestors had scouted for Custer marched with descendants of the Lakotas, Cheyennes, and Arapahos who had fought against the Seventh Cavalry. The procession ended at the cemetery's central flagpole, where Crow elders led a pipe ceremony, the first of a series to be conducted by representatives of each tribe involved in the battle. Speeches recounting the history of each of Custer's Crow scouts followed. Alma's oldest son, Ted Hogan, spoke for Goes Ahead's family.

The day was not entirely solemn, however; as was often the case in my adventures with Alma, humor became part of the experience. Following the ceremonies Alma and her family went to lunch at Putt Thompson's trading post and restaurant. When Mrs. Thompson, in a gesture of friendship, placed a vase filled with wildflowers on the table in front of Alma, Bill Snell Jr. looked at it for a moment and softly remarked, "You better be careful where you put those. Mom might eat them."

Formal events such as the Little Bighorn commemoration, informal family gatherings, and all manner of visitors to Windblowing Place became part of the joy of working with Alma. She prepared a traditional meal for the director of the U.S. National Park Service and his entourage. She gave interviews to a famous author, an ethnobotanist, a local newspaperwoman, and a young relative from Little Big Horn College who wanted to develop an environmental studies program there. Among many others who enjoyed Alma's hospitality were a German family who had visited her several years earlier, a young man from Massachusetts who drifted in from the Little Bighorn Battlefield to talk about medicinal plants and decided that the Snell's dog was a reincarnation of a golden retriever he had once owned, a group of New Agers who were visiting a nearby tourist attraction, and some Roman Catholic nuns who were on a religious retreat in the vicinity. Interestingly, the New Age group was in Alma's living room when the nuns arrived. Alma responded to the surprising situation with characteristic grace, but the New Agers departed fairly quickly.

The most memorable encounter of the summer of 1995 occurred when Alma met Sally Hatfield, Linderman's granddaughter, for the first time. Sally and her husband, Bob, had seen Alma on a video about Linderman which the University of Montana had produced in 1991, in conjunction with an exhibit on Linderman's life and works. Subsequently, the Hatfields learned that Alma was living near Fort Smith. Because she had no telephone at that time, they contacted her through Fay McCoy, the community's postmaster, and set up a time for a visit.

On July 17, Bob, Sally, and two friends from Billings arrived in Fort Smith at the appointed hour. Immediately, Alma and the Hatfields began to talk as if they had been friends forever. Sally revealed that Linderman had dedicated the book *Red Mother* to her because she was born while he was working with Pretty Shield. Bob, in explaining how they had located Alma, proclaimed that she was the star of the film on Linderman's life. We spent about two hours talking and sipping tea at Polly's Cafe. The conversation ranged from Alma's memories of Linderman through plant lore to uses of Indian sign language. As she demonstrated the signs for the Lord's Prayer while the rest of us prayed the words, I thought I detected tears in Alma's eyes. Before leaving, the Hatfields invited us to visit Linderman's log home at Goose Bay. Alma's quick reply was, "When?" She and Sally hugged each other, decided that Linderman and Pretty Shield were "somewhere smiling about this meeting," and agreed to see each other soon. When the Hatfields had gone, I asked Alma how she felt. "Very familiar," she replied. "There was something very familiar about Sally."

In two days we were on our way to the home of Faith and Jim Chosa, Alma's daughter and son-in-law, who lived near Flathead Lake. A few days later we attended a dinner party that the Hatfields hosted at Goose Bay. When Alma, Bill, Faith, Jim, and I arrived at the log house in midafternoon, Bob Hatfield bounded from the porch: "Alma, I've been waiting for this since ten o'clock this morning."

Two French-Canadian craftsmen had built the house to Linderman's specifications in 1917. The huge exterior logs are of varying sizes, the largest about two feet in diameter. Windows are floor length, and a comfortable porch faces Flathead Lake. Trees planted by Linderman shade the lawn, which stretches to the lake. In 1919, when a forest fire destroyed most of the original trees at Goose Bay, he and his friends saved the house by soaking the roof with water. Linderman soon planted new trees and decided to name four of them "Dad," "Lige," "Blue Bird," and "Mac" for characters in his novel, *Lige Mounts: Free Trapper*.[57] As we stood beneath their branches, listening to the history of the place, Alma touched those four trees, one by one. "These have grown straight and strong," she said, "just like the legacy of Linderman and Pretty Shield."

The Linderman–Pretty Shield legacy was certainly strong on the evening of our trip to Goose Bay. Linderman's imprint on the place was everywhere. Furniture, books, and memorabilia that had belonged to him fill the interior of his home. A large photograph of Pretty Shield holds a prominent place above the author's desk, which remains as he placed it, facing a window so that he could look out on nearby shrubs where chickadees lived. On a table in the living room is a copy of a guest book with entries from earlier days. In 1919 one friend, the artist Charlie Russell, wrote, "Whales are harpooned, not biscuits" – a reference to the exact words Mrs. Linderman had once used to reprimand him for reaching across the table to fork a biscuit.

Our visit lasted long into the night, as if no one wanted it to end, and conversation was as comfortable and natural as the home itself. The next

In 1995, Linderman's living room at Goose Bay. Alma Snell and Bob and Sally Hatfield examine elkweed, which is used as an aphrodisiac by some plains tribes.

morning Alma pondered what had happened and said, "I feel that my life is much richer – much richer because I have met the past. I can say that I have truly met the past."

In August 1995 I returned home to await the birth of a grandson; I wanted to be present when Frank Emmett Willis arrived in this world. Following that excitement, I completed the daunting task of transcribing the dozens of tapes that Alma and I had recorded during the summer. The following summer the work of editing this information began.

Alma and I agreed that I should follow the chronology of her life as I arranged her stories. Although Alma never mentioned specific dates, we inserted some in the narrative and included a time line of her life as an appendix. We hope that these additions will assist readers who have questions about the sequence of events.

We also agreed that I should adjust what Alma calls her "he-she" problem. During our interviews, Alma spoke in English but thought in Crow, which has no pronouns to indicate gender, so occasionally she referred to a female as "he" or a male as "she." Also, as do many Crows, Alma sometimes spoke of the past in present-tense English. I have changed this in most instances, though in a few places where it is essential to the flavor of what Alma is saying, her usage remains.

Language differences created another concern. As Alma explains it, "I can use English for descriptions, but I need to speak in Crow to express my innermost self, my gut feelings. The Crow language recognizes that everything is part of this realm of life. Even the smallest blade of grass has its place. Our language helps us to connect all things." In an innovative study of Crow ethnoastronomy, Tim McCleary gives a prime example of how the Crow language makes these connections. The Crow expression for "quiet peace or serenity" is *ihkaxáaxaaheetak*, which means "the stars are shining brightly." One elder told McCleary, "When all was quiet in the camps and peace was about, no inclement weather, then people were wont to say, *'ihakaxáaheete, ahó, ahó,'* the stars are brilliant tonight, thanks, thanks."[58]

We have no satisfactory solution for the differences between Crow and English, but we believe that it is important for readers to be aware of them. Because we also want readers to gain an appreciation for the rhythms and repetitions of Crow oral tradition, reflected in Alma's narration, we suggest that they read portions of the text aloud.[59]

Many Crow storytellers have a penchant for detail and repetition; Alma is no exception. She and I consulted on what portions of her stories to omit, in the interest of readability, and which ones to retain, in the interest of authenticity. We sometimes eliminated the word "and" from the beginning of sentences and removed extraneous phrases such as "you know." Once, when we were discussing the deletion of details, she said dryly, "Don't cut too much. You'll clip this Crow's wings." In a more serious tone, she explained that Crows like details because "you imagine history, but that's the way history is. If someone gives the details, you know they have been along the trail. They've been on the trail if they can tell you. Imagination is funny. You may hit it, and you may not. Reality is absolutely different from imagination. Details add reality." Insights such as these strongly influenced the editing process.

Alma had the final word on everything in the manuscript. We read and revised each completed chapter together. Occasionally, as we came to a particularly meaningful passage, our conversation stopped, and Alma's eyes moved away from our stack of papers toward the landscape beyond her kitchen windows. In those moments of quiet contemplation, I knew that she was no longer with me at our work table. She was in the hills with Pretty Shield.

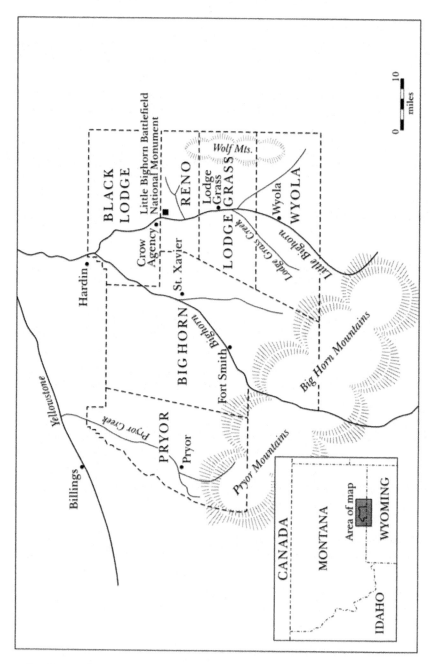

1. Crow Reservation.

1

Grandmother's Grandchild

Pretty Shield was my mother's mother. She was with me when I was born. At that time my father was working for the government, and my family lived in a large home in Crow Agency, near the Little Bighorn River. I was the seventh child born to Little Woman Goes Ahead and George Washington Hogan. I guess in all those births, my mother was pretty well undernourished. She had a hard labor with me – a very hard labor. I happened to be a big baby, ten pounds when I was born, and she couldn't, she absolutely couldn't have me, they thought. My grandmother, being a midwife, had always taken care of my mother's births, but this one was overwhelming to her. She had to call on another midwife, an old lady from the neighborhood.[1]

My brother Georgie told me that the old lady came. She came. She had a little porcelain bowl. It was tiny. She gave that bowl to my brother and asked him to go to the river. She told him to put a little fish in the bowl with some water. He went down there, broke up the ice near the river's edge (it was January), and caught this little fish. Somehow, he got it into the bowl with the water in it. He came as fast as he could to the old lady. "Hurry!" she said. She agitated the water with her finger, teased the fish so that it swam around desperately. Then she took the fish out, gave it to my brother, simultaneously pouring the water into my mother's mouth. As soon as she drank that water, my mother had me. I was born. My father, who was in the next room, praying, heard my first cry. Then the old lady told my brother to take the little fish back to the river, "Release it. Watch it. Come back and tell me what it does." He came back and reported, "The fish wobbled on its side for a little bit and then swam swiftly away." The old lady said, "They'll be all right. The baby will live." I've always had a way with water. I love the water.

Helen Goes Ahead at right, c. 1914; others not identified.

I don't remember my mother. Within a year and a half after I was born, she injured her ankle, and tuberculosis set in the bone. She wouldn't go to a doctor or to a clinic or to a hospital. She just got worse. Finally, my father persuaded her to get on the train to go to a healer – I think it was Aimee Semple McPherson – in California. When my mother got on that train, she saw some men wearing heavy overcoats and hats way down on their brows. She was afraid because she thought they were gangsters. She was so afraid, she got off the train and didn't go to California. She finally died. My grandmother then took over raising me and my brother and

The four oldest Hogan children, c. 1917: Mayme, Cerise, George, Frances.

sisters, as well as another grandson, Johnny Wilson, who was my brother in the Crow way.[2]

I have always liked to imagine how my mother might have been. I imagine that she was very attentive to her kids, very loving, very patient. On the other hand, I imagine she sort of relied on Grandma to help her if she needed advice. They worked together really well. My grandmother would ask her daughters to do something, and they would do it for her. She, in turn, did things for them, sent things to their families, something to eat or something to wear, always something useful.

I imagine my mother as a woman who loved to sing. My father told me one time when I was singing for him, "Your mother sang like a canary through the house. I loved to hear her sing." She sang Christian hymns. "Nearer My God to Thee" and "Pass Me Not, O, Gentle Saviour" were her favorites. That's what my father told me. He said that my mother sang the hymns in English, but my grandmother sang in Crow. She'd sing Indian hymns like

Akbaatatdía Aho
Akbaatatdía Aho
Chichíilak
Chichíilak
Awáss íkaak
Aho, Aho

Creator, thank you
Creator, thank you
Look for Him
Look for Him
He's looking down
Thank you, thank you[3]

Then she'd repeat it, and she'd reach upward, toward the sky, with her hands.

My father told me that his father's name was Long Ago Bear. His mother was Emma Duchien or Shane. She was half Crow and half French. Her mother was a Crow woman named Stays in the Woods, and her father was Pierre Duchien, a fur trapper. My father had two older half-sisters whose father was a Scotsman named Frazee. One was Liz (Lizzie, we called her), who married a Crow named Hawk with the Yellow Tail. Two of their sons, Robert and Tom, became well-known Crows.[4] The other sister was Mary, who married Takes the Gun. We called her "Grandma Beans" because her Crow name was *Awaasásh*, meaning Beans. When her husband passed away she had a little tent house built in Crow Agency. The floor was boarded, but the top was tent. She wanted to be near my father, so she was there. I remember Lizzie would come often and visit her sister, and they'd go over to my father's place. They loved to be together, those three. They just enjoyed each other's company because they loved each other very much. My father always said, "Don't ever do anything to hurt my sisters. Don't ever hurt their feelings." My grandmother, Pretty Shield, always gave those sisters many gifts. She treated them well for the sake of her daughter Little Woman.

I don't know anything about Long Ago Bear except what Amy White Man told me.[5] She said that he was a very kindly man, a tall man and very good-looking. He loved my grandmother and my father very much, very much. One time when my father was a little toddler, he cried for butter.[6] He liked butter, the churned butter that the farmers had. He loved it thick on his bread, and he cried for butter. The family didn't have any at that time. My grandmother told him, "There's no butter, now. You quit crying." He turned to his dad and said, "I want some butter." And his tears – the man looked at the little boy (he looked so much like his mother), and he said, "Come. I'll get you some butter." He took one of his good horses, and he went to the farmer and traded that horse for a pound of butter so he could see his little boy happy.

My father's name was Sitting Bull, but I didn't know that until I was a young lady. I had always known him as *Isáahkachiash*, which might be translated "Old White Headed Man." They called him that because when he was small his hair was very white, and they wanted him to live a long time. I have been told that he received his English name at Carlisle Indian School. He was taken to Carlisle when he was about seven years old. When the children got to the school, the officials lined them up and gave them new names. They gave the boys presidential names like Abraham Lincoln or Thomas Jefferson. When they got to my father, they said, "George Washington." A young army officer who was standing nearby said, "I like this little boy. He has blue eyes like me. Give him my last name; it's Hogan." My father remained at Carlisle for thirteen years until he graduated. He never got to come home, not even when his father died.[7]

My first memory of my father is of a praying father. I saw him praying all the time. I saw him poring over his Bible. I saw him checking up on us to see that we went to Sunday School. Even if he was working somewhere else or living with his second family, he'd always come over there where we were with Pretty Shield and make sure that we went to Sunday School. Pretty Shield caught on: "This must be what my son-in-law wants." So, always, she got us ready to go to Sunday School.[8]

Before my mother died, my father sold land and built a magnificent house for her in the Benteen area. It had everything up to date for that time, even to Persian rugs and hardwood floors. They had big fancy beds and a Victrola that had to be cranked up. These are some of the things my sisters told me about. When I came along, there was nothing in there except emptiness, it seemed. There was a big stove, a table with benches and chairs, a china closet where we kept our dishes and our staples. Going into the living room, there was a bed there and my grandfather's old rocking chair – Goes Ahead's rocking chair. Grandma wanted that rocking chair, so they left it there. Sometimes that chair moved, even though no one was sitting in it. Grandma would say, "That's Grandpa." She wasn't afraid; she just thought it was Grandpa. In the other bedrooms there were beds, but that's all. There were no rugs, nothing. According to custom, everything was given away when Mother died. People even took her dishes. To me that's a bad custom, one I wouldn't wish to hang on to. Sometimes they even gave away their chickens and other things that were for sustenance.

During my very early years we lived in the Benteen house, there in the Little Bighorn valley. That valley was always a pretty place to me. And the river was so pretty. Our house was very near where Nest Creek ran into the river. That's just about the place, where it's all beachy and rocky, where my grandma used to wash clothes. The beaches looked sandy close to the water, but about five yards from shore the rocks started to form. The small rocks were all over the bottom of the river, but the water was clear. You could see through it to the bottom, except where it went too deep to see. Upstream maybe six hundred yards were tall banks that met a whirlpool, a deep, deep place. My father had made steps in the hard clay dirt of the bank there. Those steps were strong, but when they were wet, they got slick. We used to get our water there. They tried to dig a well near our house, but it didn't work out, so we got water from the river. We'd tie a rope onto a bucket and throw it out to where the water would be more pure; then after we pulled our bucket in, we took the rope off and left it on the bank. We hauled the water to a huge reservoir on the side of our big stove in the kitchen. It held about two buckets, and that was the hot water we used. We'd have to go back and get more water for drinking and cooking.

At another place along the river my grandma had a large hole straight down below the bank. She had put rocks down there and a platform of boards. She put butter and milk and her mixtures like rose hips and tallow in that hole, put a heavy rock over it, and that was her little cooler. About a quarter-mile away was the place where she butchered. The river was very pleasant there; it was beautiful. Its slope was not harsh. It just

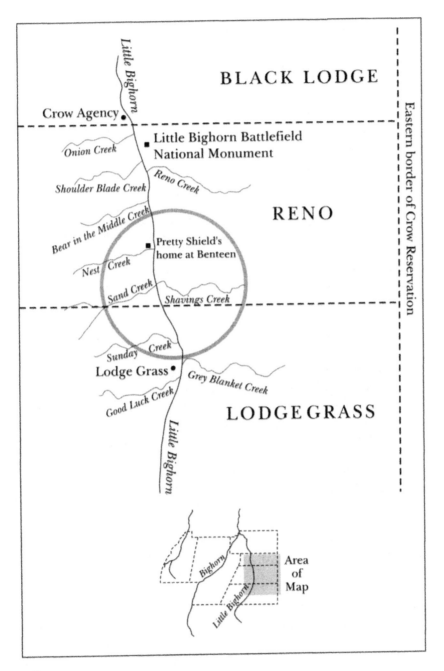

BLACK LODGE

Little Bighorn

Crow Agency •

■ Little Bighorn Battlefield
National Monument

Onion Creek

Shoulder Blade Creek *Reno Creek*

RENO

Bear in the Middle Creek

■ Pretty Shield's
home at Benteen

Nest Creek

Sand Creek

Shavings Creek

Sunday Creek

Lodge Grass •

Grey Blanket Creek

Good Luck Creek

LODGEGRASS

Little Bighorn

Eastern border of Crow Reservation

Bighorn

Area
of
Map

Little Bighorn

2. Benteen area.

gradually went down to a rocky place, then to the beach and the river. That was our crossing. I can still feel that sandy road under my feet.

We had just a wagon path to take us to the gravel road that led to Crow Agency. Of course, we didn't have a car. Very few Crow people had cars when I was small, so almost everybody rode in wagons. When we went to Crow Agency, we'd go past hills with pines on the left-hand side of us. On the right was the river with all its cottonwood trees and box elders and berry bushes. And grapes – lots of grapevines grew there. Sometimes I ate grapes until my mouth just itched. Peopled liked to hunt in through there. Boys liked to hunt through that valley. There were a lot of deer in there.

I didn't go to Lodge Grass too much. I may have gone to church services there a time or two, a special thing at the Baptist church, like a revival or a picnic. People would put their tarps out and sit on them and eat and talk. It was just a good social time. We also went past Lodge Grass and into the canyon to camp. That canyon – now you're getting into mountainous area, foothills of the Big Horn Mountains. We'd have to go through a ravine to a place where there was a spring. It had pine trees all around – a beautiful place where you could see the larger mountains all around you. We camped in the Wolf Mountains too, to the northeast of the Benteen area. The Wolf Mountains were always a beautiful place to me.

When we lived in the Benteen house, it seems like we were hard up more times than when there was plenty. When I was about eight years old, I remember that we had a little more to eat than before. Even then, when the garden dwindled down, we would collect dry peas, dried old peas on the ground. We'd collect enough for a bowl of soup, and my father knew how to prepare it. He would boil it, boil the peas, and he would put little pieces of carrots and onions with them and make a kind of gravy of it – soup, soupy gravy. We loved it. We were so hungry, I guess. It tasted like nothing else.

I remember my dad singing lullabies to put me to sleep. He liked to sing "East Side, West Side, All Around the Town."

I became what the Crows call *káalisbaapite* – a "grandmother's grandchild." That means that I was always with my grandma, and I learned from her. I learned how to do things in the old ways. While the mothers of my friends changed to modern ways of preparing things, Pretty Shield stuck to her old ways. Nowadays, we change in a few years with technology, and it was the same when I was growing up, just at a slower pace. While my grandmother was teaching me her ways of the past, how they survived and their traditional and cultural values, mothers of other girls were teaching them to adapt and the purpose of advancing. There are two different things here. A grandmother's grandchild and a mother's child were two different things – two different girls, you might say, if they were girls. A grandmother's grandchild did what her grandma did because there was nothing else to do. A mother would say, "Go play. Go play with the little ones over there, or go play with your dishes," or whatever it was. But a grandmother's grandchild never got that. A grandma always took her granddaughter with her so that the little girl could learn to survive. The mother, however – she was going to live long enough to take care of her child, so the mother didn't show the child ways of surviving; she did it for her. She did it for her.

A grandmother's grandchild did things with her, and when the grandmother grew older and was unable to do some things effectively, the grandchild was old enough to help. If the grandma wanted to lift something, the grandchild helped her. The mother did it herself – lifted or worked; the child was out playing or doing something else. I liked to play. I liked to play with the neighborhood kids, and I did when we had a quiet time, but otherwise I was forever helping my grandma and learning from her and doing with her. She was helping me, and I was helping her. Those are the differences, differences between a grandmother's grandchild and a mother's child.

Because I was always with Grandma, I was always with the old ladies. That's the security I knew. "This is where I belong, right in this realm." To me, they were always there and they will always be there. I didn't see a conclusion to them at all. Grandma and her ways built a fringe around me. It kept me in that circle. That's where I wanted to be. I always thought, "I'll do what Grandma says." It was almost as if I thought I might offend her and she would go away.

I wish I could remember everything she taught me. She said, "The earth is like our mother because it gives us food like a mother provides food from her breast." She respected it. I remember she'd say that when the farmers first came, they "cut into the face" of the earth – *iisáduukaxik.* It's like a wound there, and it hurt her.

When I was with Grandma and all the old ladies that used to go and dig turnips, I'd watch them, and I noticed that they *did* care. They all did the same thing. They had a routine about it. They didn't just go carelessly around; they did these things patiently and correctly, and they were just right at home there. They would dig the roots with their sticks; then they would replace the soil and tamp it down just like nobody had bothered it. They always said *Aho* (thank you) to the Creator, and if there were any wild seeds, they would scatter them about for more turnips to grow in another year. So I always do that now. I feel like the earth is happy when we do that. I feel like it's comforted.

In between their digging the old ladies rested and ate their lunches. When they rested, they told stories. I loved it when Grandma took out our lunch. She would tell me to sit behind her on the ground and rest my back against hers. I just leaned against her back, and she loved that. I know she loved it. Sometimes she said, "Move, move yourself a little to the left." So I did, and she worked her back and let me sit there. Then she would talk to me.

Sometimes she told me about a time when she was in the hills, mourning the death of a child, a little girl. She went into a visionary trance, and little ants came to her and took her into their lodge. In the back of the lodge, at the center in the place of honor, sat a golden eagle. The eagle did not speak, but the ants told Grandma that they were her friends and said, "No obstacle is too great. Keep working, keep doing what you are doing, and you will have what you need." So she always told us not to be lazy. "Look at the ants" is what she said. She told us how the ant people talked to her, and she said, "Don't step on them. Don't step on them if you can help it. Wherever you are, there will always be ants around your home."

When we went out into the hills to dig these roots, turnips, and she came to an ant pile, she would take out some beads from her pouch and sprinkle them on the pile. Some of them were kind of large beads. Then she'd tell the ants, "I brought you some little beads. I thought you would like them because they're so pretty. I brought them for you as a *gift*, and I want you to have them." Those little ants would take the beads, even the big ones. They'd take them to that hole on top of the ant pile. They would disappear with them, and I would just keep watching them. I sat there and just wished with all my might that I could see where they were going with those beads. In my child mind I thought, "My, they must have pretty rooms with dance halls and things like that." I used to imagine such things when Grandma gave beads to the ants. After so many years (I don't know how many years later) a ranch woman saw ants bringing beads out of their holes. She took them. She says she has a handful of them.

I *know* they're Pretty Shield's.

Once, over at Benteen, this little boy sat on an ant pile, great big ant pile. There were big black and red ants crawling all over him. Those are large ants; they bite hard. He was plumb naked. Little boy, he was, and he went over there to play with them. They just crawled all over his body. I got scared. I ran over to my grandma, and I said, "Junior, Junior Boy – we called him Junior Boy – he's in the ant pile, and they're all over his body. He's going to be screaming pretty soon from the bites." Pretty Shield said, "I know. They won't hurt him. They will not do anything to him. Let him play with them." He sat there and played with them, raised up their little hills for them. After quite a while he left, none the worse. Grandma didn't get after him or anything. She said, "They'll be good to him. Don't worry."

A long time after that, when I went to school in Flandreau, South Dakota in 1940, I took up home ec, of course; the girls had to take home economics. I baked the devil's food cake and the biscuits. That was my duty. I was working in a tea room that was a project to help fund the school, and at the same time I was learning how to prepare different things. Anyway, one morning when I was cleaning the glass containers for the cakes and cookies that we sold, I heard the teacher say, "We're going to have to do something about those ants. They're coming in here, and people will come in and see them in our cake showcase. Something's got to be done. We'll put out some poison tonight, in different corners. We'll put it there tonight and see if we can get rid of those ants." When I heard this, I thought of Grandma and her ants. I went back into a closet where there were a few ants, and I warned them: "You little ants, they're going to kill you. Tonight they're going to put something out to kill you. So you better move and get away from here." Then I left. The little ants were just there. They didn't talk to me, didn't say, "Yes, we heard you," or anything else. I just told them, and I left.

The next morning when I went to work, the teacher remarked, "We put the poison out. The boys put the poison out in different places, and we didn't catch one ant, not one." But the ants were gone. I looked all over – counters, everywhere – and there was not one ant there. I decided that they had heard me when I warned them. Later that day one of my friends told me, "I went for a walk last night, and I passed this way. I saw a column of ants moving. They were going from the tea room building right across the sidewalk, across the road toward the power house, that direction." Evidently they heard me. It happened that very day.

I didn't see my grandmother do much Indian doctoring because she had promised Goes Ahead that she wouldn't use her medicine powers.[9] But I do remember a few experiences. Sometimes she used her skills as a "pusher." Pushers helped people who had headaches, or their backs were hurting, or arms or legs. Pretty Shield would work with the spine, from the nape of the neck on down. She would go not with the clock but the opposite direction. I noticed that she always moved her hand the opposite direction from the way the clock went. She would go right down the spine and push now and then, put pressure now and then as she went along. It's just like she pushed the thing right out, from the soles of their feet or wherever she pushed it to. It seemed like they would always feel better about the fourth time. Four was always the number they did a thing. People would bring her little children who had colic, and she would also do the pressure for them. Colic was always doctored that way, but with a little pressure to the stomach, too.

In the old days, if a man had left a wife or a wife left a man, or if a man wanted a woman as his wife and she didn't care about him, they would come to Pretty Shield and she would fix something or other. I've never seen her do it except for a woman and her little girl. The woman for some reason had sent the child to live with her grandma, but there came a time when this mother wanted her child back, this little girl. That woman happened to be from St. Xavier. I remember that. My grandmother told her – these things kind of stay in my mind, these odd things – Grandma said, "Now remember, when your girl goes out in a field or some place to urinate on the ground, when she urinates, you rush over there and urinate over it before it gets cold, before the urine gets cold." Not too long after that the mother came and told Pretty Shield that she had won her child back to her. Pretty Shield said, "I was never ever to do this again, but I did it because of the child and the mother. I believe it's appropriate that I do this." The woman was very happy and gave her things. Four things.

I watched Grandma heal a spider bite on a young girl's neck. She went over, over that girl's neck, and I watched her because I knew Blanche, the girl. She was younger than I was. She had tremendously thick hair, but the spider had bitten her, and there was a rash all over the side of her face on down to her neck. Pretty Shield got some ant dust, dirt from an anthill, and mixed it with tallow – a grease of some kind; I think that she used tallow. She mixed it, and she went all over the girl's face and put this poultice on it. Then she came on down on her neck and said, "Here is where the spider bit you, right here. I'll cleanse that out." She pulled the skin up, kind of like she was taking something out of it. Then she covered it with the same poultice and sent the girl back home – told her to come back each day. The fourth day she was healed of that rash. Each day it became better and better, and the fourth day it was okay. She didn't have to use that mixture on her face anymore.

One time when I was at Flandreau, I had warts on my hand from the little finger to my wrist. There were several warts there, and I used to wash them every day because I was ashamed. The boys would see those warts, and I was kind of ashamed. Then springtime came along. One day I was in the girls' building, and I was looking out the windows in front, out to the campus. I saw lightning and heard thunder – the first thunder I'd heard that spring – and immediately, it came to my mind: Pretty Shield saying that if you have any warts, listen for the first thunder of spring and run out, get some grass, spit on it, and rub it on your warts. They'll be gone. With that thought in my mind, I rushed out as if the thunder was going to get away from me. I rushed out to get that grass, and I spat on it; then I rubbed it all over my little warts that I had kept so clean, and I never thought any more about it – I had done what I was told to do. Next day or so, I washed the green off. Maybe the second day or the third morning. I was washing my hands and started to try to scrub the warts clean again and there was nothing there. All of them had gone, and they have never returned.

Since Grandma was the main object in my mind, when I was with her, I was always attentive to her. If I was going to do something, I'd look at her to catch the expression that said, "It's okay" or "It's not okay." At any given time she would drop everything and she'd start to meditate – to pray. She could be sitting down, or she would fall to the ground. In prayer, it seemed like all earthly things were gone from her. The house, the trees, whatever was around were completely gone from her presence. She would look up at an angle, up to the top of the hills if we were in the valley or looking far off, into space, if we were on the hilltop. She would be talking, and nothing intruded in her conversation. I don't think she would even have moved if a snake came over her feet. That wouldn't have moved her. It seemed to me that she had this powerful spirit about her.

In her prayers (and I probably won't remember everything), she would say, "My, my, my," an expression like that. "Oh, how we were over this land, and we were so free. There was laughter, there was unity, and hearts were high and happy. Why is it that we were taken out of there? Why is it that this was all taken from us? But you are the one. You are the one that made all things. You are the one that made all things. Give us knowledge to this change that we may help ourselves. We don't understand. We do not understand what is to come, but you are there. In spite of all the change, you're there. You will look after us. You are the one that sees everything. You are the one. Whether we like it or not, whether anyone likes it or not, this is the way you want it. And the way it will go. But you will look after us because you take care of your creation."[10]

When she was through, her completely relaxed expression became more tense and aware now of what was around her. She'd check on me right away. When she saw me, and everything was fine, she seemed satisfied. She would either grab the end of her blanket, her lightweight blanket, or her muffler, and she'd wipe the sweat from around her face. Sometimes she would say, "It was a good thing." The prayer was good. It had been a blessing to her. She felt free.

When I was still small, Grandma and I would go out to pick berries. We'd pick berries a lot. That's when she told me how to protect myself if I saw a bear. She said, "When you come face to face with a bear, don't smile at it like you want to be kind. When you're kind to a person, you smile, you smile. Don't do that to a bear. Look at him in the eye and just stare at him just as he's staring at you. Don't give up. He's bound to walk away. But I hope it never happens," she'd go on, "because some of 'em get mean, especially when they have cubs or especially if they think you're in their territory. Don't grab a limb or pick berries. Just stand still like you're not doing anything. After he goes, you walk slowly away. He's observing you, but he thinks you're no threat."

I felt very safe with Grandma, no matter where we went. I felt secure when she was around. I guess in my child's mind she talked to the animals, even to horses, even to bulls. I was safe with her always.

One time when I was a little girl, she was washing clothes in the Little Bighorn at Benteen. She rubbed the clothes against a big white rock that was halfway in the water and halfway out. She rubbed her clothes on it; then she swished them in the water. While she was washing, I was playing. Just above us, toward the house, was a kind of plateau where my brother was throwing his arrows. He was good in the arrow game, and he was always practicing. So there he was, and I was playing with rocks along the shore. It wasn't a dropoff or anything; it was just a nice shore with rocks. I came up to this sandpile thing, I thought. I thought it was a rock with sand on it, so I got on top of it, and I was sliding my feet on it, one way and the other. I kept sliding both feet – and it started to move. I screamed, and Grandma came running over there not too far from me. She came running over there. She took me by the arm and threw me to shore and hollered to my brother, Georgie, "*Iisashpítshiile*! (That means Yellow Rabbit.) Bring your gun! Bring your gun! This turtle, *dáako*, scared my little grandchild, and I want you to shoot it!" He came with his arrows. He didn't take time to go to the house and get his gun; he came with his arrows. By that time Grandma was getting in the water to go downstream where this turtle – now it's not a little turtle, that big thing – was going. It's a big one, camp-stove size. She took off her clothes quickly (her top dress, left her underdress on) and swam after the turtle. I was betting on my grandmother.

By this time, Georgie had thrown some arrows at the turtle. I could see two arrows and a little white one stuck on his back. Those things have hard backs. Pretty Shield swam after it, but it went down. It went down, down, down. Arrows and all disappeared. After she came out of the water, Grandma told Georgie, "You should have never used your arrows because they're hard to make." But he said, "Well, I'll make some more. I'll make some more arrows. That thing could have done something to my little sister. She might have got hurt." Pretty Shield didn't say any more. Things kind of settled down, and we got through washing.

Another time, I remember, I was with Grandma and my sisters Mayme and Pearl. We were coming back to the Benteen house from the trading post in Crow Agency, carrying what we'd bought in bags. We caught a ride with someone. He let us off at the highway, and we walked about a quarter-mile or so to the gate of this bull pasture. A rancher was leasing this land, and he had his bulls in there. We were afraid to cross that pasture because of the bulls. Two of them were scratching the earth. When they scratched the earth and made that dust fly and made that noise from their throats, we were afraid of them. We hated to cross because they would gore us, but if we went clear around, that would be another two miles around that pasture to where we could cross the river.

Pretty Shield decided, "You stay right here. You stay right here on this side of the fence, and I'll go in there."

Mayme, my older sister, said, "Oh, Grandma, you might get hurt by that thing."

"We'll see," Pretty Shield declared.

She got across the fence – we helped her get through – and she went right up to this bull that was scratching the earth, the one closest to her.

Another one beyond was doing the same thing, and there were a lot of others, grazing around, over in front of her. She went right up to this bull, and to me it seemed like she grabbed its tail and wrapped her hand with it. Then she just jerked it with all her might! That bull bellowed and shot forward. Away it went, and this other bull went with him. All the rest followed. They were gone over to the side. She says to us, "Come. Come. Hurry now." So we hurried up and got our bags under the fence. We crossed the field and we went to the river. I remember that just as well.

Grandma hated fences. She'd say, "Why is it that they put up fences? If you keep something in a fence too long, it will die. Let it go its way."

She would lament, "I'm living a life I don't understand." She would be working and talking – maybe telling me stories, little stories of long ago – then immediately she would fall silent. She would continue to work, but she was silent. I would be with her, and I would sit silent and wait for her. I became accustomed to that, so I was a very quiet individual at times. I was patient. I was quiet. Then she'd come up with this sound she always made, "Hummmm, aaahh." She said it mournfully, like this thing that she was thinking about in her mind was so overwhelming; "Why has this thing come upon us? Now we are made to say 'yes' and 'no.' When the white man comes and says something to us, we just naturally say 'yes.' We are not obligated to take what he has, but my children, my grandchildren are always right there to say, 'Yes, we'll do it. We'll do it.' They seem to like to do it. They seem to like what they see. I feel like I am losing my children to this new world of life that I don't know."

She never did like fences. Everything seemed hard to her with fences around.

2

Pretty Shield and Goes Ahead

Basáakoosh
Basáakoosh
Attáxxawaachish diikaalee
Báatchaat díalaak

Goes Ahead
Goes Ahead
Many have heard the shots from your gun
What a great thing you have done

That's a Goes Ahead song. That's my grandfather's song. When it was sung in a gathering of some kind, then all of those in Goes Ahead's lineage would get out there and go around in front of everybody. Those who were his closest relatives followed him right away. Then the rest readied themselves and went on. They kept adding on to Goes Ahead's lineage. Grandchildren, great-grandchildren, they moved together as the song was sung. Then they laid something down in one place to give away to visitors, to honor him. We still do that today. Any male in Goes Ahead's family, if they have no song, they can use Goes Ahead's song. My grandfather's Crow name was *Basáakoosh*, Goes Ahead. Everything I know about him, I learned from listening to stories told by other people.

My grandmother, Pretty Shield, liked to tell me about her early memories of the man who became her husband. She said,

When I was about nine years old, I would be playing with my make-shift travois with little girls my age.[1] We would notice when the men got ready to go to war. We'd watch them, and sometimes they'd shoo us back: "Get back, get back away from the horses." But it was fun to watch them. We never ever talked about getting married, but we'd play house, and we'd move the leaves aside to make a circle. If we didn't have a little lodge to put up, that circle was our lodge. One of the girls would say, "Oh, where's your husband?" Another one would reply, "Oh, my husband went hunting, or went to battle, but he'll come back. Oh, here he is now." That girl would have a long stick taller than herself, and she'd pretend it was her man coming home – in through the lodge door. She'd set the stick way in the back of the lodge, and that was her man. She would talk to him like a wife did.

When I was thirteen years old, I still went out to play. Goes Ahead would stop by and say to me, "How are you?" I would tell him, "All right." I wouldn't stay and talk with him too much because I wanted to go out with my girlfriends and play. But I knew that this was the man I was going to marry. Goes Ahead would stand there, and he'd smile – kindly man. He'd smile at me and he'd say, "Go, go. They're getting away from you." I would take off with the girls and never pay any more attention to the man I was promised to. So this was my man. He was *eechik*, good-looking. He always kept himself neat, his hair done up, always wore abalone. He'd go away. He don't bother me. He don't touch me. He just asks me how I am. He knew this girl was his.

Grandma knew she would be married to Goes Ahead. Her dad had already arranged that. She was given to him, and she would be married to him. He was a good provider, a good hunter. He was a very kindly man but very brave. He was a good fighter and was very lucky in his hunts – never missed, that she knew of, always found something to bring home. When she turned sixteen, they had the wedding ceremony. His mother and sisters had a tipi made for her, put it up, and inside they put all the things she would need as a woman to care for the lodge, to feed the family. It was all gifted to her. The bed was made for her, and pretty robes, a buckskin dress with leggings. Later, the men of her family, her father and brothers, gave Goes Ahead moccasins, a shirt, weapons, and horses. When the time came, a crier went through the camp saying, "It is time for this wedding to take place. Goes Ahead will take Pretty Shield for his wife, and you are all invited to eat. Come along and take a meal." They had plenty of meat, pemmican, cherries, and lots of fat hanging on the racks for people to cut off.[2]

Grandma said, "It was a gala affair. It was a happy affair, but it was frightening to me. I anticipated what I was going to go through. I didn't know whether I wanted to or not. I had admired a lot of the men, boys, some of them – the way they carried themselves, their mounts, those kinds of characteristics about a man. I'd watch. I'd say, 'That is a nice-looking one, a neat one, or a grand-looking one' – just kind of notice everything about them. I noticed if they were helpful to their families or lazy to their families, but I never ever looked at one as wanting to be with him because I knew in my mind that I belonged to Goes Ahead. After I married him, I didn't want any other."

Goes Ahead was already married to Pretty Shield's older sister, and later he married her younger one. Three sisters were given to him because he was so well known for his responsibility. Grandma said something about the older one going out on him quite a bit, but the younger one was very nice. The younger one was good and loyal to both Pretty Shield and her husband. When a man wanted to get rid of a wife (if he was mad, or hurt – his pride hurt – or if his friends teased him), at the first public meeting or celebration he would give the camp crier gifts and have him go out and announce, "He's throwing this wife away. Anybody who wants her can have her." This took care of the husband's responsibility. The wife would move, probably next to her family, until another man married her. That was divorce. Women could do it, too. Goes Ahead never did that to the wife that went out on him. It may have been the influence of Pretty Shield, because she was so close to her sisters. This was a *strong family unit,* Pretty Shield and her sisters and Goes Ahead.[3]

Pretty Shield always held a sort of queen status, the queen of the lot, you might say. He always gave her his war pony to ride when he came home from battle. It was very much of an honor for a wife to be picked out of so many wives to ride his steed as he went through the village. She was very proud of that, "I got to ride his war horse every time – not just one time, all the time." She was the only one to have children, she told us. Pretty Shield and Goes Ahead had five children altogether, but two of them died at young ages. She had been told by an eagle being that she would have children but that some of them would not live long lives. *Itchish* (Good) was the only son who lived to become a man. Two girls – Pine Fire, the oldest, and Little Woman, my mother – grew into womanhood. Good was a very hard-working man. He became a farmer in the Benteen area. He put in alfalfa, put in a garden, and they had vegetables. But he died also. He died from overwork. He was a strong man, big healthy man – just overdid it. He used to carry those old plows that go behind a horse. He used to carry those from field to field on his shoulders.

Goes Ahead received his medicine power as a young man. He had a place up toward Wolf Mountains, going toward what is Wyoming today, one of those peaks there above what is the Jeffers ranch now. He would just go right up through those coulees, go on up to Wolf Mountains, to a peak there where he had made a circle of rocks. That was his fasting place, and his fasting place was known to my brothers, Georgie and Johnny. Some of those rocks are still there. He fasted there for four days, and the fourth day he thought, "Well, there is nothing. Nothing has been shown to me. No helper has come around. I guess I have just fasted, and that is it." As he got up to go, he started to look around and say the words they always said when they departed from their fasting places: "It's done. I'll go on. It's done. *Aho, Bachaáhawatash.*" (That means, "Thank you, the One Man, the One Above.") "I have fasted. I haven't been given a helper or anything. It's done."[4]

He was going to depart for home, when he looked toward his left and saw what looked like a bird coming from way off. He saw this big bird, and in his eyes it was flying in a kind of precarious fashion, unbalanced. It was trying to fly, but it seemed like its body was too heavy. It was just going all kinds of ways. It was coming over toward him, and as he watched it, he began to get excited. "This is not a bird, but it does have wings." It looked like it was hurt, and it twisted and turned up there until it fell at his feet. He looked at it. It was a serpentlike body – lizardlike, I guess – with wings on it like dragonfly wings. It had a tail to it. As he picked it up, he thought it was mighty strange. There his power was. His power was given to him there: "This is for you to use." So he picked it up. He took it home and told about it, and the men around the council thought it was *great*. (It was usually the men they told, and then the wife knew about it. It went on to where the village, everybody, began to know about it.) He had it encased in beadwork, according to how he was told to wrap it. He was *told* to wrap this thing up, and he did. He always carried it on him, or it was put on a tripod behind his tipi. He had many medicine bundles handed down to him, but this was his main medicine. We always said the butterfly was his emblem. It was like a butterfly with a big body, a long body. In fact the body looked serpentine.[5]

Goes Ahead had his medicine with him when he scouted for Custer before the Battle of the Little Bighorn. He told Grandma that Custer's spirit had gone on before him, so he had no choice but to follow it. That was in death. Goes Ahead and the other Crow scouts counseled Custer to wait. "Wait." He would not listen. When someone doesn't listen to wisdom, the Crows say he has blocked ears, like mud in the ears. That is a sign that the spirit has left them. The body is still present, but *iláaxkoolasaak* – the spirit is absent. So the Crow scouts went. They went, and they dressed for death. They took off their outer garments, the shirt, the leggings; they pushed all their garments into a hole in the side of a hill. They hid them there. Then they had their faces marked and their breechcloths on and, behind their ears, breath feathers from an eagle. They put those breath feathers there so they could float on to the other world easier. "Then we went on," he said.[6]

Goes Ahead told my father more than once about the battle and where they went afterward, and the trees – a kind of pine ridge there toward Busby – where he put his mark. My father told me about it, and I remember just where we were standing. He pointed up to the pine ridge and said, "Your grandfather put his mark up there on one of those trees when they were headed away from the battle, but I have never gone up there." Years later, I told a historian that I met below the battlefield. He went up there to search for it; he found it and took some pictures. That was this Bill Boyes. More than one hundred years ago, that blaze was put on, and the tree swelled, but the blaze was still there. The serpentine body was not as vivid as the wings were. The wings swelled up. "I believe that this is Goes Ahead's blaze," the historian told me.[7] It's right with me, what Goes Ahead said about the battle. He was a kind man, and few words. He didn't waste many words.

Another time when Goes Ahead was fasting, he saw a vision of a heavy sort of movement, coming through the valley, the Little Bighorn valley, from the north. It was going south. He thought perhaps it was a storm, but then, in his eyes he saw this vision, this heavy iron – he didn't say "iron" but called it "heavy": "It's a *heavy, moving, large, long object.*" And it was puffing out what he thought was smoke or a lot of hot steam, like a great *baaisbiláaleete baatcháachik* (that means "a great animal coming"). It went through that valley. He saw the length of it that went almost from one end of the valley to the other. He didn't see a little portion of it; he saw the whole area. Then it went past. Later he said that when the train came and had those boxes that made it long and it was puffing that steam, that's what he had seen coming through that valley. I have read in other books that some other people said a person saw that same vision, but whether at the same time or not, I don't know. It was before the train, though. He mentioned this to the council, and they wondered what it could be. When a man like Goes Ahead had a vision, he told it to the circle, all the men who held council from time to time. He would tell them of these things. When he told it, they pondered it. They pondered it very much. They were silent about it. They accepted it, but it remained to be seen whether it would come to pass. I guess Grandpa would laugh when that train would go by. He would kind of laugh and say, "That's what I saw. That's what it was."[8]

My father experienced how Goes Ahead used his medicine. He saw Grandpa working with a patient who had pneumonia, and his chest was filled up. He could hardly breathe, and he was sick. My father saw Goes Ahead work on him. The healers prayed as they worked. They continued to pray to God as they worked. Then, whatever they had to say about their power, they'd say it, as it was given to them when they fasted. Goes Ahead put a reed to the man's chest right where it was hurting worst, worst place, and he drew out – he sucked that reed. He sucked it up, and he put it away from the man's body toward the ground, and he blew it out of that reed. It was nothing but a mass of phlegm and blood mixed. My father saw this himself. Goes Ahead did that several times, then gave the patient medicine to take, and the man got well.

Headaches, severe headaches – he would work on them, too, and clear the head part where the pain was coming from, almost in the same manner. There were always these feathers that they used to pat them, their patients, in the different areas of pain – just like they were sweeping it away.

He did many wonderful, wonderful healings and helping of people. In fact, he was one of the more powerful medicine men there was, and always people came to him, and he'd tell them what to do: "Go get this kind of root – go get this from a tree or a plant." He told them how to mix it and how to take it, or he'd mix it himself and make them take it right there and come back again. Usually they'd come back about four times. With everyone who administered these medicines, four seemed to be the number that completed things.

He had many, many things that were given to him, horses and material things. He was a very prominent man, and Pretty Shield, too, received gifts because she healed people. They were considered well-off people of that time. If visitors came, Goes Ahead would immediately tell his wives to serve them. He'd begin to get his pipe out and get ready to talk and smoke pipe – a very kind man.

People liked to camp near his lodge. I have been told that when they did, he sang this song:

Ashé xaxúa biwiilápaatuuk
Ashé xaxúa biwiilápaatuuk

All these lodges are my friends
All these lodges are my friends

Absolutely not leaving anyone out.

He was an extremely lucky hunter and so were his grandchildren. Never did his grandsons come back with nothing. He told the boys not to eat kidneys, kidney of any animal: "Don't eat the kidney or you will not have good luck with your horses." It seemed to be true, too. My brother, Georgie, told me that any time he ate kidney (and he loved kidney), something would happen to his horse. My grandmother would get after him and say, "Well, you asked for it. You weren't supposed to eat kidney and you did." They still hung on to those beliefs like that.

Goes Ahead always told his grandboys to take care of their weapons and treat them like they had life: "Treat them like you would your own self or your child, and they will be good to you." He would burn pine needles on the stove or on stones. He would burn this incense from pine needles and run the gun over it. Then he'd turn it over and run it back over the needles again. He scented it real good with pine incense. Then he would say, "Don't bang it around. Hang it in a place where nobody can touch it. Don't let anyone touch it but you, and it will always bring you luck." While I was growing up, my grandmother took over that activity of burning the pine incense. Pretty Shield took over the responsibility of scenting their guns and weapons over burned pine needles.

Later I did that too, for my husband, Bill. He wanted to know what I was doing, and I said, "This is the way Grandma Pretty Shield did for Georgie and Johnny – their weapons, and they're always lucky. They brought home something each time." He kind of smiled at me, but he let me do it. Then he thought in his own mind, "Well, what a nice thing to do!" He told me, "The deer that we go after, usually the deer, are not estranged to this type of smell. They smell the pine, and they won't smell the metal or the scent of man on the stock. It's all incensed out." Naturally, he figured what it was all about. The way I thought was, "Just so we incensed it. It was great."

When the missionaries came in the late 1800s, Goes Ahead heard about the God that the Crows had always called on, the Maker, the Creator. They knew that there was a being who created everything. Goes Ahead heard that this Creator had given his only son to battle for them, to force down the evil forces, to defeat the forces of evil around them, to protect them and to give them life with him by dying, by giving his own life and being raised up again with such power from his Father. This is what I believe Goes Ahead thought:

There can be no greater power than to bring life back into a son and sit with him where his lodge is. What a magnificent place that must be – a huge lodge – a great chief's lodge, a chief who made all things, who was so powerful that he created and made the substances that keep us alive, and the shelters that we have. Then he decided that we need to live with him, and in order for us to do that he would have to cleanse us. We have such evil in our minds and our hearts that he sent his only son and said, "Die for them. Put your lance in the ground before the enemy and challenge him. Do this to save the people." And the son did. He put his lance in the ground and challenged the enemy. He even dropped his robe.

Goes Ahead was told that the son's name was Jesus Christ, *Ischawúuan-nakkaasuua*: that means "The One Pierced in the Hand." The Pierced in the Hand gave himself, saying, "Take me, kill me, and take my garments. Let my people go." That's what the warrior says, and that's what the Pierced in the Hand did. He even dropped his splendid robe when he was killed. A great warrior goes forth and says, "Take me and let my people go." And the enemy kills him and takes his robe – his fine robe. He's dead. We bury him and that's it. But this One had a *holy* and powerful father who brought him back to life and said, "It's finished with you, now. It's finished. It's done." To his followers, the father said, "Don't cut yourself or pierce yourself or hurt yourself because my son did all that for you. He's done all that for you. And I have taken him with me. He's sitting at my right hand." With Indians, the right-hand place was for their son, always. "Someday he will come after you and take you to be with us; whatever we have is yours. You are the heirs."

Goes Ahead said, "What greater thing can anyone do for any people – for any people? This day my heart bows before him, and I will take the cross that he asked us to carry. I will carry it from this day forth. Those of you who wish to do the same can follow me. I'm going to that place where they teach about him, and I'm going to tell the missionary that I'm going to be a part of that now." Some of the people cried because he had thrown all the medicine bundles and things that he inherited from bygone days into the Little Bighorn River. He did it in the month when the water was high and swift (that's probably March), so that it could take them away quickly. He threw in pieces of animal fat with them, as was the custom of the people. Some of the people cried and said, "What are we going to do now? Something terrible is going to happen to you for doing this. You can't do this." They cried; some women wailed. But he had this great spirit that came forth, and he was baptized. He was absolutely committed to Christianity after that. Some of the people followed Goes Ahead, and some did not. He was posted as the first deacon in the Baptist church in the Reno District. There were people turning to Christ in other districts, but this was in the Reno District, there at Crow Agency. My brother Johnny told me that this picture of him with his suit on was taken when he became a deacon. Pretty Shield was under his influence that she must do what he did, so she was converted, too; she was baptized at the same time he was. As long as there was an interpreter, she attended church every Sunday. She called the missionary "Great Boy." When she wanted to give money to the church, she would untie the corner of her muffler, and there would be a few coins. She'd stand at the churchyard gate and call "Great Boy" from his study, which was near the gate. Then she'd give him the coins and say in Indian, "This is for the Lord." I've seen that happen more than once.

I think my grandma may have been a little slower to give up her Crow powers than Goes Ahead was. My brother told me a story about a time before I was born; it must have been about 1916. Pretty Shield and Goes Ahead lived in a log house near Benteen – not the one my father built but an earlier one. In my mind, it seems to me it was a two-room log house, and there was a shed with it. In this shed Pretty Shield would store her dried foods like jerky, roots, and berries. Well, this one time the cupboard was bare, you might say. The government had given the men rifles, but they were without shells, so they couldn't go hunting. Georgie, my brother, a young boy, ran in and said, "Grandma, have you got any bread to eat? I'm hungry." Grandma said, "We haven't got a thing left here." Georgie insisted, "I'm hungry. I want some bread." She picked up her blanket, her little cotton blanket. She threw it over her shoulder and

Goes Ahead and Pretty Shield together, c. 1895. He is wearing his presidential medallion, and she is in an elk tooth dress.

said, "I'm going to the trading post. *Hám biiwáaaachilee.*" That means, "I'll ask for some luck so I can get some things." Maybe she was even going to ask if they would give her something until she could pay later.

She caught a ride on the road between Lodge Grass and Crow Agency. It was a gravel road. Someone picked her up and took her on in. She got off at the store. It was early in the morning; the storekeeper was just opening the door. He saw Pretty Shield there, and he let her in and said, "Good morning, Pretty Shield. I'll get this till ready in a little bit, and I'll be right with you." He started counting the money that he was putting into his till – going all through it. While he was doing that, Grandma stood there with her fists clenched. She just kept them clenched, while she was concentrating on what the man was doing, putting the money in the cashbox there. All at once she felt something go into her right hand. She kept it there. She didn't even open her fist. She didn't look. "Okay, now, Pretty Shield, what do you want?" the man asked. "I want some good meat, and I want to pick it out," Grandma told him. Her right fist was still clenched. He took her back there into the walk-in cooler. She pointed to the hindquarter, part of the hindquarter of a beef up there, and said, "I want some of that." So he cut it up for her and wrapped it up and gave it to her. "What else?" She got flour, grease, baking powder, sugar, hardtack. When she got done, the storekeeper said, "Now wait a minute. I want to see your money before I sack it up." So she opened her fist. There was twenty dollars. She used part of it, and she kept the other. The grocer put her food in little sacks for her, and she caught a ride home. She went in and cooked – cooked the meal. Goes Ahead asked her, "How did you get this? Where did you get the money?" She wiped her face. Georgie said she took the end of her scarf and wiped her face with it and said, "I got it with the storekeeper's own money." Then she told Grandpa what happened. Goes Ahead knew her powers. He said, "I told you not to ever do these things again." She said, "I know you did, and I'm sorry, but my grandchild was hungry. I had to do something." That was Pretty Shield.

When Goes Ahead became ill in body and knew that he must go, he saw a vision of Jesus Christ and the evil one. He said there was an evil one there, and they fought, they fought a fierce battle over his soul. He said, "I watched, and in the end, the Son of God won. He was victorious, and I was happy. I was glad. Now," he said, "it won't be long until he'll be coming after me." He seemed to know, so he wished to have his lodge put right next to the Little Bighorn River, where the bridge now is on the main highway – just down there from the bank, the south side – that's where his camp was. There Pretty Shield and he stayed until he passed away. That was in 1919. He died in a tipi by the Little Bighorn River, which he loved. He loved that river so much.

Grandma was a widow for twenty-five years. There were other, older men who wanted her. This one man said, "I have no heirs. If you marry me, then I'll take your grandchildren as my own. My land will be yours and theirs." Still she said, "No. It's not that I dislike you. I appreciate your concern and everything, but I belong to *Basáakoosh*. I want him to see me as he left me."

After Goes Ahead died, Pretty Shield received a pension check from the government because he had scouted for the army. It wasn't much, maybe thirty or thirty-five dollars each month; she used it to help feed her grandchildren. She couldn't read the calendar or anything like that, but always when a moon, a month, had passed, she heard this song:

Baawaaláache húuk
Biiwiiíkaak húuk
Biiwiiíkaak húuk
Baawaaláache húuk

The paper is coming
It sees me, it's coming
It sees me, it's coming
The paper is coming

She had a song for everything. My grandma had a song for everything.

3

My Camp Is in a
Different Place

When I was about eight years old, Grandma gave me a new name. She thought I was sort of sickly all the time, and she changed my name. She didn't have a ceremony. She did it at home by herself, and a few people in my family were there. My first name had been "Lady That Searches for Rocks with Holes in Them," but *Biá Asíitash*, meaning "Well-Known Woman," became my new name. Later Grandma would laugh and say, "It's good that I changed your name. You are feeling better, and your name is better, too. If you had kept that old name, people might have shortened it to Looks for Holes." She was always saying something crazy. I was glad she changed my name.[1]

I started to school just about the same time that Grandma changed my name. When we went out in the hills to dig turnips, I knew I was missing school, but I didn't care. Neither did Grandma. She always said, "Well, you know what to do. You know how to pick this food. We know the foods that we eat – the berries, all these things. Learn them and learn them well. And sew, sew moccasins and garments. Learn how to sew and cook and keep a house well. That's what you will have to do as a woman. Let the boys go to school. You don't have to go to school. Just keep your lodge good, and plenty to eat in it. That's your job." I said, "Yes, yes, Grandma." I agreed.

The school officials came to her. They came to her many times, and I'd play sick. I'd scratch myself, really scratch myself until I almost gouged my skin. And I'd say, "I'm getting chicken pox." Grandma would say, "She's sick." She told the school people I was sick, and they'd be kind of afraid, and they'd say, "All right. We'll check later, but she's got to start to school." I was eight years old before I started to school. We got away with it so long, Grandma and I.

Before I went to school, Grandma had to make two trips a day to the highway so that the older kids could catch the school bus. Every morning she harnessed the horses to the wagon, crossed the Little Bighorn River – drove those horses right through the water – and went on, maybe about two miles, to the Old Bears or the Yarlotts. There she let the kids off. The bus stopped there on the highway. She'd go back home, free the horses and hobble them until time to pick up the kids. Then she'd throw the harnesses on the horses again and go back to the highway where the bus stopped. Twice a day – it was a tremendous undertaking for an old lady, now that I think back. But then I thought, "Grandma's capable. She will do anything. She'll last forever." I'm very awed when I think of my grandmother's life.

When I started to school, Grandma decided to move to Crow Agency so she wouldn't have to drive the wagon every day. It was a big change for us. To Grandma it was *bashannáshe iiháatdeeluk*, meaning "my camp is in a different place." To me it meant I was growing up in a little town instead of the country.

Our place in Crow[2] was a frame house covered with tarpaper, brick-looking stuff, around it. It was nice, a warm place, but it was just the one big room. It wasn't all that huge either. I remember the look of the door, when I think back to it. It was a light green, rough-like door. Had a screen door. Inside to the left was a makeshift cupboard, probably orange crates that were nailed in there, to put a few things in. Then the washbasin and the water would be there. I remember the dipper that we used to drink out of. It was above the basin, hung up on the wall. Right next to it was a big homemade table, not great big but big enough to seat all of us around it when we were there. There were benches rather than chairs – always slid under the table. Maybe there might have been a chair or two around, but those benches were under the table to make room. Past that table was a corner that had different boxes or suitcases to contain our clothes. Also, they slid some footlockers or suitcases under the bed. That bed was for us girls. Right in the middle of the room – a Monarch stove. It had the warmer and the place where you heated water and a large oven. Behind that Monarch stove, in a corner behind the door, was my grandmother's pallet bed. It had a mattress, and it had a buffalo robe, always. She liked to sleep in a buffalo robe. She had her own pillows that she used, too. That's where I slept most of my young life. She always told me stories, and she would tell me to answer her with "Eh, eh," that sound, so she would know I was listening. When I stopped saying, "Eh, eh," she knew I was asleep. Then she quit telling the stories.

Most of the stories we'd hear quite often, but there were times when she'd reminisce about her own life. "When I was a little girl like you," she'd say, "I had my own mother but I was given to my aunt to comfort her. She lost her little girls and would not be comforted, so I was told to go with her. Oh, how I longed to be with my mother, but then I had my business to do with my aunt. I had to heal her heart before I could go back to my own mother. My own heart was longing for my own mother when I was with my aunt. Oh, but I also loved my auntie. She treated me well and I learned to love her. When I grew older, and her heart was comforted, then I got to live with my own mother quite often. But my aunt was always there, and I always took her as a mother."[3]

This aunt had bear cubs for pets because bears were her medicine. Grandma used to tell us about when she had her own bear cub. She took care of him, and he meant so much to her. He became almost human. He did the human things that they did, tried to help with his mouth. If they were dragging wood, he tried to drag wood. He would mess up a tarp because he wanted to help lay it out. When they had to get after him, he would pout. She said he'd sit over there and pout, and they'd all laugh. Pretty Shield laughed when she was telling about it. She still laughed at it. The bear sat with them when they ate. They sat on the ground, and he sat next to Pretty Shield and ate out of a dish, a bone dish, ate like everybody else. He even rode Pretty Shield's horse with her. Finally there came a time when she noticed the bear was growing up. Sometimes he would come when they were sitting around the tarp, but sometimes he wouldn't come; he was venturing out someplace. Once in a while he came and sat by Pretty Shield, and she said, "I looked up at him. Now I had to look up to the skies to see him because he was so tall." That little bear was so tall, so tall even sitting there, he just towered above them. She had to let him go. It really broke her heart.[4]

Another time she had a little buffalo. The little buffalo she had was motherless. They fed it, and it got used to being around their camp, and everybody always knew that little buffalo. It hung around the camp, and the kids played with it. They went round him and chased him, and he didn't even pay attention to the kids. She loved that little buffalo so much. She would have it grazing nearby while she was working. He would graze next to her and she'd talk to it. He would go, "Ump! Ump! Ump! Ump!"

She said, "I knew it was trying to tell me, 'I hear you talking.'" So they laughed at him because he tried to talk and couldn't do it.

When the little calf grew up and was getting pretty big, her dad told her to let it go with a herd of buffalo that was nearby. He said, "It doesn't belong here, and it may be going into its season of being a young male. Let it go or it will get mean." She let it go. She whipped it. They whipped it for her, over toward the buffalo herd. It would look back, and she'd look at it – just as if they were both crying. It was making noise with its mouth, and she had tears dripping down her face. The next morning they got up, and there it was, standing in front of her tipi. It came back and stood in front of her tipi. She was glad; she said, "I went and put my arms around him and I was so happy. He was doing that little 'Ump! Ump! Ump! Ump.' It was happy also, but they drove it off again." Finally it went with the herd, and she said as they watched it go, it grew. It grew right in their eyesight and became as big as the others. She said that her dad told her it was a buffalo with powers or a phenomenal animal. "It's a strange buffalo," he said. She never saw it again after that.[5]

Usually, there were three or four of us who lived in Grandma's little shack. Cerise went to boarding school and then got married not long after we left the Benteen house. She went to live with her man in a nice home in Wyola. Frances got married and went with her man to Wyola, but she wouldn't stay there, so they fixed up another little shack, next to Pretty Shield's, and came back to live. My brother Georgie married Mary Anne Reed, and they lived in other places. Later, their daughter Etheline came to live with Grandma. My brother Johnny Wilson got married and didn't have a place to live. There was no room in Grandma's house, especially for a man and his wife, so they decided to go look in the shed. The coal shed was made of ties from the railroad, ties that had been pulled up and left. They moved all the coal dust to one side and piled it there. They put a curtain between that and where they stayed, and right down on the ground they made their bed. They lived in the shed until they were able to find a place that was better.[6]

During the day, Grandma was outside our little shack in Crow most of the time. She liked to work outside if the weather was good. She had a place for a fire and a large stone where she could pound meat or berries. Usually one or two other old ladies came and worked with her. Our little shack was right in the middle of the neighborhood. Behind us, against the highway, was a space where people lived in more of these tarpaper shacks. Old Horn lived there, Hattie Old Horn. Next to her was a filling station that they called George's Place. Up there was a water pump, next to his station, where we got water sometimes. Then there was Amelia Passes, and next to that was Howell Hoops, who had a sprawling shack house. It had been built onto to make a little church. It was the Four Square Church. Beyond that were the Yarlotts and the Old Bears and Jack Stewart and his family.

Across the road that ran through the village, Max Big Man and his family lived in a large home that looked like a log house to me. That was a big family, and Cordelia, Max's wife, was an industrious woman. She could take a saw and a hammer and put up a house like anybody. I think that's how she got her nice big home. It was her doing, and it was goodly built – a strong house. Next to her was Dexter Williamson, who was a shaman. Next to Dexter was the John Deernose place, which was an excellent home. He had a nice big home there, and I loved to go to that home because it was so grand. The Real Bird and the Medicine Tail families lived north of the Deernose house, and the Dave Stewart household. To the left of our shack was Frank Shane. He was my uncle – my father's uncle, so he would be my great uncle. He had a nice frame house, nice and white. The sheds – in those days we had outhouses – were always painted white, too. He had a pump right outside his house where some of the neighborhood people went to get water. That's where I got water for Grandma and me. As long as I lived there, I hauled water – *buckets* of water; I liked to do it because it made me strong. Then the Baptist church completed a kind of circle, and across from it lived a bus driver named Al Steen. He was a white man. His wife knew my mother, said she was a friend of hers. I wish I could have asked her questions about my mother, but I didn't.

Those are the families I know of that made up that community. It was on one side of the Little Bighorn River, the north side of the river. Most of us who had these small houses there had homes in the country that were built pretty good. On the banks of the river, where we used to play, there was a lot of willow and some box elder trees. There were chokecherries and a lot of bull berry along that river. Mint grew near the water's edge, the kind of mint that we would use for tea. We gathered it sparingly because others wanted it, too.

A short paved road led from our neighborhood to the main street of Crow Agency. It was just one main street with business establishments. The ones I remember were a lumber and hardware place, an ice cream parlor, and a mercantile place. Then from the mercantile store was the

Blue Front Garage – the Blue Front Garage, we called it. On down was Johnny Burns's Confectionery, and next to him was a cafe and bakery together. Also there was a pool hall for the men to gather and talk; then the Richardson and Small Trading Post. I believe that might have been the first trading post at Crow Agency.

Across the way was a park which was a rectangle, probably a couple of acres, with a cement sidewalk around it. It had benches and a pavilion where they could have programs. Not far from the park was a large gymnasium or community center where dances or basketball games were held. At one point my dad bought an old movie projector and showed movies in that building. He showed Disney movies, and people paid five cents to see them. The hospital and lots of government buildings were beyond the park, and on one side was a flour mill. That's where people who had grain leases could get flour. The Campbell Corporation leased Grandma's land. They would give her part money and part flour for the year, so when we ran out of flour she would go to the mill to get some more.

The depot and the railroad were on the western edge of town. The Crow people liked the railroad because they could go to Billings on the train. When they got their lease checks, they liked to go shopping in Billings. The women would go to the dime stores, and the men would buy hardware, gloves, tools, things they needed. That was Billings then. I went to Billings so few times in my childhood that I barely remember it.

Near our neighborhood, in the Little Bighorn River, there was an island where people lived. They camped there. I remember a lady called Eliza. She and her children were Crees, and they came to camp there. They had a relative that married into the Crows, so they followed him, I think. She had a couple of big boys and a girl named Mary. They lived in a tent, and they were very poor. Eliza always had a kind of roll-your-own cigarette in the corner of her mouth. Even if it was not lit, she had it there. She used to cook outside. She had this great big deep frying pan with a long handle to it. She'd fill that with potatoes and she'd add water every now and then until they were cooked. Even though we had something to eat at home, I would long to eat Eliza's potatoes. I'd go over to the island, and I'd wait and wait and wait there, and when they'd start to eat, she'd give me some, and I thought I was in seventh heaven. She made "push bread," too. She had nothing else. But the way she fixed that bread – I relished that. She just mixed flour with water and baking powder, then she let it sit next to a warm fire. I'd see her turn the bowl now and then so one side wouldn't get too warm. After it sat there about an hour, she

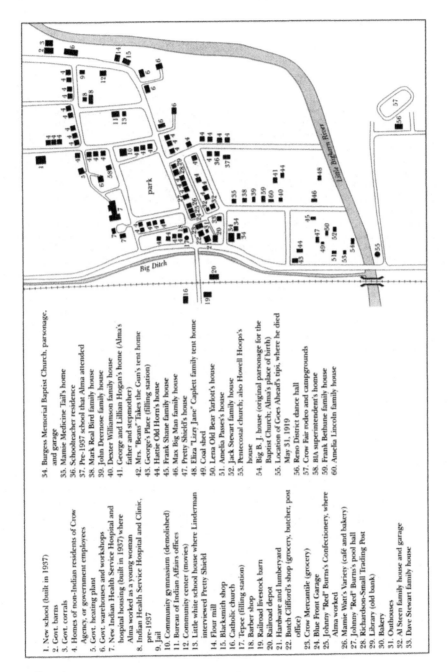

1. New school (built in 1937)
2. Govt. barns
3. Govt. corrals
4. Homes of non-Indian residents of Crow Agency, or government employees
5. Govt. heating plant
6. Govt. warehouses and workshops
7. New Indian Health Service Hospital and hospital housing (built in 1937) where Alma worked as a young woman
8. Indian Health Service Hospital and Clinic, pre-1937
9. Jail
10. Community gymnasium (demolished)
11. Bureau of Indian Affairs offices
12. Community center (movies)
13. Little white school house where Linderman interviewed Pretty Shield
14. Flour mill
15. Blacksmith shop
16. Catholic church
17. Tepee (filling station)
18. Barber shop
19. Railroad livestock barn
20. Railroad depot
21. Hardware and humberyard
22. Butch Clifford's shop (grocery, butcher, post office)
23. Crow Mercantile (grocery)
24. Blue Front Garage
25. Johnny "Red" Burns's Confectionery, where Alma worked
26. Mamie Watt's Variety (café and bakery)
27. Johnny "Red" Burns's pool hall
28. Richardson-Small Trading Post
29. Library (old bank)
30. Bakery
31. Outhouses
32. Al Steen family house and garage
33. Dave Stewart family house

34. Burgess Memorial Baptist Church, parsonage, and garage
35. Mamie Medicine Tail's home
36. Schoolteacher residence
37. Pre-1937 school that Alma attended
38. Mark Real Bird family house
39. John Deernose family house
40. Dexter Williamson family house
41. George and Lillian Hogan's home (Alma's father and stepmother)
42. Mrs. "Beans" Takes the Gun's tent home
43. George's Place (filling station)
44. Hattie Old Horn's house
45. Frank Shane family house
46. Max Big Man family house
47. Pretty Shield's house
48. Eliza "Lizzy Jane" Caplett family tent home
49. Coal shed
50. Lena Old Bear Yarlott's house
51. Amelia Pases's house
52. Jack Stewart family house
53. Pentecostal church; also Howell Hoops's house
54. Big B. J. house (original parsonage for the Baptist Church; Alma's place of birth)
55. Location of Goes Ahead's tipi, where he died May 31, 1919
56. Reno District dance hall
57. Crow Fair rodeo and campgrounds
58. BIA superintendent's home
59. Frank Bethune family home
60. Amelia Lincoln family house

3. Crow Agency, 1930s

Crow Agency, mid-1920s. The Burgess Memorial Baptist Church stands out in the center.
Photo by Laura Bentley; used by permission of Myrtle B. Hubley.

kneaded it, then made it into rounds that were as big as a skillet. She put
a forked stick into a hole that was in the side of the skillet, and she pushed
it against the hot coals and turned it until all the bread was brown and
nice. Eliza called it push bread.

She and her children coughed all the time. My sisters told me, "Don't
go over there. They have tuberculosis." TB was rampant in those days. I
went anyway.

I remember in our neighborhood, anyone who was out of sugar, flour,
lard, the basic things, would send a cup or a little jar by one of their
kids to say, "Could I borrow some sugar or flour or tallow for cherries?"
There was no hesitation. We knew that they were going to pay it back, so it
was always given to them without any questions. They shared. When they
were in good, why, they'd pay it back. What they borrowed was always paid
back. I've seen my grandmother give her last biscuit to a visitor. While
Grandma was pounding meat or pounding cherries, she'd think of one or
two of her friends, and in her little work area there she'd put a couple of
handfuls aside, and she'd keep on working. She'd say, "That's for Lizard
That Shows," and she'd pound away. After she got a little bit more, she'd
say, "Well, maybe I'll take this for Beaver That Passes. I'll put a little fat
with it and they'll like it." And she did. She wrapped it up in a little cloth
with a piece of fat in it, and she gave it to them. They would say, "*Aho,*

búchilee hŭk – Thanks, you have blessed me." Grandma gave and gave and gave. She prayed and she ministered to people. As long as she was doing for someone else and as long as she was needed, she was happy.

There was an old lady in the neighborhood who called me when she wanted to have a laugh. Lena Old Bear Yarlott, old Lena. She wasn't able to see too well. She'd say, "Will somebody tell Pretty Shield's granddaughter that I want her to come and visit me?" My grandmother would say, "Go and sit with her, " and I'd go. I'd say, "I'm Pretty Shield's grandchild." She'd laugh. Maybe she'd give me a little something to eat, maybe prunes or berries. So I'd be eating it, and she'd talk to me, and I'd answer her. She only wanted to talk with me and hear me talk because I pronounced my Indian words funny. It wasn't that I had a speech impediment, but I used the wrong sound: I'd use the sound of *g* instead of the sound of *b*. Old Lena was one of the encyclopedias of the Crow language, and she'd laugh when I said something wrong. If she wanted to laugh, she called for me. That's one thing they did; they longed to laugh sometimes. They'd think of something to laugh about, so Lena always called for me, and when I pronounced my words, she laughed. When she got enough of her laugh, she'd say, "Go play. Go play, I'll call on you later." She always gave me a little something. I'd go and tell my grandma that I sat with Lena, and she'd say, "Good."

Grandma liked to laugh. She'd break out with a song and make everybody laugh because of what it might be that she was singing about. I don't know where she got tunes that were so different from one another, but she had them. It's hard, it's hard to get those tunes. She always had different tunes. When she went to get groceries, she teased the storekeeper. She might say something about the garment he had on. If he was wearing a vest, she'd look at it and try to pull it together. She'd say, "*Eelásh bachhíisaak* – it is too small for your waist." "Hey, Pretty Shield," he'd say, "are you going to tie a string to it and pull it together?"

She spoke no English. Nothing. The storekeepers knew Crow, or sometimes she pointed at what she wanted. Then they would say, "Let me see your money. Let me see if you can cover this." I think the storekeepers were honest with her. In fact, they tried to help her. They lived in the community, too. When Grandma finished shopping, she said "*Aho.*" Then the grocer would say, "You're welcome." If it was the other way around, if he said, "*Aho,*" she would say, "Eee wahken." I always wondered what she meant by that "Eee wahken," because I always heard her say it. Quite a while afterward I realized she was saying, "You're welcome."

Grandma didn't always have much money to clothe her grandchildren. So the storekeepers sold her things that were sort of going out of style but still usable, still new, to try to help her balance her budget. My little girlfriends already had little oxfords and sandals, but I was still wearing high-top, laced-up, pointed-toe, leather, bootlike shoes. Those were my new shoes, and the children knew it. I think their parents knew that Pretty Shield, "she's an old lady. She's not working to make any more money." They told their children, "Now she's got new shoes, but not like yours, so don't laugh. She has to wear them." Most of the little girls I played with would say, "Oh, you got new shoes." They'd rub their hands on them and make me feel good. I liked those shoes. They wrapped around my legs and protected my legs while the other girls were getting thorns in theirs. At times they'd even say, "We want some shoes like hers. We want some like hers because she doesn't get hurt."

Before we went into shoes, Grandma made moccasins for all of us. We had good pairs of moccasins. They were plain. Once in a while they had a few beads on top. They were pretty plain. She was glad when she didn't have to keep making moccasins for us. I knew some girls, much older than I was, who were still wearing high-top moccasins to school. They had manufactured dresses, but they wore moccasins.

Grandma wore long dresses. They were doubled; maybe she even wore three skirts. I know for sure there were two, two on top of one another, made of cotton. She always had her medicine with her, like bear root.[7] She tied that up to her belt. Then, she'd lift up her first skirt, and there was her money pouch underneath that skirt. I guess she was kind of hiding it. She'd have her blanket and her muffler. She used her little blanket for a pallet on her stomach, against the digging, when she dug. She went without panties; older ladies didn't wear panties. And when girdles came out, she said it wasn't good to have them. She didn't think you should have girdles. She always wore moccasins, but she appreciated very much the overshoes for wintertime, for wet times. She said it saved the moccasins. She liked some other modern things, too. She thought that those manufactured combs with big teeth were better than porcupine tails, and she really enjoyed eating canned tomatoes mixed with macaroni.

She was glad when needles came in, but she never used thread on her moccasins. She said, "No, I have to have sinew." She would take her moccasin off and she would examine it all over, all along the edges to see where the sinew was weak. She took a needle and split the sinew. She pulled it through her mouth to wet it a little bit; she rolled it on her leg, rolled the whole thing on her leg, kept rolling it until it did look like thread and all the rough edges were gone. Then she threaded her needle – they weren't very long pieces – and repaired her moccasins. She would go over, over, and over again until she used this thread up. Then she'd take the needle off and make a knot there. If she came to the end of the thread and had to have more, she did the same thing again. She tied the new piece to the other thread and continued to go on until she finished. It seemed to me that anybody who used sinew threaded the needle quite often because the pieces were short, and they had to keep threading the needle with a new piece. I used to watch her do that, used to watch her do that. I even can see, I can even see her mouth, the way it went when the thread went through. I'd *watch* my grandma, watch her repair her moccasin. She took a piece of thick – the thick part of the hide of an animal and put it around her finger for a thimble.[8]

Sometimes Grandma massaged my feet. She rubbed her hands all over my foot, underneath my foot, and over it. It felt so good. Then I would say, "Grandma, I'll do that to your feet." That's when I used to see her cotton stockings with the toes and heels cut out. The old ladies cut the toes and heels out of their stockings. They were the first ones to wear stirrups.

I was thinking about all the things she did to feed us. She never quit looking, looking, looking. In the winter she was always sewing, or fixing meat that my brothers brought her, or dressing hides. Oh, it was just a tremendous going-on. She was happy when she worked with meat; it seemed like she never tired. But when she worked with a hide, scraping it, toward the end of the day I would hear her say, "I'm wasted." She didn't say tired; she said, "I'm wasted." That meant that she had to let it go and rest a bit. She said it like the strength was gone, so, "I'll quit now." Even though she didn't want to give way to the feeling, it was "I'm wasted," meaning "The strength is gone."

She always told us, "Don't sit around! It's worse than working! You think working is bad. Sitting around is worse, and if you sit around, you get nothing done. You have nothing to eat. You have nothing toward your house. You have no wood. You have no food. To sit around is worse than working. I don't like to see myself or my children sit around. They should be doing something."

She always said, "Don't waste the day, because it's not a long day. When it's night you rest. And don't keep lying on your back all the time. Some day you're going to lie on your back forever. You'll sleep forever. You'll

Pretty Shield working with meat.

sleep forever, so get up and do something while it's still day." She splashed water on our faces when we didn't get up in the morning. She called us and called us, and if we didn't wake up, she'd say, "I'm bringing the water." If we were still in bed or covered our heads, she just tore the blankets off our faces and sprinkled our faces with cold water. She dipped her fingers in cold water and splashed our faces with it. We got up then. I saw her do that to Pearl a lot of times.

Crow Agency is not the same today. Even the trees seem sad. If they could tell stories, they would tell about the once happy times, I believe. And the lanes and trails we used to take – why, I could tell you almost every trail where we went to get wood. I always went with Grandma to gather wood. It was one of our chores. We went walking, and we gathered up sticks and limbs that had fallen off trees. She stacked them up, and I helped her. We piled it along the river or around the town in Crow. When she got ready, we went back to pick it up. Then we put it in her blanket; we wrapped it up and tied it into Grandma's blanket. I helped push it onto her back. Then she caught the blanket and pulled the corners together. I walked alongside her, and when it was sagging, I'd push it up for her again. It's a funny thing – as I got older, I never tried to shoulder any of it; I just put it on her. Then, if a few pieces dropped out, I would put them back in her blanket. I knew how to do it. I knew just what kind of stick was a good burning stick. When we got home, she chopped it, but when I got bigger, I did the chopping.

We had our tools out under the trees. Those cottonwood trees seemed like they really strengthened their muscles to help us when we put our hides on them to scrape. I remember we scraped deer hide and elk hide, and threw the scrapings out to the dogs. The dogs would clear up the place. Sometimes my grandmother put money in a Calumet baking powder can. She sealed it, and she put it in a hole under a certain tree. Nobody knew it but the two of us. She left it there until she was in real need; then she would go and get it. She would tell me, "Don't follow me," or "Don't tell anybody where I'm going." I knew what she meant. I knew where she was going, so I didn't tell.

Grandma still washed her clothes in the river. When we went swimming, she had Fels Naphtha soap with her. Before she could get soap, she had used sand or even dirt to clean a stain, but she started using soap. She soaped the garment as she rubbed it against her leg. Then she rinsed it in the river, wrung it out, and threw it over branches to dry. Sometimes she put it on even though it was only half dry, kind of damp. "It's good. It keeps you cool," she said. Later, much later, she bought a washing machine. Pearl and Mayme operated it. Grandma bought it with her lease money. They went to Hardin to get it; it was gasoline operated. We

Pretty Shield with firewood on her shoulders.

didn't have electricity then, either. We had lamps and candles. When the
oil ran out, we went to candles.

They kept that washing machine in the house, but when they used it,
they put it out the door so all the putt-putt noise and gasoline would be
outside. It had a hand wringer, so they pushed the clothes through the
wringer into the rinse water, which was in a galvanized tub. Pretty Shield

would not touch it. She would not touch it. She still washed her own garments in the river as long as Mayme let her. Finally, Mayme did all the laundry.

The Little Bighorn was not muddy like it is now. We used to be able to see little minnows and rocks, right to the bottom. Grandma showed me how to dog swim, dog paddle. She could make that Little Bighorn seem small. She took that dog stroke and hit her foot, splashed the water with her foot, and boy, she shot out there about five feet each stretch. She was really fast at that kind of swimming, and that's the kind of swimming I learned from her. She used to put a red mark on my leg before I went swimming. She prepared her red paint with grease, and she put it all along my leg, the outside of my leg. She talked at the same time she did it, prayed that I would be all right, safe, and that the water animals would see it and leave me alone. She said, "Never go swimming until you tell me." She didn't want me to swim without it. When Pretty Shield went swimming, she took some tallow and gave it to the river and asked the river people to "please ignore us. We're just swimming." It was a ritual that she had.

If there were just girls at the river, we swam bare naked, but we also had our swimming dresses. We swam with dresses on, maybe no sleeves, but they would be long and loose. We swam all over the place in those dresses and dove, too. When we made the water come underneath our dresses, it made big bubbles in front, as if we had big bellies. We floated around like that. Going home, we just left our swimming dresses on. We put on our shoes and went home. The dresses would dry. We'd hang them someplace in the house. My place was on the bedstead. It was a special dress for swimming.

Before we went swimming, Grandma always said, "When you go in the water and you see otter, come out and let them have the water. Don't let them brush past you – your body." Shes told us that many times, because "if one of them slides against your body and touches you that way, it means bad, even death." I remember one time when we were in the Benteen area, Cerise brought a friend with her. She was part Crow and part white, a very beautiful girl. They were swimming in this big, deep whirlpool place where we were advised not to swim in the first place. While they were swimming and playing around and laughing, being careful that they didn't go into one of these swirls, an otter came, and it brushed the body of this friend of Cerise. They hollered and got out, excited by it, and told my grandmother. Grandma said, "It's bad when they do that. They don't come around usually. If they come around and do this to you, it's usually bad. She should have her folks ask someone to do a cleansing." Of course, they didn't believe it. Maybe it was within a month, she was dead. The doctor told them she might have died of pneumonia.

One time, I had to be cleansed. I guess I was about six or seven years old. There was a bag that hung above the bedstead. I knew it was a holy bag, a sacred bag; Grandma had told us, "Nobody ever touches that bag. Nobody ever brings it down." But I was a child. I was curious and wanted to know what was in it. I got up on the bedstead, and I climbed up there to this bag. I don't know the design it had. It was tied, flapped over and tied, then it had a string to hang it by. I opened the flap and looked in. There were more bags in there. So I opened one, and there was another little bag. I opened the little bag, and that's when it blew in my face. It just went "Wooosh!" About that time, Pretty Shield caught me. She jerked me off that place, and she was yelling all the time. I was on the floor. I wasn't hurt, but I was very bewildered. I felt this stuff on my face. It felt like when you get dirt on it. I thought, "It's on my face. I'm frightened. I'm frightened because it itches." I said, "Grandma, it blew in my face." She said, "You could go blind from this." She had me wash my face with water. She put some cedar on the stove, a handful, and it started to give out smoke. She grabbed a cover (it may have been a tarp, because it didn't feel like a quilt to me), and she put it over me. Then, with a little coal bucket shovel, she brushed in that incense.9

She was *praying*, and she was whipping me with the smoke. In her prayer, she said that I was a child, a very small child. She said, "You have to forgive her for this because children can do anything. Without guidance, they'll do anything. If you forgive her, I'm cleansing her, and I'm asking you to be kind to her. Be kind to her." Then she said, "*Aho.* Thank you," as if it were already done. There was so much of that smoke under the tarp that I had my eyes closed. I didn't want to cough. When I came out, I opened my eyes to see if I could see, to see that I had not been blinded. She sat me down. She said, "When you're talked to by anyone who *knows* about something, believe it. Do it. Keep it here." She pointed to her chest. "Keep it here and remember what you're told not to do or what you're told to do. Keep it here, and leave things alone." She talked for about an hour. I don't remember what all she said. I do remember she said to obey those things.

In the summer, we went to the Benteen area sometimes. My dad did some ranching there.10 He had some Texas longhorns. He used to butcher them, and maybe once a year he butchered for Pretty Shield. I remember that was a real happy time. There was a gathering of our family and friends, and Grandma went to the stream and cleaned everything. She was very happy doing that, cooking, boiling meat, and feeding people. She was preparing things she liked to prepare. When the Crows first got beef, she could hardly eat it. She said beef stunk. She said, "Beef stinks so bad. I never really thought it would replace buffalo. When I first tasted it, I wondered why white people liked it. It almost made me sick." She even hated the texture of it. But after a while she was right there having fun, too, because she got accustomed to it. When she was fooling with meat, slicing it for jerky, she was happy. She always had a smile on her face then. When Pretty Shield was happy and merry, I was too. I liked that.[11]

Another time she was happy was when they had hand game. Maybe the old ladies in the neighborhood would get together and have hand game. Grandma was happy and playful, and she tried to outdo the others. She was a good player, and they were always leery of her in the hand game. She sang,

Baaxshéesheweewaawaam
Baschíimmeeleeduuk

I can't help but win
I can't help but beat you guys

That song. I could hear her singing that song, and she'd laugh. She and her friends had these little bets, maybe a little cup, or a blanket, or dress goods. First they laid their bets down. Then they had this little bone, and each one in her turn moved it from hand to hand. The other team had to say which hand the bone was in. They kept a tally of little sticks that they moved around here and there until the game was over. Grandma said that she watched the eyes of the one with the bone; she watched the eyes very closely and the eye seemed to twitch over the hand that held the bone. She liked to gamble.

Grandma liked talking to Linderman, too. She was overjoyed when he was going to come: "Oh, my friend is coming. My friend is coming. Sign Talker. Sign Talker is coming. I have to be ready." He brought skins for her – deer skins, elk skins, all tanned – and she made dresses for her grandchildren. Plus the silver dollars, those silver dollars that he gave her.

The place where I remember Linderman and the two ladies, Pretty Shield and Kitty Deernose, the interpreter, was mainly in this little white house, a schoolhouse. There was a potbellied stove in there for heat, with a table right next to it and shelves behind it. Many times they sat around that table, next to the heat. There were trees around there that I used to climb, way up on top, and just look all over and wait for my grandmother while she was talking to Linderman.

When he came, he was in a car that looked like a Model T Ford. Sometimes he had a horse. Whether he borrowed it or not, I don't know, but he rode it around there. I remember his slick boots, his shiny boots, kind of brown and up to the knee almost. He had pants that were not like jeans, like today; they kind of puffed out a little on the side. He had a vest on, a leather vest. I saw him that way. He had glasses on, and he had a pipe. In my mind's eye, I have seen him while he was talking to Pretty Shield put one leg on a chair, next to the table, and he would have this pipe. He would clean it by banging it on a wooden bowl, clean it out while he was listening to the interpreter. It seems to me that he wasn't always sitting there, taking notes. Pretty Shield and Kitty Deernose would tell so much of what he wanted to know, then he wouldn't ask any more; the two women would be visiting, and he would take his paper and write down all that they'd just said. Many times he did that. Other times he'd turn his back on them and look out the window.

I'd watch this man because he was so different, different from other men. He was very kind to us. He would take time to talk with us and ask us little questions and make us feel like we were wanted around him. But other times he paid no attention to us, and this is when I would be watching him. I guess Ruby Deernose was with me, or Agnes Old Bear, and Pearl. We knew that when he closed the door to that little schoolhouse, we were to stay away.

He was a pretty laid-back person. I mean he wasn't what you'd call anxious about anything. I have seen a lot of men jump up and walk back and forth, then sit down. He wasn't that way. He'd look outside for quite a while, then he would turn back to the ladies. They would quit talking and pay attention to what he wanted to know next, as if it was a cue that they must now listen. He'd ask questions. He would bring up some remark or question, then Pretty Shield would start in.

When he was in the park, I think that's when he wanted to be out in nature. He wanted the feel of nature; he wanted to allow Pretty Shield to be enthusiastic about what she was saying, so he sometimes took her to a

Frank B. Linderman, much as Alma remembers him. Courtesy of Linderman heirs.

place where she would feel more free to talk, instead of being hemmed in by four walls. I remember him walking with Pretty Shield to the store from the park or the little schoolhouse. When they were walking, I would be thinking, "He's going to give Grandma some money." So I was happy. I was happy for Grandma and I was happy for myself, too. Sometimes he'd give us a nickel to go to the ice cream place and buy a cone.

I liked him because I know he liked me. I know *like* from discipline. A lot of people would discipline us and then talk to us, but he'd just come to us as we were. He talked to us in our environment. He just let us continue to play – let us continue to try to climb trees, but he'd be talking to one or two of us. Then he'd pull out lollipops, and he'd give us those candies. I imagine that's what we were kind of halfway waiting for. I just loved to be around him because his personality was so touching. He looked at us like he wanted to know all about us. He was good. *Everybody*, in fact, loved him – all the people that knew him, that got acquainted with him. There was no bad word about him. He was good. He was absolutely a man that the Indians loved to have around. He cared.

I picture Pretty Shield talking like this about Linderman: "I wonder what he's going to do with this writing." Then she'd kind of leave it, kind of stay off of it. I remember when they presented her with one of the first books. She took it and held it to her breast, close to her, close to her like it was important. My sister Cerise says that after a time Linderman came and gave Pretty Shield a copy. He said, "You can have as many books as you want, if you want them for your grandchildren." She said, "I want just one. When each one reads it they can tell me over again."[12] Linderman turned around to Cerise and asked, "Shall I send you one?" She said, "No, if I'm going to get one, I might as well buy it because that's what you're in this for, to sell the book." (She's kind of educated.) He said, "Pretty Shield's grandchildren are all of the same trait. They were raised by the same kind, motherly, caring woman that I see in Pretty Shield."[13]

While we lived in Crow, Grandma joined the Crow Women's Club. It had a state charter and was part of the national organization. Kate Stewart and Minnie Enchoff were the leaders. Some of the others in that club were Olive Vann, Stella Deernose, Sarah Shane, and Lorraine Real Bird. Sometimes Grandma traveled to different places around the state with the Women's Club leaders. They went to Helena, Miles City, Billings, and Livingston that I know of. I imagine she told a lot of stories in the Women's Club. When she went on these trips, I was always put into my brother's hands or one of my sister's: "You take care of her this time. You take care of her now." When we were all together and most of them were single, there was no problem. But when they started getting married and going off and I was left, it was just like I was running out of a mother again. I longed for Pretty Shield to come back when she went off somewhere.

As a young woman, when I got lonesome, I thought of that little corner where my grandmother slept in her buffalo robe and I'd get in there with her. That's where I wanted to be. If that little house remained and there was nobody in it, I would probably go there now – anytime I became very, very lonely or despondent. I would go in there and at least pray. I'd sit there and pray until I worked it out. That would be my place, if it was still there. The buffalo robe will not leave me. Many times, I feel it around me. I feel like somebody has their arms around me, very tenderly. It's comforting.

4

Turning the Storm

Every morning, every morning of the world, Pretty Shield went outside to pray. Sometimes she went into the hills above Crow Agency; other times she stayed near our shack. It was still dark, maybe three-thirty or four o'clock. Sometimes I felt her leave the buffalo robe, but I knew where she was going, so I'd go back to sleep. If I slept a long time, then woke up, and she was still gone, I'd get up and look out the door. I could see her still in prayer, and I'd go back to the robe and sleep some more. In her prayers Grandma asked for protection for her grandchildren and for strength to help them grow up in a world that was hard for her to understand. Now, every morning, I go out and pray like Grandma did.

There came a time when Cerise had to go to school in Oregon, to Chemawa Indian School. My Grandma was *very distrusting*. She asked, "What are they going to do with our children? Are they taking them away so that they will never come back? This is a faraway place. It's going to be hard for anyone to reach that place. Yet they're sending them in trains. Off to school on a train." When Cerise left, Grandma ran down the railroad tracks, following the train and crying. She was sure she would never see her granddaughter again.[1]

After Cerise had been gone awhile, Grandma felt like it was time for her to come home. She said, "It's time. It has been some time now. I am lonesome, and I can't see her. It's time. It has been some time now, and she's not back yet. I'm wondering if I'll ever see her again."

With that, she went up in the hills – just bare hills. She went up there to cry and pray and let her feelings out because they were pent up in her. They were boiling up in her, so she went out in the hills and cried unto God, "Where is my child? Why isn't she back?" She cried. She cried her name and said, "I'm lonesome. I'm lonesome." It was like she was talking to Cerise. Then, while she was doing that, she heard this music, and she silenced herself to listen. She said it came through the air. It was a tune that she heard. When she tried to say the words that had come, she couldn't repeat them, but she knew the words told her that Cerise would be home soon. It was something like "I'm coming back to you." Grandma came down from the hills and was very happy. She fixed food for us and announced, "Eat. Cerise is coming home soon."

"Grandma, how do you know? Who told you?" I asked. She said she heard this song. Then she told us the story, told us what she went through, and she sang this tune. I remember Mayme said, "Oh, that's a pretty tune." Nothing more was said about it because we knew Grandma. Cerise did come back not long after that.

In the course of her vacation, one day Cerise was busy at the dishpan, and she started singing some of her school songs. Among them was "Oregon days will soon be o'er. I'll come back to you. When clouds are vanished and skies are blue, I'll come home, dear, to you." As she sang those words, I exclaimed, "That's the one Grandma heard!"

"Grandma doesn't know that song, little sister," she said and laughed.

I said, "Grandma, that's the song you heard; come here and tell Cerise." So she came and sang the tune. Cerise just dropped her mouth and looked at Grandma. She went over there and put her arms around her and kissed her.

"Grandma," she said, "you mean to tell me you heard this in the air?"

"Yes, I did," Grandma answered. "Because I was lonesome for you, they made me hear your song." So the words told Pretty Shield that Cerise was coming, even though she didn't understand them. She knew Cerise was coming to see her soon.

One summer Pretty Shield was living in the Benteen house (she liked to go back to Benteen when I didn't have to go to school), and we were there with her. It seems like three of my sisters were there, Frances, Mayme, and Pearl; Cerise was already with her husband by then. My brother Johnny and his family were about a half-mile away from us. Johnny, from his house, had listened to the radio and had heard that a storm was coming our way. (He had a battery radio.) When he went out to look at the sky, he heard the roaring of a freight train.

My grandma heard it, too. She looked and shouted, "I must holler to your brother Johnny and have them come! We have to go in the cellar." She got out there, and she hollered, "Johnny! Johnny!" Her voice just carried for miles. "Haaay!" she says, and calls his Indian name – Battles along the Camp Lodges, that was his name. It was a hollering, a desperate hollering to be heard. Johnny came out and waved his arms, so we knew he'd heard. She said, "Come!" several times. "Hurry and come!" So he gathered up his family, and they were coming. They were coming. We started to get ready to go over across Nest Creek. On the other side was an alfalfa field where my father had been farming. There was a cellar built there, a good cellar. So we decided, "That's where we're going." When we went in, at first we looked around; we looked around with a flashlight for snakes. There happened to be nothing. We were sitting inside on the edges of an embankment thing that they had fixed where people could sit or put boxes. Johnny arrived there as the wind was blowing. The sound was getting harder – the roaring like a freight train coming through.

When we went in, I saw that my grandma didn't come in, so I sneaked out the door. The wind was blowing the trees until they were bent halfway over. There was a lot of noise in this storm. The air was filling up with sand, just kind of golden earth in a cloud. I peeked over to see where my grandma was. There were walls on each side of the steps going on up to the entrance part, and then way below that was the door. I hung on to the rail and looked at my grandmother. There she was – standing against the storm with her hand reaching up, her garments being whipped off her by the wind. Her hair – I could see her braids going almost straight out. She was up there. She was praying unto God in a loud voice. She was asking him to spare the house that her grandchildren were living in. "That's all we have," she pleaded. "Spare the house that my grandchildren are living in." She stood there and waited for it to happen, and it did. It shifted. She was facing northeast – it turned and shifted west. It went by us that way. It turned, and the trees just came back up. I was observing all this and concerned about my grandma. "She might be blown away by the wind," I thought.

Somebody jerked me into the cellar. I sat there, and I waited. I was thinking about my grandmother. The storm was still fierce. We could hear it. There was an air vent up above, and the girls – I could hear them praying. When the storm seemed to have subsided some (it was just moving the trees around like it was on its way out), Johnny went out, and he said, "It's gone. It's gone over toward the St. X area."[2] I came out. I came bounding out of there. I looked for Grandma, and there she was, sitting on the ground, just exhausted. I ran over to her. I sat against her back, like I always do. I just sat there, and I could hear her, "Hunh," breathe hard every now and then. She said nothing. She was getting her bearings back, I guess. I sat against her for a long while. The kids were already returning home, but I just watched them. Johnny stuck around and talked to her a little bit. Pretty Shield said she would be all right, "I'll be all right." So they all went over to the big house, and I stayed there, of course. She didn't tell me to go away.

Finally she got up. She got up, she took my hand, and we went. She said she saw the storm turn, turn absolutely, and "the Great Spirit has spared the house. Now my children can live in their home, and I thank him for it. *Aho! Aho! Aho!*" she said as we went along. "*Akbaatatdía, aho!*" She reminded me so much of the Old Testament in the Bible. I didn't think it was unusual for Grandma to turn the storm. Seeing Pretty Shield doing these things, I thought, "It can still happen. It's still the same, and we can be as close to God as the Old Testament people were. We can make things happen if we rely on his strength, his spirit to help us."

I have seen it in my own day. When I was married and living in Fort Belknap, we were trying to save our crop. It was late in the summer of 1947. I heard a hailstorm; it was coming right over our place. I could hear the graveling sound in the cloud, and I knew it was hail. So, again, I thought of Pretty Shield. I put my hands up like she always did. I thought, "My grandmother used to do this. I'll do this." I cried unto the Lord to spare our crops. I just prayed that it would not hail upon them and destroy them. It went over us – went over our community – and never dropped a thing, although we could hear it. Then it left for way over there. I said "*Aho!*" because Grandma said, "*Aho!*" I felt very, very vulnerable, but I also feel very secure that someone is, someone is listening.

I believe that before the knowledge of the Bible came to the Crows, before the missionaries, when Pretty Shield prayed to the Creator, she was praying to the same God that I pray to. They, the Crows before the missionaries came, believed that all things were created by the *One Man.* But saying "One Man" does not mean a physical man. To them, it meant one great power, Creator, so they prayed to him. It's One Man.[3]

The missionaries sacrificed a lot to teach us.[4] We don't appreciate them as much as we should. After I finally started to school, I made three grades in two years. I attribute the knowledge I had to the Sunday School I'd attended. The teachers helped us learn to write our names and to say the ABCs and 1, 2, 3s. It helped when we went to public school. At first the Sunday School teachers were mostly white; later on, Crows taught, too.

My father taught Sunday School, and later I happened to be one of the teachers.

When the missionaries came to visit our house in Crow, my grandmother always wanted them to have a good place to sit. She would tell us, "Give them the best place to sit. Give them the best food." She had respect for the missionaries. When I saw different young missionaries come, mostly women, they were beautiful. They had shining faces. They were bright and loving, smiling all the time.

Now that I look back, I think they were probably smiling through hurts. Those missionaries had hard lives. They sacrificed everything to go out and tell people about Christ, but they were there to teach us and to make us feel loved. I thought how unselfish they were to give up all, even their family lives, even to staying single for the longest time, serving. I admired them, and I wanted to be like them.

I wanted to be like them because I knew that I couldn't ever be like Pretty Shield or anybody in the past. "No more," the missionaries told us. "That was done. Over. You're coming into a new society, and you must learn all about it."

Old Indian men like Deernose agreed: "That's true. That's true. It's gone. It will never come back the way it used to be." My grandmother also often repeated, "It is no more."

In reservation life there was not much left for men to do but sit around and reminisce. But we had to have activity. We had to have hope in something. There was none in our old religious ways. There was none – no buffalo even. That was the end; when the buffalo went, that was the end. People needed some kind of hope, and Christ promised it all. He even said, "I lived that you might live – there is hope. I will provide a place for you." The missionaries would talk about it. Many, many times they called it a happy hunting ground. The missionaries told us, "Perhaps you might think of it as a happy hunting ground because you like to hunt. You like to do this, but there is so much more for you. You cannot fathom it. I cannot fathom it." They would say, "He lives. He went away, he rose up from the dead, and he went away to his father in heaven where he is looking down on you."

Then the old men like Deernose would say, "That's true. That's true. It's gone. It will never come back no matter how hard they try. It will not come back the way it used to be. Therefore, don't toy around with it." They believed. They believed *that* with all their hearts, and when they believed it, they believed it in spirit and in truth.

When they were baptized, it was something else to see. They went to the Little Bighorn River, right in Crow there, or maybe it would be in some different areas of the reservation that this would take place. When they were lowered into the waters with Jesus, they said, "Buried in depths below, that I shall walk with the master, white as the beautiful snow." They're brought up from the water with that song, singing that song. When the Indian was lowered in there and brought up, before the water ever left his body, he was singing Indian hymns to the Creator for making a new life for him – and that he would walk in it.

I wish I had been there to see the first Crows that were baptized in the Little Bighorn River. The old people always told me about how the first converts were lowered into the water, and when they were raised out, before the water dripped off, before they even dripped all the water off, they were singing a new song. Some of the Crow hymns that we sing all the time come from those songs. As they were baptized, the Crows came out singing, praising God in song, that they were new people. They understood that. These new believers never condemned their old way, but they said it was no use to them anymore.

Right at the turn of the century, though many white settlers were kind, we were sort of like prisoners of war. That's why the elders like Deernose insisted, "Our way of life is gone." To me it's like reaching for a twilight star – it's impossible. Our hope shifted to a bright and morning star, Jesus Christ. He tells us, "I am preparing a place for you." In our minds, it was almost like the happy time we knew before. That is why our hope is on the Pierced One. We are still Indian, whether we practice religion from way in the past or not. We are still Indians. We still have extremely good knowledge of nature itself, and we can provide that pride to the world.

I suppose, putting all that together, I thought that becoming a missionary was the best way I could go. I was baptized when I was twelve (in a baptistery, not in the river), and about that time I decided that I wanted to be a missionary. I even asked the preacher at that time, Mr. Bentley, if he would send me to a place where they would teach me to be a missionary. I wanted to serve people and tell them about Jesus Christ. Even at that young age, I felt so in love with the Christ that loved me so much, I wanted to work for him. I was very young, only twelve, when I thought this; it might have been a fantasy. Mr. Bentley spoke to me about school, going to school. He said if I felt the same when I finished high school, he'd see what he could do. I never accomplished that desire.

Baptism ceremony, Little Bighorn River, 1924. The Reverend Chester Bentley is leading a woman into the water. Photo by Laura Bentley; used by permission of Myrtle B. Hubley.

The Baptist church, Burgess Memorial, was almost our second home. Every activity that they had, we were there, and in every class. At Christmas we all went to the community tree at the church. It was always big doings. They always handed out candy. Later, people brought a couple of gifts for the children. Because of this, the older people there in Crow called Christmas "Tie-it-to-a-pine-tree day." In the summertime they had classes, vacation Bible schools, singing groups, choir groups. There was a cookie time, and then Indian parents would send things for lunch – cakes, or pies, or fry bread. It was a jolly time.

We played games in the church hall, even had square dances. Old Dave Stewart was the master of ceremonies. He made us laugh because he sang the square dance songs partly in English and partly in Crow. He would say, "Turn your partner halfway round. *Iichick diikuusiih*, go around." Everybody laughed. Mr. Bentley learned some Crow Indian hymns. He could sing a whole Indian hymn in Crow. Also, there would be outdoor get-togethers for adults in the pasture area around the church.

Each family would bring little card tables with chairs, or tarps so they could sit on the ground and eat. I loved to do that. I was there constantly. It was something for me to do, and I felt like I belonged. When I was in church, I felt like I was accepted. They loved me, they showed love toward me, and I wanted to be under that arbor all the time. We were Christ-centered: when we were there at the mission, playing with the kids, joining every activity, Christ centered our lives. We were taught to pray before we ate, pray when we played, pray when somebody got hurt.

We had a bunch of swings that Reverend Bentley put in the big cottonwood grove that was growing right in the church's yard. There was a limb that went out, a big husky limb, so he put swings there. We went to play there, with the Bentley kids. We took turns, took turns swinging on them. I remember many, many times we played with those kids. When they were ready to eat lunch, Mrs. Bentley would say, "Now, you can go home, and you can come back in about an hour." So we'd go and come back. Sometimes she fed us – peanut butter sandwiches, jam sandwiches, and milk. The Bentleys had four children. Marie was the oldest one; she was my age. I used to roller-skate with her, on her roller skates. I didn't have any, so she let me use them. I never was too good at skating, but I always tried. We also played softball. Marie was not a noisy child. She was a very responsible child, always kind of watching out for her two sisters, Myrtle and Florence, and Charles, the little boy. When we went to school, she was there, but she would go right home. She didn't hang around or go swimming like we did. We would holler at her, but she'd say, "I have to get home and help Mom."

I sort of took Mrs. Bentley as a mother. Mrs. Bentley was everybody's mother, even though there were mothers around. She was a very good, clean, neat woman. She was from New England, and she planted lilac bushes in her yard. She would let Pretty Shield get bunches of lilacs to put on Goes Ahead's grave. She was so patient. She was so patient with the people. She had a layette for any mother who had just had a baby. They came and picked it up, or at times she took it to the hospital so the little baby would have something to wear home. The women had a sewing circle and made these little layettes, and they packaged them and put them away. They put blue on it or pink on it, so they would know if it was a girl or a boy package. I remember that.

Mrs. Bentley taught Sunday School and taught a class for women called the Philathea class.[5] She was the influence of our life, it seemed like, while

Baptist ladies' sewing group, c. 1940. Left to right: Dora Old Elk, Mabel Bravo, Evelyn Old Elk, Stella Deernose, two unidentified, Caroline Other Medicine, Kate Stewart, Mary Ten Bear, one unidentified. Photo by Laura Bentley; used by permission of Myrtle B. Hubley.

we were going to church there. She laughed a lot. She didn't have a jolly countenance, she had a very serious look about her, but she laughed a lot at what the kids did. She knew we were learning. She always had a couple of other missionaries there, usually ladies. She was very instrumental in all the activities that we had in the springtime and in the summer. She disciplined us, too. She wasn't harsh about it, but she'd say, "No. No. Don't do that. Don't do that, now. It'll break if you do." She didn't jerk anything from anybody. She went to these little children, if they had something they shouldn't, and she said, "Let me have that now." The little kids obeyed her. We must have played around there and done things we shouldn't have, but she disciplined with, "Oh, no, no." I never ever knew her to lay a hand on one of us.

I remember when I was older and Mrs. Bentley would come around to visit us in our homes. Maybe there might be four or five of us girls there, just gabbing. If one of the girls had a cigarette or a magazine that we weren't supposed to look at, somebody would say, "Oh, here comes Mrs. Bentley!" Boy, those things went underneath the bed, and

The Philathea class, c. 1940. Left to right: Evelyn Bird in the Ground Old Elk, Pearl Deernose Backbone, Mamie Stewart Medicine Tail, Lorraine Real Bird Moccasin, Mary Ann Bends, unidentified, Louella Charges Strong Wilson (sister-in-law of Alma), Laura Bentley. Alma recalls: "At one time there were thirty or forty women in the class if you got them all together." Photo by Laura Bentley; used by permission of Myrtle B. Hubley.

they were trying to fan the smoke outside, whip it out. I imagine she knew, but she didn't say much. She used to teach, "What if it was Jesus that came in? Would you hide anything from him?" She approached it that way.[6]

We treated the Reverend Bentley like a reverend should be treated. We were always glad when he came to see us at home, to see how we were getting along. Then he would go on to the next place. He's the one – he's the only preacher I know of that Indian parents allowed to discipline their children. He might say to them, "Now, if you parents cannot discipline these kids to stay in their chairs and be quiet while the church service is going on, then I am going to discipline them. I may send them out." The parents told him, "Go ahead." So when he was preaching and the kids were noisy, he would say, "All right, boys." (It's usually boys.) "I'm talking now. If you want to talk, you get up here and talk. I'll go sit down there and listen to you. Do you want to come up here?" Every little head went back and forth, as if to say no. "All right, then. Be quiet," he said. The

Memorial service, Baptist church, honoring James Burgess (portrait at left), c. 1930. Chester Bentley is in the pulpit; Pretty Shield and George Hogan (Alma's father), standing. Photo by Laura Bentley; used by permission of Myrtle B. Hubley.

boys looked, some of them, looked back at their parents. The parents just looked straight ahead at the reverend. The kids knew they were not going to get any help from their parents.

For a long time the church used Indians to interpret the services into Crow for the old people who didn't know English. Grandma went to church as long as this was going on, but when they stopped having interpreters, she stopped going. She said, "I don't understand the words, so I get sleepy." One of the interpreters was Kitty Deernose, the mother of my friend Pearl. Often, when Mrs. Deernose was called to interpret, she began by saying, "We're here because we're not all there." Everybody laughed; then she gave her testimony.

Sometimes the missionaries had things to give the people, garments, things like that. Maybe Pearl Deernose and I might say to Marie, "We'd sure like to have another one of those little shirts they gave us." Then

TURNING THE STORM 87

she'd say, "Wait. I'll see if I can get one." She would go over there and ask her mother, and Mrs. Bentley would give them to us. We'd thank her. We brought her things, too, maybe candy, maybe a box of chocolates. We made our own little boxes, and we put a few chocolates in them. She was so glad to get them. I'm sure that other people, like the Deernose family, gave things to the Bentleys, and Pretty Shield might have given them gifts, too. It was kind of up to the people to give them things like blankets or dress goods.

I believe the burden was heavy on Mrs. Bentley. It was always one problem after another that she had to deal with, and then raising her own children, too. It was a lot on her, but she always kept the same cool. Something happened that I will always remember. When I was a little bigger, Mrs. Bentley said to me, "Alma, why do people say they love the Lord and come to church when they need something, but don't come at other times? When people need coal, we usually let them have it. We share our coal, maybe we give them a half a gunnysackful to tide them over." Once, she said, a woman came over and wanted some coal, but "we didn't have any. I told her we had just about a bucketful that we were using right then, but we're hoping to get some more. We just have to wait. We don't have any." The woman said, "Well, I won't come to your church no more, then." Mrs. Bentley asked me, "Why do they do that, when they have committed their ways to the Lord?" "Well, there are some people," I replied, "that don't seem to reason or don't want to."

White neighbors came to that church, too. I guess, with Sunday School, maybe two hundred people came, and about a third of them were white. Farmers, ranchers, they would come with their families. In fact one of them taught Sunday School for a *very* long time. Her name was Mrs. Pitsch, Mrs. Billie Pitsch. When she left, the Indian ladies put their heads down. They wouldn't see her go. They wouldn't see her go. So she said, "Aren't you going to bid me goodbye?" They just put their heads down. She, in turn, got hurt because they just ignored her. She cried, she cried and said, "After being with them so long, they didn't look at me. They put their heads down and wouldn't look at me." One of the Indian women told her, "That's the way Crow people do. When something breaks their heart, they just don't look. They just don't care to."

Indians have a way of discerning what kind of people come to them. Their judgment is pretty accurate. When they don't like somebody, they send them off. They say, "Get away from us. Go." But they seem to know when a person has a good heart. So when these missionaries came and told them that things were going to change, people like my parents thought, "Now here are some people that are going to help us learn their ways. We are stepping into a world that is not our own, but we have to adhere to it. These people are showing us the way, but the main thing is that they want to save our souls, through the Pierced One, the son of the Creator."

Every summer the Baptists had a camp. We camped out for about two weeks, way up in Lodge Grass Canyon. We pitched our camps there; the Lodge Grass Baptists came, too. I was able to visit with my relatives from that area. Joe Medicine Crow, Lorena Mae Yellowtail, and others from my dad's family were there. I believe that the church did this just to allow the Indian people to enjoy themselves out in the wild. It was a merry time. Grandma went, and she put up our tent. She usually stayed kind of close to the tent, but she did go to services. I loved to see the fireplaces in the morning, early. Reverend Bentley would have fry bread in his hand. Somebody had been fixing fry bread, so he picked it up and went from door to door with the fry bread in his hand, eating it. Mrs. Bentley stayed where her camp was. She hung around there and got food ready. She managed the kitchen. I made a poem about him and her – her patience and him with a piece of fry bread in his hand.

We played games out there and had races, with little prizes for the winners. People went out to see if there were any berries they could pick, but mostly it was all singing, a lot of singing and being happy together in the outdoors. In the evenings they had services, and then campfires. Some family would start theirs, and we'd all kind of venture over to it. Maybe somebody was telling stories for the kids. Maybe it was scary stories about being chased by a bear or a bull, something like that.

I remember one time around a campfire, a missionary asked the children, "Now what do you think the Lord Jesus would do, if he was twelve years old and he was here with you?"

One of the kids answered, "Oh, I bet he would dance."

5

Womanhood

I have always had a strong imagination. When Cerise was a young woman, I wanted to be like her. She and Agnes Schaffer and Evelyn Old Elk were the noted girls in the community. They were so pretty, and they loved to dance. These young white boys would come dance with the Indian girls. I never remember too many white girls, but the boys came. I think one or two white boys proposed to Cerise.

Cerise and her friends had to have a different dress every week. They probably bought them with their lease money.[1] When she wasn't at home, I tried on her dresses and played in them. I remember a silky pink one that I liked a lot. I put it on and swirled and swirled. I wore her high heels, too, and painted my cheeks and lips, pretending like I was a princess. Cerise had her hair cut short, and she applied makeup so that she looked just like the movie actress Myrna Loy. Some of the girls who were Cerise's age tried to look and act like movie stars. They even smoked.

One time I thought I would smoke, too. I was spending part of the summer with my dad on the Benteen ranch. (At different times he'd take one of us kids to the ranch to be with him.) On this particular occasion I got some little strips of driftwood, rolled them up, and lit them. My dad caught me – he caught me smoking that wood and told me if I smoked, I would end up in hell. I've never smoked since then.

When I was maybe nine or ten years old, Grandma always braided my hair. I must have seen some of the other girls with nice long hair – older girls – so I tried to copy them by letting my hair hang loose. When I went swimming, I liked to let it float around in the water. My cousin, Agnes Deernose (we used to call her Aunt Agnes in the Indian way), told me, "If you can't keep your hair in braids, cut it. Have it cut." I agreed, "Yes, okay," and went on my way. Maybe I kept my hair braided for a while, but then I let it go again. One time she saw me. She ordered, "Come here." So I went over there to her, and she tried to run her hand through my hair. It was kind of snaggy. She took me by the hand, and she marched me right over to the barber shop. It was where the post office is in Crow today.

I knew I was going there, and I protested, "No, I'll braid it. I'll braid it."

"No," she replied. "This will be good for you. You won't have to care for it so much."

She had them give me a shingle bob. That was kind of the style. It was short, and I got to like it, but I hated to have Pretty Shield see it.

When she saw me, she just looked and asked, "Where is all your hair?"

"In a barber shop," I answered.

"Why did you do this? I've taken care of your hair all this time, and braided it. Now, why did you do this?"

"Agnes took me and had it cut off because I didn't take care of it right."

So my grandma said, "Well, when it is your mother" (they considered the older women mothers), "when it is your mother that takes you there and does that, there's nothing I can say."[2]

At nine years of age, I began to detect blood on my pants, and I got scared. I thought something was desperately wrong. I was going to die. I'd throw those pants away, down the toilet hole in the outhouse, and I'd put on another little pair of pants. It wasn't that much, just a spot of blood, so after that was over, I'd throw those pants away, too. I'd be happy again until the next time, but finally I'd run out of little panties. Mayme said, "I've washed our clothes, and I am missing your little pants. Where are they? I want to wash them." "Oh, I'll go get 'em," I answered. "I know where they are." Then I ran over to the missionaries, and I asked for panties. So, they looked around and found little panties, maybe four or five of them, and I took them home and told Mayme, "I have my panties. I have all these."

One day she declared, "Okay, but I want the ones you have on, because I'm going to wash." I argued, "They're clean." I was going through that – I didn't know it was menstruation. I didn't know. I raised my skirt slowly, slowly, slowly, and I said, "See. They're not dirty." She looked and she saw a spot.

"What's this?" she said.

I cried, "Uh, I don't know what it is. I'm scared, and I was afraid to tell anybody. I'm scared, and I'm ashamed."

"You should have told us because that's the way girls do," she replied.

So she told me about it. She never had thought to tell me before, because I was young. They got me a little belt and some small Kotex and showed me how to use them. I guess from then on the missionaries were happy that I didn't keep coming for those panties.

My sisters told me that when we had our menses, we weren't supposed to go in front of men; it weakened the body – weakened the man. I had only two brothers and they were married, so we dealt with women mostly, and we had no problems. But if my brothers came to our house, if they were sitting down, we should not step over their feet at all. We were not to serve food or water or anything to any men that might be guests in our home. In fact, if men were visiting, we stayed away from our house. We went to sit with our friends or went walking until they left. There was something about menses that men avoided. They avoided it because it sapped their stength. My grandmother always said to keep to yourself while you're having menses. Men also told the younger generation not to have intercourse with a woman while she's in that way. In my day, a girl might be called outside by a boy who said, "I want to talk to you." She would say, "I'm sick at this time." He might decide, "That's okay. I just want to talk." Maybe after they talked, he would take a sweat bath.

Pretty Shield told me that a long time ago, women took soft deerskin and stripped it, then tanned it soft and cut it into long pieces, put holes on the ends of them. A buckskin was tied around the waist and through those holes. They washed their pads in the river real good and tanned them over again to make them soft, and so it went until they had to make new ones. Later, women used flannel sheeting that was given to them. They washed it like diapers until the next time. That's how they got along in that era. Women didn't bleed much. They were exercising all the time, so they didn't bleed much. Grandma said she never knew of a woman to go beyond three days of the menses. They did not step in water or get chilled when sitting on the ground. In fact, they wrapped themselves from the waist down. If a woman didn't take care of herself, she might get female sicknesses. After their menstruation was over, they always used flat, sweet cedar for incense to smoke the lodge and to smoke themselves.[3]

When Kotex came along, women thought it was a good thing to have those pads – how good it was that you could use them and throw them away. They were pretty flabbergasted when the tampons came along. They just couldn't believe that; that was too much. They didn't even want to think about it.

Crow Agency Public School, c. 1930. Photo by Laura Bentley; used by permission of Myrtle B. Hubley.

Going to school was a hard adjustment I had to make. When I started school, I don't know why I should have been so bad, but I was. I was reluctant to do anything that they told me to do. Finally, one teacher slapped me across the face. She was so determined that I would listen and do what the rest were doing. My nose bled, so I kind of paid attention after that. When this nosebleed stopped, I felt a little wet on my head where they had put water on the top of my head and at the base of my neck with a cloth to stop the bleeding. When it stopped, I felt more like, "Well, they do care." When they were taking care of me, I was enjoying it, and I was happy about that. I went back to my desk, and I paid attention for the first time in that class. When I got going with this learning, I skipped over the second grade and was sent to the third, so I never knew what the second grade was like. I picked up the third grade pretty easy, too.[4]

None of the teachers was Crow. Everything in class was in English. I have never known a teacher to say, "Don't talk Indian," but we were to

School bus, mid-1920s. Students and teacher unidentified. Photo by Laura Bentley; used by permission of Myrtle B. Hubley.

talk English in class. We spoke English so that others could understand, because the classes were mixed. Out on the playground it didn't matter if we talked Crow. The white kids and the Crows kind of played separately, except for Marie Bentley; she was always with us. I remember one time when the Old Bear boys got into a fight with some Russian kids from out in the country. It got to a high crescendo. I went home for lunch, and when I looked I saw Arthur Old Bear coming from the woods with a big limb on his shoulder. He was going to use it against those kids. There was racial prejudice there. We always felt it. The Bentleys told us, "Don't think anything of it. Just pray for them, and one day they'll quit."

There were a couple of us who were kind of instigators of game playing. Games like "Pom, pom, pull away, if you don't come, I'll pull you away," and tag, and red rover. I wanted to run, run, run. Maybe I was a tomboy. I liked to fight. It seemed to me that the girls came to me and pushed me to be a leader, encouraged me to do things. I felt pretty big about it, so I did them. There was a lot of jumping the hurdles, and I was good at that.

Then the high jump – I wasn't a tall girl, but I jumped high. There was a black girl from over toward Hardin, named Ethel English, in our school. She could beat me in the high jump, but I could outrun her. She was always kind of alone, but she was my friend. In races I always came in fast, pretty fast, first or second. One time, when my father went to Washington DC as a delegate for the Crows, he brought me back a tennis racket and balls. He wanted me to learn tennis. He thought that I had the potential of being a good tennis player. We never had a court, so we just played around with it, especially Marie Bentley and I.

I became pretty good with a rifle. One summer I was living at Benteen with my dad; I must have been twelve or thirteen at that time. Dad had a garden and some chickens there, but he didn't want to kill the chickens because they gave us eggs. I was very hungry for meat, and there wasn't any. I found a twenty-two rifle and looked around for some shells. I looked and looked until I found one bullet for the twenty-two. I found it in a nail can. I told my dad that I was going out to shoot a rabbit, and he cautioned, "Well, be careful." So I got on my horse (it was as tame as any kid's horse could be) and rode out into the fields. Finally, I stopped, tied my horse to a tree, and sat down and waited. After a time some rabbits came out from the underbrush and were playing around.

I waited for a chance, and there it was – a rabbit, right in front of some sagebrush. I got my bead on it; I got it. I went over to pick it up, and I saw another one – another rabbit – on the other side of the sagebrush. It was dead, too. The bullet had gone through the head of the first one, through the sage, and into the shoulder of the second rabbit. I tied the hindquarters of the rabbits together, threw them over my saddle, and headed home. When I showed those two rabbits to my dad, he was so surprised.

"I thought you only had one bullet," he said.

"I did, Papa," I answered. "I just had one bullet, but I got two rabbits."

He laughed. "We are blessed. When you left, I prayed for you, but I was praying for your safety. I didn't pray for two rabbits." My dad was a good cook. He fried one rabbit and used the other one for rabbit stew and rice.

That summer, when I was with my dad, I was still in a kind of fantasy mood. Some of Cerise's dresses were in the closet there, and I still put them on and played pretend games. There was a woman's hat there. I put a rag around it and pulled it under my chin to look like a bonnet. I would look at myself in the mirror and think, "My Prince Charming is going to come." Sometimes I would ride my horse to a favorite meadow, sit under a tree, and have an imaginary conversation with Prince Charming. One day I was doing this when I heard somebody say, "Hello." Standing in front of me was a man. He had a beard and wore a black hat and a vest with Bull Durham tobacco strings hanging from his pocket. When I saw him, I jumped on my horse. He called, "Don't be afraid. I'm just your new neighbor." But I rode away from there as fast as I could. Sometimes that's the way a fantasy ends. Reality comes and you run away from it. The real world is not as cozy and beautiful as you want it to be.

I liked to be in plays at school, maybe because I liked to pretend. I learned poems and things fast. I learned by reading them three times; then I could remember them. When I was about thirteen, *Cinderella* came along. Our teachers wanted us to perform that play, and we thought, "Oh, it would be great to see *Cinderella* performed by us all." We were mixed, Indian and white in there. They chose Dean Naylor, I remember, for the prince, Prince Charming. After that I idolized him. He was not Indian. He was a farm boy that lived just below the Custer battlefield. The Cinderella was Lois McClain. Her dad was working for the Bureau of Indian Affairs, and she went to school there. I was a fairy. I wanted to be Cinderella, especially with Dean Naylor. Some of my friends said, "You're so beautiful. You should be Cinderella." Lois was one class above me, and she was probably more mature than I was. She did a good job; she was a good Cinderella. I became a little frost-patch fairy with a few others, and we had little songs that we were very happy with. Then there was another play that needed a nurse, so I was the nurse. I performed it so well that the Crows said, "Is she a real nurse?"

Miss Slater was a teacher who was always taking up for me. She was a tap dancer, so I danced. I took tap dancing under her. Mr. Metzer, another teacher, was a tap dancer, too. He and Miss Slater were kind of sweet on one another. They'd dance together, and I loved to watch that drama.

Then I took opera from the sixth grade teacher, Miss Klein Heflin. She was teaching music and she took me apart from the others and said, "I'm going to teach you voice this year. I want you to keep it up. I, myself, would like to stay here, but I'm going over to New York City and try my luck in opera there." We were all just fascinated with her. She taught me how to count, hold my voice, breathe. After that I was in every glee club, every choir, everything that involved singing. Later on I became part of a quartet. Pearl Deernose sang alto (she had a beautiful alto), her sister

Stella and my sister Pearl did the medium-range singing, and I was always first soprano. We harmonized, and sometimes at community activities, if they had contests, we sang together and we won. I won a few awards and contests on my own. But I never really fully carried out Miss Heflin's wish that I be an opera singer. I always wonder if Miss Heflin made it. I loved her; I loved her so much.

Some other teachers I liked a lot were Miss Fraitas and Miss Yetty. They supervised our Girl Scout troop. We used to be in Girl Scouts, all of us. We learned how to make knots, how to cook outdoors the way they do it, camping out. We learned how to roll up our bedrolls and put them away, and learned how to pack – pack and walk. We would go into the Lodge Grass Canyon area and walk ten miles one way. We camped there, and did what our teachers taught us – campfires, stories, wiener roasts, games. We had a lot of actvities, and the next day we would hike back ten miles, which made it twenty miles. We walked, walked, hiked, hiked, and we had little mottoes to learn, and the Girl Scout pledge. I reached first-class Girl Scout. We had little scout fixings that we had to buy ourselves, so our folks got money for us, and we gave the teachers our sizes, and we had little green dresses with yellow scarves. Sometimes we were asked to join parades and things like that.

Miss Fraitas and Miss Yetty were our basketball coaches, too. When I was older, we had a girls' basketball team. We were good. I'm telling you we hardly missed a shot; we put it up there. We got to be so advanced in the game that we played independent games, independent girls' teams from Hardin and other places. They were older and bigger than we were, but they came and played against us, and we went and played them. It seems to me we would beat them. Stella Deernose, Pearl Deernose, my sister Pearl, Irene Carlow, Lorraine Morrison, and I were on that team. We played by girls' rules then, and we always wondered, if one fouled out what would we do?[5]

I remember one time some Hardin girls got mad at us because we were making baskets and getting ahead of them. This one girl scratched my arms while I was holding the ball. She just came and scratched up my arm. I let that ball go to somebody, and I slapped her. I hate to tell that story. We were both put out of the game and had to sit on the sidelines and watch, so that was good for both of us.[6] We played so much ball and practiced so hard, I sort of overdid my heart. It had a flutteration to it, and the doctor told me I mustn't overdo it or get tired, so I had to stop playing basketball.

Pretty Shield didn't come to my plays or games at school, but my sisters did. As Grandma got older, Mayme took on a lot of jobs for her. She took care of her business, kept her money, budgeted it out – things like that. When Pearl was old enough to drive and I was four years younger – Pearl might have been sixteen, and I was twelve; the year was 1935 – Mayme and Pearl and Grandma put their lease checks together and bought a car. It seems to me like it was a Ford, a blue-gray Ford. It was sitting out there, and we were so proud of it. Pearl knew how to drive, or they could always find a driver around in the neighborhood to take us to Hardin, take Pretty Shield to Hardin to get groceries and other things they needed. Hardin was a shopping place that was rather new to us – some of the stores, dime stores and like that – so we liked to go there. Nobody drove the car, otherwise. They always parked it.

Now the scene began with Pearl asking for the key so she could drive around Crow a little bit. She said, "I'll go up the street and down the street and around the block and come back." Mayme told her, "No." She didn't want her to take it because she wasn't so sure that Pearl was a really dependable driver yet. Pearl insisted, insisted that the key be given to her. In the meantime, I was waiting, too, because if Pearl happened to get the car, I was going to jump in. I thought I would jump in and go, so I was waiting for the outcome.

Pretty Shield was in her work place, pounding food on her stone, with her cloth there. Pretty soon she wrapped that food up, and she got up. She got up, and she said, "Give me that key." Mayme was shocked. She thought Grandma was going to give it to Pearl. Again, Grandma said, "Give me the key." Grandma took the key; she went out, got in the car, turned the ignition on. It started. She put it into gear, and it's a good thing it wasn't facing the house directly. When she started out, she ran into a galvanized tub, a washtub that was lying halfway down against the wall. She ran into that and flattened it out a little bit. Then she went toward the woodpile. There was almost nothing but kindling there, and she plowed through that. She came on, and she ran into the coal shed, the door part of the coal shed. She crushed it. Before anybody could say anything – everybody was screaming around – she opened the door, which was still able to open, and got out and slammed it. She slammed it and said, "There it is. That's what I'll do." Everybody was wondering if she was hurt. She walked off. The car was dented a little bit, and I believe that my father came and straightened it out. I don't remember how it got fixed. That was the only time Pretty Shield ever tried to drive. I think she did it on the spur of the moment.

About that same time, I got to the age when I wanted to fool around more than I wanted to study. I was in the sixth grade. I must have done something, thrown a spit wad or something, and the teacher sent me to the principal's office. The kids called his office the rubber-hose room. When I got in there, he took this rubber hose, and he held my hand out so that I couldn't pull it back. Then he whipped me across the palm of my hand. When he got through with one hand, he went to the other one.

"Are you going to do that again?" he demanded.

I said, "No."

He said, "Well, see that you don't," and he brought that hose down on my hand. It was hurting bad – burning. He went on, "Now you make sure you do your work. And quit sassing the teachers."

I replied, "Yes. Yes." I wanted to get out of there.

When I did get out, instead of going back to class I went home. I went straight home, and I showed my hands to Grandma. She looked at them and asked, "What caused these ridges?"

"The principal beat my hands with a rubber hose," I answered, "because I did something, and they sent me to his office, and he told me not to do it again. I said I wouldn't, but he kept hitting me."

"Well, let's go see if he can take his own medicine," she announced. She grabbed her blanket and tied it around her waist. She strapped it around her waist, and she tucked it right in the center, and she stuck her hatchet, the one she used for chopping wood, against her side, and away we went. When we got to the school, we had to go upstairs, one long flight of stairs and then a short one to get to the principal's office. She made those stairs look like nothing. She went in the door; she didn't even knock. She just walked in, and he said, "Oh, hello, Pretty Shield." She took my hand and she showed it to him. He said, "Yes, she was a bad girl."

"You bad," she said. "You bad." She clenched her teeth, and her eyes looked fierce. Grandma's eyes can look fierce. She took that hatchet, she put it over her head, and she went for the principal. He got out of his chair and ran around his big desk there, and she went right after him.

I was really betting on Grandma.

Some teachers heard him hollering and rushed in. They said, "Now, Pretty Shield, don't do that any more." She showed them my hands, and they told her, "All right, Pretty Shield. This won't happen again. But you talk to your little girl – grandchild."

Grandma talked in Indian. She declared, "If it happens again, it will be worse than it is today. I don't like to see my little grandchild's hand all ridged. She can't even write." She picked up a pencil and said, "No."

The principal said, "I didn't hit her very hard."

"Well, there *are* ridges there," Mr. Metzer told him. "Those hands are getting swollen, and they have ridges in them."

My grandma took me by the arm, and out we went. The teachers were still talking. I heard them say that the principal got carried away. He never did use that hose too much after that, I understand.

Pretty Shield must have been kind of a feminist, because she liked to take things over. She wanted to be boss. She could *do* a lot of things without a man. I think they were more feminist then than they are today. They recognized the male's power, but they were the ones who did the work, who preserved food. They even helped bring it in. They tanned the hides and made shelter. Everything the family needed, the woman did, except hunt and battle. I believe that as far as battle was concerned, they could fight just as hard, but it was not their place. Their place was to keep the lodge. And that was very important for survival. They had to be ambitious, they had to be strong, but they held the men like glass in their hands. They knew they had to, because the men had to face danger. They defended the camp and hunted the buffalo. They had to be fierce. Women *kept the lodges,* but they *pleased* their men. They knew that was important. They understood the importance of their existence. We warred; we were ready for war if it happened. We fought; how many times did women count coup? We hit them without killing them, that's for sure! We relied on the men for strength and power, but we did our best in using that kind of energy, too.[7]

Sometimes I would be with my grandma and other women, and I noticed that they enjoyed being together. They enjoyed each other. They teased and told jokes, and the joke would kind of catch on, and it would go from one to one. But if someone came in, they got quiet. It's as if they were always anticipating something – like in the old days watching out for the enemy. They were always watching out, watching out and always in prayer and asking each other to pray. Their friends were very close to them. I don't feel that we were savages. We were in a savage land that made us hard, but we were not savages. Savages today are different, different in all ways. Their savagery is done in technical ways, so they are not called savages anymore. I don't know what savage means, really. There are good and bad in every race. There are traditional values that are good and bad.

That goes for anybody. Speaking of savagery, there was great love in the hearts of the people for their families.

Crow men were the voice in the families, but behind them women were talking, constantly talking to influence their men. We held the men like glass in our hands. I guess it's because they were the warriors. They were the ones who went out to get the food and protected the camp, although we did our part as lodgekeepers. We did a lot more than they have ever talked about. They just didn't talk about the women as much as they should. Grandma said, always she would say, "The men never talk about what we do – what we women do – and they should talk about this." Linderman was the only one, but he had her talk about only the women and not the men. I wish he had asked her to talk about the men and the relationships. Grandma told about a woman who went out to kill a buffalo, and her steed was gored, so the buffalo came after her. She went down into a crevice, and she stayed there. The buffalo kept jumping over her until he fell and died.

Killing. Killing bear. Killing deer. I've known in my day, I've known Indian women, braids and all, to shoot a deer and skin it. In ten minutes or so they'd have it hanging out there, curing. The men would come back from hunting, and they'd laugh and tease about it. They'd say, "There we were looking for meat, and she had this all ready – good woman. This woman brought meat to the house – did it all. She's a brave woman."

I know a story about a brave woman. It's handed down from a long time ago. It's a real story. To the Crows that means it isn't a made-up story. I heard it many times. I asked an old man named Hank Bull Chief to tell me the story so I could tape-record it. These are his words, which he learned from Hugh Holds the Enemy:

There was in the camp of the Crows a beautiful woman named Comes along the Shore. She was so beautiful that many of the young men desired her, but anybody who asked for her hand, she turned down. Knife was a good-looking man also, and very brave. He was bringing horses and bringing horses, so he went and talked with Comes along the Shore. He commenced to propose to her. She said, "Talk on." He finally came to the point where he said, "I want you to marry me because I'd like to have you for a wife." She said, "No. I do not want a husband."

He just wouldn't listen to her. He always brought her a bunch of gifts, fresh kill all cleaned and everything, to her family door.

Even the entrails of the animals he would clean until they were just almost transparent. And he would bring them to her. Everything was "No. No. No." I guess then her brothers talked to her and actually reprimanded her and said, "We'd love to have those horses that he brought. We eat his nicely cleaned food that he brings to the lodge all ready for us, but you will not. He's a good man. He's brave. He is one of the most handsome men in our tribe." "No," she said. "I do not want to get married."

I guess he was so crazy and possessed by her, obsessed with her, that he just kept it up – kept it up. This Knife had a friend. Whatever they did, they did together. They went out to get horses, and they got a lot of horses that they had taken from the enemy. The friend said, "Let's go through the camp with our horses so they can see us." Knife said, "Just wait a minute. I want to wait another few hours. I want Comes along the Shore to come view this great deed." So they waited overnight.

"Get up, get up," Knife said. "Morning. We must go into camp so that Comes along the Shore will see me bring these horses." Then they saw a man leading his horses to water. They asked him, "How's everything?" He said, "We're all here. We're all here, but there are some young men that went to battle. They went against the Piegans. I don't know whatever possessed Comes along the Shore to go with these young men. She wanted to be a part of it. For what reason, we don't know, but she went with them. There was a great battle going on." "What happened to her?" Knife said. "Oh, my," he said, "it's terrible! When they penetrated the Piegans in battle and some of the Crows were killed, the Piegans took Comes along the Shore with them."

Knife said to his friend, his best friend there, "You take these horses that I have and give them to my sisters. I'll stay back." He took the knife that was hanging in its sheath on his belt. He put his finger to a rock and chopped it off – his forefinger. He cut his hair like in mourning, in grief. There he cried. He let a loud cry out. He rode toward the mountains with his forefinger bleeding, his hair all cut off, in great grief. He headed out toward the mountains. For several days he was up there, then he came back. He came to camp, and he was there. His friend came to see him.

After so many days, he went to his friend's lodge and said, "My friend, I have something I have planned. Let us get together and get our good steeds and carry enough lunch to take us to the Piegan country. Let's go look for Comes along the Shore. I wish to talk to her." This friend of his could not refuse him. They were such close friends that he said, "All right, I'll go with you." They packed their lunch and they got ready. When nighttime came, they headed out. I don't know how many times they slept along the way to reach the Piegan country. Finally, they came to this river, and all the Piegan camp was on the opposite side from where they were – across the river. Many, many camps were there.

It was toward evening. Knife said, "This is the place where the women come to get water. We'll wait here for a little bit. Then he hollered. He hollered several times. The women kind of came running over to the shore. "Oh," he said, "you captive ones, are you still there? Come closer. I want to talk to you. I want to speak to you." After a while there was an old lady that had been captive ever since she was young, and she was still there. She said, "My children, I am still here. And we are still here." Then Knife said, "I wonder if Comes along the Shore is with you there in camp." The old lady said, "Yes, she is indeed here." He said, "Tell her to come closer. I want to speak with her." She said, "Wait. I will get her." They waited. She went back to the camp. After a while the old lady said, "Here she is. I have brought her."

I guess the water was high and there were limbs floating down the river. It was that time of year. The flooding was taking place. But he hollered over the river, and he said, "Comes along the Shore!" "Yes, here I am!" she said. Knife said to her, "You have caused me great misery. I wanted to marry you and you refused. I have brought you many good pieces of meat for your lodge. I have even brought you delicacies like the entrails that I have cleaned so greatly for you. I wanted to marry you. You have refused every time. You have taken my forefinger. You have taken the greater part of my hair. You have caused me great grief."

Then the old lady said, "My children, you must get ready and run. Go! I see them crossing up above, to come after you. They might wound you – kill you." When they turned to go, Comes along the Shore wept bitterly as she returned to the camp of the Piegans. Then the boys, after several days, came back to the Crow camp.

In the meantime, the main chief of the Piegans took Comes along the Shore for a wife. I guess she was in a very, very large and beautiful lodge. One day the men were going to go after meat, and this chief decided that he wanted to go along with them and wanted – whether he wanted it or she did, they both went. Why she wore her buckskin dress and her great beautiful earrings, no one knows. The best horse that there ever was, that the Piegans ever knew and some of the Indian tribes around, belonged to this chief. And that's the one they rode to go hunting buffalo with the men. So they searched for buffalo. Perhaps it took a few days to find them, but they found them. Then there was a lot of shooting going on. The chief, he got his; he got one of them. He started skinning it – started cutting it up, butchering it. He brought the delicacy and cleaned it real good in the river and brought it to Comes along the Shore. She was eating, yet she kept her garments clean. We don't know why she wore this in the first place to go there. Then she said, "I am very thirsty. I've got to have some water to drink. I'm so thirsty." So he said, "Let me go and get you some water from this creek over here." It was quite a ways. The little creek was quite a ways. Then he went.

As soon as he went out of sight, she looked around and there was nobody around. So, she took this big horse. This big horse, a pinto, was standing there all bridled up. She took the knife and a hatchet and she jumped on this horse.

Right here Hank Bull Chief got away from the story and said, "If any young woman her age tried to do this today, they wouldn't get to first base." Then he continued the story.

She kind of observed the territory, and she looked toward the mountains and said, "That's my only hope, those mountains right there." So she headed over that way. This man, the chief, after a time came over there to where she was supposed to be, and he couldn't find her or his steed. He looked around for a little bit. Then he realized that she had gotten away on the pinto horse – his mighty steed, along with his mighty wife. He started hollering, as they do. He tried to get the attention of some of those who were around there, even though they must have been busy butchering. A few of them came, and then he started shooting off his rifle, so they came over to him. They said, "What is it?" He said, "My wife has escaped." They started following her, tracking, and they went and went and went. They seemed to know about where she went, so they went in that direction also.

Oh, I guess this horse was something else. She got to the base of the mountains, the foothills, and she looked back. She tied her horse, and she went up a ways herself and got up high and looked down toward the valley. Those that were tracking her came to the foothills where she was. It was getting dark. They said, "We can't go up into the mountains in this dark and look for her. We'll never find her. Besides, she's got a great steed, and our horses will never keep up with her. So let's return. Nothing we can do." So they turned around and went. How was it known that they said this? Comes along the Shore had made out the sign language of their conversation. She was very tired. Comes along the Shore was very tired. She tied her horse sort of low to a branch. He must have slept standing up. She kept it there. She herself lay down and went to sleep and rested.

Early in the morning, as soon as the light broke, she rode and rode and rode. She began to get hungry. She came upon some buffalo. She was encouraged to get one of these because she was so hungry. This horse that she had made it easy for her to get next to a young buffalo. She took her tomahawk and hit it right square in the forehead as her steed rushed by. This buffalo fell. So she went. She finished him off. She carved till she got enough meat to sustain her. She took a lot and kept going. She got to a river. It was deep. She took her moccasins off, tied them high, and she started to go through the water with her steed. They reached the other side in a short time because of this great horse. They rode, and they rode, and they rode some more.

After going for quite a long time, she reached camp. She began to hide on the edges of the camp. She waited until darkness fell. She came to the very edge of the camp. She tied this great horse there, and she looked for Knife's lodge. She came to this lodge that belonged to Knife, and she stood at the back part of it where his bed would be – still standing outside. He was lying there. She realized he was alone, that he was unmarried. He was lying there. Since he was always going to battle, he was singing about it to himself. She came along. She heard. She said, "Knife." And called him again, "Knife." He said, "What?" She said, "Come here." "Huh!" he said. "Even if I go out to you, you wouldn't be the likes of Comes along the Shore, so why should I?" His obsession was great on the woman. "Well, come on out here. It's me," she said. "It's me. I'm Comes along the Shore. Come on out here." He said, "It may be so," and he got up to go out. When he went out, there she stood, beautiful as ever.

He said, "I'm amazed that you are here. How did you get here?"
They decided together they were glad to see one another. She was
willing toward him now, as she never was before. He said, "She has
come to me." Now, he sings a song. He sings a song. He's telling
them in that song what has transpired, and that it makes him want to
laugh. He said, "My poor people, I want to tell you that Comes along
the Shore has returned to me. I would ask you all to come and see
her, for now she resides in my lodge." They came to see her. From
everywhere, they came to see her. She sat in an honored place in
the back of the lodge, and the lodge lining, the flaps and the lining
were raised up, halfway up, so that everyone could see her. I guess
they brought them food – Knife and his new bride Comes along the
Shore. So they began to eat dinner together. Then the people asked
Comes along the Shore to tell the story of what happened. She told
all that happened to her. I guess they all went home then, after a
long time with them. Then, she took Knife – "Come here," she said.
"I have something for you." He got up. She led him out of the lodge
over to where she had tied her steed. She untied this horse and led
it to Knife. He took that horse, and with great pride he led it. Right
direct to her mother's lodge. Her brother came out. With great pride,
Knife said, "Here are the reins of this great horse that she got for us.
Take it." The brother-in-law took it.

She said, after a time together, she said, "Knife." He said, "Yes, I'm
listening." She said, "You have asked me to marry you, and it's not
that I didn't like you or desire you, I just did not like to have crusted
dress around my breast, where I feed the baby. I hate that, and I
didn't want to ever have it, so that's why I always refused marriage."
When women have a baby, they invariably have that mess around
their armpits on their dresses. Well, so long afterward, she had a
baby from Knife, and what she didn't like happened to her. There
it was. She had this baby. She was crusted under her breast on her
garment. Knife looked at her, and he said, "Comes along the Shore,
what you told me – the story about yourself – you are that way now.
So, take up anything that you have here, that belongs to you, and
leave." So the great love story ended.[8]

She should not have told him, but that's the way men are. It's men's
egos that drive them to possession and obsession. My grandma always
told me, "Do not look for a man yourself. Do not try to win them over. If

they see you and they like you, if they desire you, they will come to you themselves." I waited. I thought, "If someone came and desired me and wanted me, they would love me always." And it happened – it happened with this guy, with Bill.

Grandma also talked about what a wife should do if her husband went out on her. She said, "If you're not going to leave him, don't say anything. You're just wasting your time. You're just wasting your time. If your man goes out – and men will, there are very few men that will not – if he goes to another woman, and you know it, don't go after him. If he's yours, he'll come back. If he don't want to, there's nothing you can do about it. When he comes back, lay out clean garments for him. Feed him good, and don't ask him all kinds of silly questions that you might be imagining yourself. Let him forget. He'll settle down, and pretty soon it's you he'll be watching." There was a kind of discipline there. There was discipline. There were societies that were well respected. There was also competition among the women, and the men, too. They always tried to better themselves through competition.

In the old days, women sometimes had to worry about tipi creepers. A tipi creeper was a man who would crawl into a woman's tipi at night when her husband was away. I have heard where women tied their dresses against their knees together when they slept, because they didn't want anyone to bother them. My mother-in-law told me about an Assiniboine woman who tied her dress together, and this man came. She was asleep, and he tried to get between her knees. He pushed his hand through that tied place, and the woman woke up. He couldn't get his hand out. She thrashed him good. Later, when she told it, she laughed. She said, "I wonder if he ever had a whipping like the one I gave him." That's a true story.

6

Loneliness and the Night Sky

Not long after the rubber hose incident, the principal called me into his office. I thought, "Uh, oh, here we go again. I didn't do anything."

"I'm going to see that you pass the sixth grade," he announced to me. "I'm going to see that you pass the sixth grade with good grades because I want you to go to Pierre, South Dakota, to the Indian school. You're a smart girl, and you'll make it, but if you don't go, I'll fail you."

So I said, "I will go." He wanted me out of that school. I told my grandma, and she didn't like it. Mayme, my sister, tried to explain to Grandma, tried to tell her that it would be better for me to go. She said, "There's nothing for kids to do around here. All they will probably do is get in trouble. At school, they will teach her how to make a living, and when you're gone, she'll need that."

Pretty Shield said, "I understand. Now, I'm beginning to understand what it's all about. They want *all* our children to be educated in their way – the white man way. I know there's no stopping it. That makes me sad because I am going to have to let the old ways go and push my children to this new way. It breaks my heart to do that." She told Mayme, "I'm too much a part of the past. I'll continue to live that way. I have no reason to change, but looking to the future, they must go. They must go. When one of my grandchildren leaves me and goes somewhere like Cerise did, it tears my heart out. It hurts. It hurts, and I feel so helpless. It's just as if I'm nothing. I'm nothing no more; where I was capable, where I prided myself in keeping my lodge, here I am at the brink of no more. It makes me look vacantly out into the future. My children are snatched from me and sent away to learn this new way which I fear. But they must go. It's the law. They do what they want to us in spite of our protests, so we just have to try to suppress our emotions and harbor them in our hearts and hope for the best."

They got me ready to go. We went on buses, different tribes took their own buses to haul their own students. But the Crow bus was full, so I rode in a station wagon with some elders. They must have been the chaperons. They talked to me about the sights along the way, Devil's Tower, all these things. I remember them talking, but I don't remember what they said. My mind was full of "I want to go home. I want to go back." I just wanted to go back. I hated this country. I thought, "I'm going someplace – who knows what's there, what's ahead of us?" I even hated to think of what we were facing. I thought it was something dreadful, that nobody would know what was going on in that place. And how would a person tell, if something was going on?

The school at Pierre looked like a BIA compound. It had two huge dorms, one for boys and one for girls, and an administration building with things like a bakery, laundry, and tea room spread out behind it. Later, I found out we would learn to do different kinds of work in those buildings. As we went through the gates, we saw the administration building first. Some of the kids were so small, maybe as little as second grade, and many different tribes were there. Most of the Montana tribes had students there.

They sat us in our rooms. It was a dorm. They said, "This will be your bed," to one, "This will be your bed," to another. There was a little table next to each bed. That was for what we had ourselves and to put our lamps on. Downstairs were locker rooms, like the sportsmen have nowadays. The lockers were all lined up, and each one had a girl's name on it. We had keys to them, and we put our clothes in there, what we wanted to hang up, and shoes and things like that.

First of all, we were assigned those living places. Then they said, "Line up where the matrons are standing." I asked, "What are they going to do?" They said, "They are going to put kerosene or Cuprex in your hair." Oh, the fright went through me – "Oh, my God, it's starting." I left the line and ran right over and said, "My head is clean. You can look through it if you want to, but I don't want that stuff on my hair."

Miss Carter, who was the more reasonable of the two matrons, explained, "It's just orders that we're taking. We have to do everyone, see."

I said, "But Miss Carter, I don't want that on my hair."

"I know how you feel," she said, "but just get it over with, and once you get it over with, you'll feel better. You'll feel much better when it's over with. See those children out there? Well, they went through the same thing, and unless we find something wrong with your head, you'll never have to do this again."

So I got back in line, and my head was doused with it, and everybody else's, too. Oh, it smelled bad. They told us not to get it in our eyes, and we tried not to, but the smell of it was overwhelming. We had to leave it on for a while, not really long, maybe twenty minutes or half an hour; then we got to wash it. Boy, did I wash mine. Oh, I wanted every little smelly place out of my hair. Some of the girls that I knew didn't have anything in their hair had to go through the same thing as I did. To watch them going through the same thing helped me. I thought, "Well, they're going through it. They look like they are clean people, and they're going through it." I began to realize that there were others who were hurting in their pride just like me. They had to give up and put their heads down into a basin and let somebody put that stuff on them. Their pride was hurt, more than the actual operation itself. The boys must have gone through the same thing, but no more was ever mentioned about this to one another.

We never talked about it. It was too shameful. We were too ashamed. We wanted to forget it.

We had a regular routine. Every morning we fixed our beds like the military does. We went downstairs, washed up, took our showers, got dressed, and got in line in the basement. The matrons were there and they examined us with their eyes, up and down, our hair. When they came by, we showed them our hands, mostly for the nail part, I think. They looked at our shoes to see that they were shined up. We had these government-made shoes, and we called them stogies. All of them were black, and they were just like oxfords, only made by the government. We shined them up and made them look good. When we dressed up we could wear our own shoes, and when we played ball we had to wear tennis shoes, but those stogies were assigned to us. Since my feet were small, mine looked pretty good at that time.

We marched everywhere. In the mornings we marched to our dining room. The boys and girls ate in the same room, but we didn't sit together.

One time we went to breakfast, and worms were in the oatmeal. I asked the girls around me, "Do you find any worms in your food?" They said, "Yes, yes." The worms were dead, but they were there.

I told the matron, it was Miss Livesey, "There's a couple of worms in my oatmeal, and I don't want to eat it. Is that all right?"

She said, "You sit there, and you eat that oatmeal before you leave this place." We had to eat everything that was given to us.

"I can't," I replied. "Can I eat some of it?"

Miss Livesey huffed, "I don't want to see one piece left in that bowl." I put the oatmeal in my pocket.

The rest of the girls ate theirs, and they didn't show any worse for it, but I could not, knowing that there were worms. They were little white ones with black faces. I knew they were in there. They were dead, they were cooked, but they were in there. I asked the others for their used napkins. I put the oatmeal in the napkins and the napkins in my jacket pocket. Miss Livesey came, and she looked at all the bowls, and she looked at mine, and there happened to be a little piece in there.

"What is that?" she asked. I said, "Oh," and I took the spoon and ate that. She complimented us and then asked Miss Carter, "Do you see any worms in here?" Miss Carter usually is the good one; she looked and shook her head and walked away.

So Miss Livesey said to those who were still eating, "I don't want to see a bit of this oatmeal left. You need to have it. We have got to keep you healthy." When I left the dining room, I went and put my oatmeal in the toilet and flushed it down the toilet. Then I washed my pocket, and I thought, "Boy, I hope I never ever have to eat oatmeal again."

Sometimes, the matrons would say, "If some of you girls want to skip breakfast and catch up with your homework, you may." Sometimes I did, because I was afraid of oatmeal. What I did, though, was in the evenings, if we had beans or something like that, I'd put some in my cup and I'd mash them up. I'd mash them up, and I'd put that between bread and wrap it up and put it in my pocket. I saved that bean sandwich, and when I didn't go to breakfast, I ate a bean sandwich. Oh Lord, what we didn't go through, it was so militarylike.

At night, sometimes, I went down in the basement of the dormitory and looked out the window. It was square, this perfectly square window on the end of the bathroom. And there was the evening star. I would look at it and say, "Star light, star bright, first star I see tonight, I wish I may, I wish I might have the wish I make tonight." I looked at the star, and I cried. I said, "I want to be home. I want to be home. I know Grandma's lonesome. I know that she's praying." I was so lonesome for her, for home – just to be there. Even if it was not a beautiful home, I wanted to be right there with the person I loved, that I was longing to be with.

I kept writing home. I kept writing home for them to come after me: "I want to go home. Send some money. I want to go home. I'm lonesome." Mayme would write back and say, "You'll get over it. You'll get over it. Just stick it out. Finish your grades there. You'll make friends; it won't be long." She would tell me that. She used to write real pretty, and I just looked at her handwriting and longed for her.

But I did make friends. Not only did I make friends with the girls; I made friends with the laundry matron. She always liked to have me come and visit her, but I didn't like to do laundry.

There was a girl named Mary, and I asked her if she would do my laundry. I told her I would give her a brand-new coat if she would do my laundry for me all year. Mayme had sent me a new coat that was a little big for me. It always seemed to me like when Grandma or Mayme bought clothes for us, they bought them a little bigger, a little bigger all the time. They were thinking of the future, so this coat was too large for me; it hung kind of long. It was a beautiful coat, gray, but I had a coat that would pass. Mary said she would do my laundry, and I gave her that coat, and she was very proud of it. It fit her just right. She was my friend after that.

Some of the kids at Pierre were very poor, much more so than we thought ourselves to be. At least once in a while I got a little money in the mail. I'd have to turn it in, though, to the matrons. We turned our money in to the matrons, and they kept it. When town day came, we went to the office to sign out, and we told them what we needed, and they would add a little movie money and popcorn money to it. They kept a record of that. Sometimes when one child, a friend, wanted something really bad and didn't have enough money, we would give our popcorn money to her so that she could have enough to buy these stockings or underwear or whatever it was she needed. In the end, she would do something for us. If she got a little money, she'd pay us. It might not always be the right amount, but we were satisfied. Maybe I might lend her twenty cents from my popcorn money, and she would give me back fifteen cents. That was okay, that was fine with us. We were still pretty much living a social life like in the Indian communities – sharing, like in our neighborhoods.

All the students had jobs and received a little money for doing them. We worked in the bakery; we worked in the kitchen; we worked in the laundry. We were assigned to different places like that. I had a job at the superintendent's home. I'd rush over there and change my clothes. I couldn't work in my school clothes, even to dust or vacuum. If it was fifteen minutes that I would be there, I had to wear a little black-and-white uniform, a little apron. I always had to put my headband thing on, white with a black strip through it, across my forehead. I went there and made lunch or did something that was assigned to me. Sometimes I made sandwiches and decorated them. I was good at that. Mrs. Calhoun, the superintendent's wife, loved it, and she loved to show me off to her guests. I would make a little bow for them.

In the mornings, when I was assigned to that place, I did Mrs. Calhoun's face. She lay down in kind of a barber chair thing. She had her box, and I would open that box, and I would clean her face, then put grease paint on – it looked like grease paint. She'd lie there with her head wrapped up and she'd talk while I did her eyebrows, her skin, and made sure her rouge blended and her lips were lined. Then she'd be so satisfied: "Oh, how you can please my heart," she said, "when you do my face and put my makeup on." She lay there like a movie star. Her daughter did go to try for movies. She had a bright red convertible car, a shiny one. Mrs. Calhoun had oil wells, I think, in South Dakota. She had a maid that lived in an apartment above the garage, and another girl from the school worked there also. I worked for Mrs. Calhoun through the school year. She liked to have me with her. She was lovely, very charming, and she would play the piano for me.

I finished the seventh grade at Pierre. Then, when I went back the next year, there were too many eighth graders, so we were given a test. I advanced to the ninth grade after that. We had classes in math, English, history, penmanship and writing, glee club, and art. I liked penmanship and writing. I excelled in that. The others were just kind of average; I did enough to pass. Math I didn't like. History I was not too enthusiastic about, but I did "oh and ah" about what happened and what people were like in all those different places. I liked "Cinderella" and all those tales: "Snow White," "Sleeping Beauty," "Rose Red," and King Arthur.

In my second year at Pierre I became a dorm officer. Dorm officers were kind of policemen. We were supposed to look around, keep the students from fighting or running away; we just had to be on the lookout.

When I tried to break up a fight one time, I had to get stitches. Two girls were fighting in the basement, and I was up on the first floor. One girl came running to me and to the matron and exclaimed, "There's a fight downstairs!" I was in our game room, and Miss Livesey said, "Alma, go down there. There's a fight in the basement. Break it up." I said, "Yes, ma'am." I ran down there, and these two girls were fighting. They were going at it. I hollered at them to stop, and they wouldn't. So I got in between them and stopped them. This one girl stood aside and quit, but the other one really hauled off and hit me on the face with her fist. Right

Alma as a young teen.

on the cheek. I got ahold of her, and shook her up and threw her to the ground. She said, "This is my second fight. That's why you can do this to me." She had been banging that girl with the heel of her shoe, but when she hit me, it was with a doubled fist.

She said, "I'll see you tomorrow, Hogan. Right down here in the locker room. I'll see you here."

I retorted, "Any time. Now, you behave yourself. I'm an officer, and I'm trying to stop this fight, but if you're going to be that way, I'll be here in the morning."

The next morning I went down early. I went on downstairs, and to the right was her locker, and she was sitting right in front, at the end of the lockers. She was sitting in a chair there, and she looked like she was sewing a garment. I came, and with heart pounding I stood at the door, and I looked at her. She said, "I've had enough, Hogan." Within my own self I thought, "Oh, glory be." I didn't want to fight, but I was going to whip her if I had to, to kind of bring her around.

Miss Livesey fell in love with my dad.

She was always picking a little bit on me. She was a pretty woman. She had long bright and light hair. At night she'd put on her nightgown and her housecoat, and she'd have her long hair down to her seat, hanging behind her. She would come into the dorms and walk around to check. I always thought, "Ooh." I think I went back to my fairytale time, and I thought she was one of those fairytale characters.

There was some kind of performance in the auditorium, and all of us kids went. This man who was on the stage was a magician. He called out, "Can I have your prettiest girl come up here?"

"Hogan! Hogan!" All the kids started hollering, "Hogan!" So the man asked me to go up there on the stage. He looked at me. "So this is your prettiest girl. I can see." Oh, he was just bragging and flattering around. Finally, he got his trick over with, and I went back and sat down.

Now, Miss Carter was really good to us. She didn't care who was pretty or who wasn't, but Livesey seemed like she did. After this magic show, before we went to lunch, she came into the locker room and told us, "Line up. Line up. Let me see your hands and nails." She came by me. She looked at my fingernails, and she said, "Prettiest girl, huh? Humph." And she went on. Some of the girls told me she rolled her eyes at me. So I stood in line. I never said a word, because if I did, I'd catch it. She made little remarks when she had a chance. She always made little remarks.

To top it off, the boys in the town of Pierre – they were not Indian boys – came on horseback to the campus. Two of them were under my window. The girls said, "She's in there." Those boys started hollering at me, "Hey, Hogan! Hogan!" So I looked out the window, and I saw these two boys. I happened to turn, and they said, "She moves! she moves!" "What are you up to?" I asked. They waved at me, and I said, "Hi." They got all tickled and everything. Then the boys' adviser came and told them to get off the campus. They said, "Okay, okay," and left. Miss Livesey didn't like that attention I got.

It was after all this that my dad came through on his way to Washington. He stopped at Pierre to see me; I think he was traveling on the train. I remember he gave me his wallet, and he said, "Take what you want." I took some money, and one of the matrons said, "I'll keep it for you. You can get it whenever you need some of it." Dad talked with those matrons, and they told him my situation, how far I was advanced and all that. I remember this distinctly: when my father left, Miss Livesey came down, came through the line like she always did, and she said, "Have you met Mr. Hogan?" to all those in line. They said, "Yes, ma'am." I could hear some of them say, "Yes, ma'am." She said, "Now we know where she got her good looks. Do you agree?" Everybody clapped, so I looked back at her. She went by me, and she smiled at me. She said, "Your father and I had a very nice visit." I said, "Yes, ma'am."

She wrote a letter to Dad, and she proposed. He showed it to me. He said, "She is a nice woman, nice-looking, a pretty woman, but I already have other ideas." She put in that letter, "I will bring her up. I will tend to her, and she will have the best education anybody could wish for, if we could get married. I am very willing." But Dad went home, and later he married Lillian.

I left that school, too, about that time. I came home for the summer, and the next year I went to the Indian school at Flandreau, South Dakota.[1]

That summer at home in 1940, I began to become a little more interested in this boy-girl thing, but Grandma really kept her eyes on me. Toward evening, Pearl Deernose and I liked to go over to town and go to the confectionery and get some candy. We went walking and ate. One time we had just come out of that store when Thomas Medicine Horse, who was older than we were, came up to ask us if we had seen a certain somebody. We said, "We just came from the house, and we didn't see anybody." About that time Pretty Shield came around. We were standing right between what is now the laundry and the Crow Mercantile. Well,

Pretty Shield came around that mercantile store from the south side of town.

Pearl saw her first: "Uhhh, your grandma."

I looked and thought, "Oh, she's going to chase us home."

Thomas, in the meantime, ran across the road. He ran across the street, and there were a lot of sunflowers and tall weeds around there. Grandma picked up a rock, and she threw it at him. That rock – I could see it hit him right on the calf of the leg when he was running. It threw Tommy right into those sunflowers, and he went rolling.

I said, "Oohh, Grandma's mad! We'd better get on home." We went around that place where the laundry is now, and we headed toward a bakery that was near the Baptist church at that time. Behind that bakery were toilets, outhouses. Pearl said, "Let's go hide in a toilet." We ran in there; we closed the door. We thought, "Boy, she will go on – right past. Maybe she'll go in front of the bakery and go home." Pearl decided to sit on the pot. She was sitting on the pot, and we were real still, when the door flew open. I don't know what happened to Pearl. I stood there, and Pretty Shield, she slapped me. She slapped me right across the ear part, and boy, did my ear ring. It just rang. I turned around and headed home. Pearl Deernose headed for her house. Her head was shaking, too, just like it was jelly or something.

When I got home, I hid again. Grandma found me. She caught me someplace, and I said, "You hurt me." She said, "It's better to hurt you than to let you chase wild. You have no ears for me, for my words, so I have to let you know that what I tell you, I mean." For a long time after that, if I asked her if I could go to town and get some candy and visit with friends, she would say, "No."

Pretty Shield was so afraid that she wouldn't be able to control us kids. She thought it was her responsibility. When we were small, she disciplined us by telling us stories, but she had no stories, no analogies, for the things we ran into as we grew up. She whipped my sister Frances one time. That's the one she told Linderman about.[2] She didn't like the white dances, the drinking, the smoking. She said, "We are coming into a time where everybody's ears are hard as rocks."

7

Assiniboines Have
Strong Medicine

Grandma always wanted our dresses below the knee quite a ways. I had kind of straight dresses, but they were long. Maybe I'd have a belt to go with them. She wanted us to wear that kind of dress. In Pierre, almost all the girls had the same kind, so it didn't bother me too much.

When I went to Flandreau in 1940, the style was different. When I first got to school, there was a place to register, so I went there, and I noticed that nearly all the girls had on either short dresses or kind of thin slacks. I had my dress on; I didn't feel bad in it, so I started into the registration building. All the old-timers, the kids that had been there before, were sitting on some high benches like bleachers. They saw me coming, and they said, "Wow! Oh!" I thought, "Well, boys are that way." They called, "Hey, Cherry!" I said, "Don't you dare call me Cherry." They said, "Oohh!" like that. I went on in, and later I found out that "Cherry" meant a girl was a virgin – innocent. They teased me about it after that. When I went to Flandreau, I was truly very unfamiliar with that kind of lovemaking.

I wanted clothes that were like what the other girls had. So after I got settled in school, I either cut my dress off to a shorter length and hemmed it up or traded something I had, maybe a pair of shoes or a sweater, for a short skirt. Then Mayme sent little woolen skirts that were kind of short, and I was so glad, glad I could wear that kind. Of course, she knew Pretty Shield wasn't around to see me, because Grandma wouldn't like it. And she didn't like it; when we got home, she thought it was terrible that we showed our knees. But she got used to it, I guess, or she ignored it. I think she was very sad about the changes that were coming over us. She didn't feel that our skirts were modest.

At Flandreau the girls had their own building, and the boys had their own building and their own supervisors. There were rules that contained us. On the campus, in the buildings, in the dining room, in the kitchens – wherever we worked, there were rules we had to go by. We had better go by those rules. It was very much run by the staff – and very well, too. We learned as we lived on that campus; it was Flandreau Indian Vocational High School. It looked like a college compound, much bigger than Pierre. It was a pretty, well-kept campus. I think it helped us to get over our depression. The plants, the lilacs – these were good for the senses. We had a little rock garden and a pond with cement benches where we could sit.

Kids from reservations all over the country were there. When we first arrived, kids from the same reservation kind of hung in cliques, but afterward we got to know different tribes. Different tribes got along, seemed to get along.

There was an oval there, a walkway around the rock garden. Toward evening, different kids or couples went out and walked around it a little bit. Sometimes we went and sat in the garden and just reminisced or visited. Once, in the fall of my first year at Flandreau, some girls said to me, "Let's go around the oval to see what's going on." This one evening I saw a crowd gathering around somebody who was entertaining. It was noisy; there was some music. I walked over, and there were these two guys. I watched them. It was Bill Snell and another guy named Rusty, but I didn't know either one of them then. Bill was playing the banjo, and Rusty was playing the guitar. Then Bill played the banjo by himself. They were playing and singing songs that kids requested. Kids threw them change to sing their favorite songs. So they played, and they made a little movie money that way. When I was there, I asked them to play "Stardust." That was my favorite at that time. What I threw out there, I don't know.

I looked at Bill and I thought he looked like "Li'l Abner" because he had a perfectly white shirt on that fitted him – his muscles. His pants came up very high on his waist (that was the style then), and he wore suspenders. I used to like to read about Li'l Abner and Daisy Mae in the comics, and I thought, "Well, he'd make a good Li'l Abner with his black curly hair." But I didn't think too much about it. That's the first time I saw him.

When he saw me, he said to himself, "There's the girl I want." Of course, I didn't know this. "When you walked into the dining room with the rest of the girls," he later told me, "all the football boys were sitting together at one table and commenting on the girls. When you came in, that was it. That's all she wrote. I said, 'That one's for me. I think Hogan is the best-looking one.' I was just following you as you went by, and you looked at me, and you smiled, but you just swung your head like, 'Oh, well.' I thought, 'She's acting cute.' "

Bill sent for me. He sent for me that same evening I saw him singing. When I went back to the girls' building, he sent his cousin after me.[1] She said, "He wants you to come out and talk with him." I said, "No, I don't think so." I really didn't have a boyfriend at that time. I didn't care to. I wanted to go home. I wrote letters that I wanted to go home, but they wouldn't let me. So it was me and the girls. I loved to hear their stories. They sat around and talked about their experiences. I liked the talking back and forth, so I'd be one of them. I was a good listener. Here came this girl and said her cousin Bill wanted to see me out there. I said, "Who is he?" "My cousin," she said, "the one that was singing." I said, "I don't care to." Days went by, and the cousin came back with the same question. About the third time, maybe a couple of weeks later, she asked, "Why don't you just go, go round the oval with him and then make up your mind?" I went outside then. He was just tickled.

I said, "Hi." He said, "Hi." We walked around the oval, and we talked and got acquainted. I found out he was from the Assiniboine tribe at Fort Belknap. Pretty soon, toward the last, he asked if he could hold my hand. I said, "I guess so." So he held my hand. He had great huge hands. He doubled up my hand, and he put it into his big hand like a little ball. I noticed that he held it like that, and we walked around. Afterward, I asked him why he'd held my hand like that. He said, "I don't know. Maybe I was a little nervous. I guess because I play ball all the time." We laughed about it, but every time after that when we walked around, I gave my hand to him in a little ball form. So, he just got kidded from then on. But it got so that I was coming out to him and walking around.

One time, after we had been seeing each other for a few months, we went to the show, and Bill got in a fight with a Cheyenne boy, Kenneth Bear Tusk. I had never gone out with him or anything, but I had known him a while. When I finished at Pierre, this Cheyenne said, "Alma, why don't you go to Flandreau? It's a good school. You'll like it." I said, "Oh, well, I'll think about it." He said, "You do that. Maybe I'll see you there." That was just a passing thought. It was the school people, the government people, who tried to encourage us to go to Indian schools. I picked Flandreau because I thought it was closest to home. I didn't even see Kenneth Bear Tusk when I first got there. Later he would smile and wave. He was a senior. Boys made fun of seniors who went out with the younger girls.

The time of the fight, Bill was running the movie projector. When I came out of the show, Kenneth was going to walk me to the dorm. Bill came out, and they got into a scuffle. Bill didn't hesitate at all. He was going to finish Kenneth right off. I ran. I ran from there and started toward the dorm, but Bill caught up with me. I said, "What did you do that for?" He replied, "Well, he likes you." I said, "I have nothing to do with him. He is not my close friend. He just wanted to walk me home. You were busy."

There are so many memories of my husband before I married him. At Flandreau we became noted for this little whistle we used to do. When I crossed the campus, Bill wanted me to know where he was, so he made this little bird whistle. I could do it, too, with my fingers in my mouth. I would answer him, so he would know where I was.

When summer came, we left school. Travel was impossible in those days, for us, at least, and Bill was way over there at Fort Belknap. I thought, "God knows where that's at." I never knew where it was then; I never was familiar with it. I was full of adventurous ideas in my mind. I read a lot of books, and I acted a lot in my imagination. I was getting to where I was a young lady, and I knew that girls my age were about ready to get married, but I actually didn't ever think of marriage. I wanted to live in a fantasy world. I did not want reality. I wanted to stay young and childlike forever, if time could stand still.

When I got home to Crow, every day I went looking for a job, just a job to get me over the summer. I dressed up for it. I dressed really clean, and when I went to a place and asked about a job, they would say, "Well, come next week" or "Come in a few days." So with that, I would leave and go on a walk. I walked down Main Street, or I went to the park and walked around. It was one of these mornings that I was going down the streets of Crow Agency, I went to this little place, confectionery place. I had worked there before, and they liked me. That day they told me, "Don't give up. We need you. We're going to get you." I said, "Okay." Then I went east down the street.

I heard this whistle that we used in Flandreau. I thought, "That couldn't be Bill Snell." As I was approaching the mercantile place, I noticed that this whistle came again. I looked toward the park, and he came from behind some trees out to the opening, and I thought, "Aahh." I was just surprised to see him there in Crow Agency. He had his arms out, and I ran. I ran across the street. Then I fell into his arms, and we stood there for a long time, just happy to be together. He said he had come on a freight. He caught the freight from Great Falls.

"You're here," I said.

He nodded, "Yes, I had to come."

We went on home to meet Grandma; he walked with me. I told him, "This is my home. It's this little shack."

"I'm afraid. I'm a little afraid to go in," he admitted. I brought him in anyway and introduced him to Grandma, and Grandma was hesitant about it.

After the visit, Bill said, "I'll see you because I'm going to have to look for a job." So he went into Hardin looking for a job. When I came back to Grandma, she declared, "He is not going to stay here with you. He's another tribe. He is not of your own. You might as well know that right now."

I felt bad. I felt very bad. I'd thought perhaps my grandma would make a cot for him, because the girls were gone, and she and I were the only ones there. I told Bill, "I don't know what to do," and he said, "Well, I'll find a place to stay. Don't worry about it." When he left, I said a little prayer, asked God to find him a place. I didn't know it until he told me later (after several days), but he stayed next to the depot where some telephone poles were stacked on the ground. He lay between them and slept all night. He would tell me, "I'll be at the depot." So I took BLTs to him – bacon, lettuce, and tomato sandwiches. That was our favorite. I sneaked that to him almost daily.

In the evenings I charged food on Pretty Shield's credit at the trading post. I got wieners, mustard, buns, and I took those to a place under the bridge there at Crow – that railroad bridge. Maybe a couple of my friends would join us, and we had wiener roasts. These girls brought a little something with them, and we all got together and fed this man, Bill Snell. They liked to be around us because we were funny. We were having fun. He joked a lot, and I did funny things. They thought he was really something – masculine. At that age, I thought he was the most masculine person I ever saw. It was from hard work. He had worked since he was eight years old, hard farm labor, by hand, by sheer force. When he was twelve years old, he looked like he was seventeen years old.

Before summer was over, Bill sort of won Grandma's approval. He chopped the whole woodpile and stacked it up in her house for her, where she always stacked up her little woodpile. He stacked it real neat.

There was so much of it, and she watched him all that time. Then she did say that he was a good man. She still didn't let him stay with us.

Finally, Bill got a job in Hardin, mixing grasshopper poison sprays. He met this man there who was from Crow, married to a Crow woman. That man was from another tribe, too. He told Bill, "You can stay with me. I'll fix you a cot where I live." He also had two small buildings like Pretty Shield had, two small shacks. He made a cot for Bill there, so at least he was out of the weather. This man had a couple of nice-looking daughters who were maybe a year or two younger than I was. They really liked Bill, but he had eyes for no one else.

When he would come back from work, it would be toward evening. We went swimming because he needed to have a bath – he stayed in a place where there was no bath. When we went swimming, there was no one else around, so we said to each other, "Don't look!" And we slipped out of our clothes and went into the water. We really played in that water. We didn't dare go up on the banks, though, and slide down like beavers do. We used to have slides like that. There was always this old Crow man swimming there with his neck sticking out of the water. He sat there, and he thought we were crazy I guess, but we'd say, "Don't look! I'm getting out." We did as each other said.

I actually didn't know what being in love meant. I don't know why, but I didn't have that understanding. I guess I was a pretender because I was always saying, "I'm supposed to do this. I'm supposed to do that, so I'll do it. I'll do it the best I can. This boy likes me. He loves me. What am I supposed to do? I'll let him love me because he's good to me. I like the way he acts and treats me." I began to love his ways. One night, beneath the cottonwood trees that grow in the churchyard, I learned what it meant to make love. Bill and I both learned. We were so innocent; we learned together.

We were so much in love that many noticed. This one lady was just happy for us. She said, "You kids want to be together all the time. Are you marrying him?" I answered, "Yes, we're going to get married." She went on, "That's good. I have a building right over there and I'll let you stay in it. There is nothing in there; nobody lives in there. You can live in there. You can stay there if you want." We thanked her. We thanked her and Bill stayed there, and I went over. One night, he said, "You know, there are bed bugs in there." I said, "What's that? How do you know?" He said, "They bite all night." I said, "Oh, my word." I was frightened about it, so he said, "We'll leave this place." So he went back to the man that had first given him a place.

Not long after that the police came to him and said, "You're going to have to leave because you're under age." He was seventeen; I was eighteen. So they told us, "You're going to have to go back home. You kids will see each other again at school. You're going to the same place." I said, "Yes." The policeman told Bill, "You wait until that time because her grandmother is concerned. There's a drifter that came in and is hanging around another girl here who is under age. We're sending him out, too, not that you're like him. But you're just going to have to go back to school or either home and wait for one another."

So, Bill left. I remember crossing that Crow bridge with him. We were way over on the other side of the river, and I was crying. He was sad, too. He took the freight again and went on to Flandreau. That's when the sun-dance thing came in.

When Bill left, I told him I would be true, I would wait for him, so I stayed home. I didn't go any place. Then it came time for Crow Fair. We camped there, and that was a happy time for all of us because camping was part of us. Grandma put up a tipi and a big tent.[2] I borrowed my brother Johnny's battery radio. It was in our tipi, and I played that thing. I listened to music that was familiar to us, to Bill and me. I just stayed there, washed dishes, prepared food, kept things clean, but I wouldn't go any place. I was waiting for the bus to come and take me to Flandreau so I could see Bill.

Pretty Shield said I'd been charmed by love potions. She said, "This tribe – the Assiniboines have strong medicine." So she said, "I'm going to take you to the sun dance that is coming up." That was the first year it came back, kind of revived. The medicine man was from Wyoming, and his name was John Truhujo.[3]

I got scared. Pretty Shield told me, "It's starting, it's opening tomorrow. I want you to go down into the river and cleanse yourself. I'll have your dress ready. You cleanse yourself. You come back and go to bed."

I went to the river at that time to cleanse myself. I went down to the river. I remember going down to the river and crossing it, heading for my dad's home which was on the other side, on the Crow Agency side. I went right to him, and I fell on my knees by him. He was sitting on a big chair under a shade behind old Deernose's place. "What's the matter?" he asked. "What's the matter?"

"My grandma's going to take me into the sun dance," I said. "I'm scared to death." He said, "Don't be afraid. Don't cry. Don't be afraid, I will pray

Crow Fair, 1947. Photo by Laura Bentley; used by permission of Myrtle B. Hubley.

for you. You do as your grandmother says. She raised you, and you have always done her bidding and what she told you to do. Do this. I will be praying for you."

So I felt much better, and I went back and I swam around in the river for a while. Then I got out and went over to the tipi and told Grandma that I was bathed. "All right," she said. "That's good." She fed me, and I ate. I stayed mostly in the tipi all the rest of that day, and that night I went to bed.

Next morning, I woke up and I thought, "Well, here I go." I was very sad because I didn't want this to happen to me. I don't know if I believed that the sun dance would kill this infatuation or love I had, but I didn't want that to happen.

I got into my dress, and I waited. I could see the sun dancers going and lining up against the side of a hill with the medicine man right ahead of them, leading them. Then he was standing in front of them, looking toward the east where the sun would come up, and sure enough, when it showed, the whistles went, the eagle bone whistles. They whistled and whistled and whistled and whistled until the sun cleared the horizon. Then they all marched back, with the medicine man leading, toward the sun lodge. They were out of sight from me, but Pretty Shield got up and said, "I will go and see how this is done – how it is conducted. I cannot let you go in if something is amiss. It's more dangerous to go in when it's improperly done than not to go at all." So I waited, breathlessly. She was coming, and I thought, "Oh, she is coming now. I'll probably have to go with her now." To my surprise, she sat down at her work. I think she was pounding meat. She would always kind of wrap it up, fold it over and put a weight on it. She would leave it and then come back to it after a while and pound some more. So, she sat back down, and she was doing this. I was waiting, and finally she said, "Ama." (She calls me Ama.) "Ama."

"Yes, Grandma," I replied. "Come over here," she said. So I went to her, all ears, because I knew I didn't want to miss any instructions she might have.

She said, "Sit down." I sat down beside her, like I always did, and I leaned against her, part of my back against her. "You're not going in," she told me.

"Wow, that's a switch," I thought.

Then she went on to say, "I looked for strips of buffalo tongue, and it was not there, not hanging up there the right way. Not at all." It was very important. It did not appear right to her. She said, "I'm afraid, so you don't have to go in. Something terrible might happen because it's not done properly," according to the way she knew. I was so relieved that I put my hands up toward the sky and I said, "Oh, thank you, Lord." At one point she said, "I don't want you to go into these dances ever, because it will never be the same. They are not doing according to the way they had done it before." So I took her advice.

When the bus came to take us to Flandreau, there was one day of the fair left, but it didn't matter to me. I was on that bus first thing. I had my bags packed. I kissed my grandma and told her, "I'll be all right, Grandma. I'll write to Mayme so she can read my letters to you." She said, "Go."

When I got off the bus at Flandreau, there was Bill, waiting for me at the bus stop. So Bill and I were in each other's arms again. We were happy, but it didn't last long. In November, Bill enlisted in the marines. They promised boys that age that they would get a higher education if they would go into the marines, and Bill did get this electrician background from there. He was a journeyman electrician when he came out.

Then came Pearl Harbor. I remember we all started packing our bags. We were going to go home. There was crying everywhere. Pearl Harbor was miles away, but we thought it was right upon us. We wanted to be home when anything happened.

I think the whole football team went into one service or another. It was a very lonesome time. I cried and I cried. Bill said he could see me crying through the screen door of the tea room where he left me.[4] When he walked away, I thought, "Maybe I'll never see him again. Maybe he's leaving me now. Why is it that we were so close, we couldn't wait to be together, we accomplished it, and now we have to be separated?"

I finished that year at Flandreau, then I went home to Pretty Shield. She was beginning to feel ill in health. The doctors said it was just old age and that she needed a rest. They couldn't find anything wrong with her, but after I started going away to school, I think she kind of gave up. More and more, I saw her counting the elk teeth on the dress she wanted to be buried in. She wanted to be buried in that dress because Goes Ahead gave her some of the elk teeth. Later, my brothers Johnny and Georgie always gave her elk teeth. She saved them and washed and dried them to put on her dress. She would lay out her dress with the arms outstretched. She'd take matches, large farmer matches. She counted five, then ten elk teeth, and she put a match through a buckskin loop. She counted elk teeth. She loved to do that, even though she knew how many elk teeth there were – I don't remember; I think it was more than five hundred. She was a big woman. She wasn't fat, but she was husky. The elk teeth on the dress would almost come to her knees. She wanted to be buried in that, so Goes Ahead could see her in that dress.

One day, I was showing her my school pictures. I had a lot of them, and she was going through them with me. I said, "That's my girl friend, this is the girl that worked to fix hair, this is our matron." I was telling her about the pictures, and she looked at all of them. She looked at the boys, too. I had pictures of them, classmate pictures, and she was looking at them. She came to this one picture and she said, "This will be your husband." It was Bill. I thought, "Oh, how could it be? How could it be?"

I didn't know if I would ever see him again, but Pretty Shield knew. She knew.

Bill was my first and really my only love. Grandma believed that the man who first made love to you was your husband. If you did not remain with him, if you went with someone else, well, that someone would be your partner, but the first one was your husband.

8

A Bad Time
in My Life

In the summer of 1942 I worked away from home for the first time. I went with Agnes and Donnie Deernose to the state of Washington, to that rich agricultural area around Toppenish. Donald had a truck, a racehorse type of truck. It had stalls, windows on the side, and that big gate thing that opened in the back. He was taking his wife, Agnes, his sister Pearl, his brother Ted Deernose, and some others. They were going to travel in that truck, then live in it when they got to Toppenish. Pearl was my friend, and she wanted me to go along.[1] Grandma thought I would be okay, because Agnes was going to be there. Agnes was always another mother to me. Pretty Shield was happy that I could go and make a little money, but when we got there, it wasn't so easy.

When we got there, some other ethnic people and some white people also were in these fields. We had to sign hiring papers; then they decided that Pearl and I would go out in the cornfield. I didn't mind because I was used to picking that kind of stuff, but I didn't realize that I could overdo it with my hands. We had to go down those long rows of corn, twist the ears off, and pile them up at the end of each row. My hands began to get sore, but I kept going on, row after row. Pretty soon, they were bleeding. I didn't have money to get gloves, but I'm sure that if I had gone to the boss, he would have gotten me some and deducted the cost from my pay. I didn't know that. I just was out of my cozy place at home, out in a place where I didn't realize what I was doing.

They took me out of the cornfield, and the boss said, "I think I'll put you in the dining room where you can wait on tables." So they took me over there and gave me all the instructions that I needed. I was good at taking instructions. I went around to the different tables; I poured their coffee, poured their water, or whatever they wanted. I worked hard at

Alma believes she was "maybe nineteen years old" when this picture was made.

pleasing them because it was my job. Two or three days went by. When I went in with the coffee, the men started calling to me, "Over here! Over here! What size dress do you wear? What kind of flowers do you like?" All this stuff. So after I got through that day (I got by as well as I could), I told the boss, "I'm afraid of those men." I was as innocent as can be. I didn't know anything about men. I told him, "I'm afraid," and started to cry. He said, "Why don't I put you in the kitchen. You can help in the kitchen." I was kind of a rookie in the kitchen, but I said, "Okay. Fine." They put me in the kitchen; I didn't see those guys anymore.

In the kitchen they brought me fifty pounds of potatoes to peel. They didn't have a potato peeler. I wondered if they had a peeler like the Indian schools I went to; they had potato peelers. But there I was with fifty pounds of potatoes, and a little knife. I sat there and peeled as fast as I could, took the eyes out of them, and put them in this big pan. Then they were washed and put through a slicer, then we filled up the frying pan and we fried potatoes. The frying pan was as big as my kitchen table. I thought to myself, "I wonder if this is what they have to do when they say they have KP duty in the army."

Finally, the boss came in (his nature reminded me of Linderman, quiet, soft-spoken). He announced, "I'm going to put her on the belt in the corn cannery." So they put us in real heavy rubber aprons, and we had to put on gloves. My friend Pearl was there, too, beside me on that belt. She was about as young and about as green as I was. We were supposed to take that corn, use these blades in the machine, and cut off the bad parts. We did that, and we did it well. It's funny, but when we got our checks, it seemed to me like we didn't get very much. We paid for our food, our board and room. We paid Donald Deernose, and we didn't have much left.

In fact, his sister, my friend Pearl, said, "I've got my check, and I got some money here, but I must get to my boyfriend, Frank Backbone." He was stationed at an army post not too far way. She said, "I got to get there." I asked, "How much do you need?" "I need ten dollars more to make bus fare and a little something on the side to eat with," she answered. So I gave her ten dollars, and that left me short, but I did it for her. She was going over there to marry him. She went. Then when I returned to the truck, Agnes said, "Where's Pearl?" I said, "I don't know. I think she might have gone to the store or something." Agnes said to me, "You know where she is. Tell us." She kind of felt uneasiness about my conversation, I guess. So I admitted, "Well, she got on the bus and went to Frank Backbone."

Anyway, it was too late for them to try to stop the bus. She was already gone. I really missed her.

I slept on the part of the truck where the horses feed. Agnes fixed me a bed, rolled a bunch of blankets up in that loft thing. Agnes did the cooking. She had a gas hotplate there in the truck. She looked after me while I was there.

We worked a while longer; then it was time to go home. I came home with just my last check, which was almost nothing at all. They didn't pay us much. We were kids, and we let it ride like we were told to do. Pretty Shield said, "You've been gone all this time, and I've been concerned about you, worried about you." I said, "This is all I have." She said, "Ohhh, you've been gone too long to have just this much."

I detested being gone. There were some mean people around that place in Toppenish, too, people I was not very fond of. I mean women that drank and wanted to fight. An Indian woman wanted to fight me because she thought I was interested in her husband. I didn't have anything to do with her husband. I didn't even know who he was. I ran. I took off, not knowing what for. I went under a porch that had a lattice around it, and I watched her and her friends look for me. I was afraid that they would kill me.

Not long after I returned to Crow, my sister Pearl asked me to come to Tacoma, Washington. She was working in the shipyards there, and she needed a babysitter, so in the fall of 1942 I went to Tacoma. There were quite a few Crow people working in the war industries there, and other Indian people, too. I went because I wanted to be nearer to San Diego. That's where Bill was. He was going to ship out, any time, and we wanted to get married before he left. When I went to Tacoma, I sent him my address and told him, "As soon as I hear from you, I will come to California." He mailed a letter to Tacoma, Washington. I kept asking my sister, Pearl, "Where is the letter that I'm expecting?" She said, "I don't know."

But she knew. My older sister, Cerise, was in Tacoma, too. She came to Pearl's apartment, got the letter from Bill, took it and read it. The letter said, "Come immediately. We'll get married." I was waiting for that letter. Being kind of mothers to me always, those sisters had the idea that my business was theirs. So, Cerise read the letter. "Oh, no," she vowed. "I'm not going to let her marry a different tribe. Oh, no. I'm not going to let her marry a different tribe." She threw the letter in the heater at Pearl's apartment. She threw it in there and burned it. She burned that letter up, and they never told me until way afterward. Pearl told me, a long time later, after my children were born. I even cried then, when she told me.

I stayed with Pearl for a time, then I went home. I was forlorn, I didn't know what to do. I got a job and tried to make my own money.

Bill, in turn, said, "Well, if she didn't answer me, I guess she doesn't want me any more." He got drunk. He and his friend – they had the attitude, "We're going to die. We're going out to die, so we might as well have fun, now." So they went to a dance hall, where they met these two girls. They got drunk with them and got married. Bill told me, later, "I don't remember even putting the ring on her finger. Then we shipped out. And before we knew it, when the paperwork reached us, we were giving some girls part of our checks. I felt like I had sinned." He wrote me and told me what happened, but I felt like it was too late. I heard from him two or three times, telling me he had made a terrible mistake. He still had my photo. Before all this happened, I had sent him a picture of myself and had signed it "Dew Drop." When he first left Flandreau, he said he dreamed of me; he was chasing me and calling me "Dew Drop," so I signed the picture "Dew Drop." He told me he put my picture in a photo contest that his platoon had, and it won first place.[2]

I didn't lack for friends, for male friends, during this time, but Bill just stayed on my mind. I remember one time I stepped off the bus at home, and Frank Yarlott saw me. He looked at me and said, "Well, there she is. The belle of Crow Agency." I went to work at the confectionery shop again, cooking hamburgers and hot dogs. A lot of people came to eat there, and Johnny Burns, the owner, had a record-playing machine there – a nickelodeon, we used to call it. And people would come, and some would dance. We congregated there.

Now Johnny Burns and Mary Kate Reed, an elder and a prominent person in town, decided that I would represent them in a bathing beauty contest that was going to be held in Hardin. Girls were going to put on their bathing suits and go around a swimming pool to be judged. One of the kids came running over to me and said, "They're coming to see you. They're going to enter you in the bathing beauty contest." I was afraid. What I was afraid of was the bathing suit, actually. I hid under the bed in Grandma's house, and I said, "Tell them I'm not here."

Mary Kate Reed came. She said, "Johnny Burns sent me here because we met and decided that we want Alma to represent Crow. We want to sponsor her in the bathing beauty contest. She'll win. She'll win." My girlfriends said, "We don't know where she is." My folks didn't know that I was under the bed; I had only told my girlfriends, "Don't tell. Tell them I'm not here." So one of my friends said, "We'll tell her when she comes." Mary Kate said, "Well, you be sure. You make sure she comes over to Johnny Burns's confectionery. Now we want her real bad in there." I wouldn't. I just refused to go. It was the bathing suit. I didn't want that bathing suit on. We went swimming in our dresses.

We were forever trying to go to some social event during that time, about 1943. They had dances. They had local talent, Indian people, that would play saxophone and piano. They played waltzes and the fox trot. We loved to dance or watch other people dance. They had the dances in a big recreation hall right there where the BIA buildings are now. We had push dances just across from town, just across the bridge there, where there's a little building over to the right.[3] It had a little potbelly heater system that used wood, and the boys went over there early and got the place all warmed up. The musician for the fiddle was a boy we called Fred Takes the Horse, and other people played other instruments. We also had Indian drummers and Indian singers. Sometimes some of the boys would do a kind of war dance, and we'd have to go along with them.

We never had road scrapers to clear the way when it snowed, so if the weather was bad, and everybody heard there was going to be a push dance, we went in knee-deep snow to get there. When we got there, sometimes we took off our socks and shoes and put them by the stove until they were kind of half dry. Then we put them on and danced anyway.

I needed more education, so with two other Crow girls, Alice White Clay and Annie Big Man, I went for training at the National Youth Administration in Helena.[4] There were whites and Indians there. Those two Crow girls told the whites that I was an Indian princess, the daughter of a chief. I told Annie, "Your dad is always saying he's a chief. You should be the princess." She said, "No. We've told them it's you, and they believe us."

Another funny thing happened while we were in Helena. A young Crow who later became a distinguished elder wrote us love letters. He was off somewhere – away from Crow – and he wrote each one of us a letter, sent it to our addresses at home. Well, the letters were forwarded to Helena, and when we got them, we compared them. They were absolutely identical. He wrote the same thing to each one of us. They were nice letters, said things like, "I've always liked you. I hope you'll write to me. I'd like to have a date with you." The three of us got together and wrote him

one letter in reply. We all signed the same letter. I have always wondered
what he thought.

I began to be friends with this white boy who lived on a ranch not far
from Crow. We visited with each other, and one day, he asked me to marry
him. I said, "No. I can't marry you, because my family is Crow, and yours
is white." He said, "Our families would not be getting married. It would
be us." I didn't want to be intimidated by his family. I had seen Crow girls
marry white men, and they had to give up their ways. I knew I couldn't
do that, so I told him, "No."

I know what discrimination feels like. One time in 1944 I was with a
bunch of Crow young people like myself in Sheridan, Wyoming. They
said, "Alma, you go in there and get us some hot dogs." They gave me
ten dollars, I remember. "Get it all in hot dogs and bring 'em out here,
and we'll eat." I said, "Why don't you all come in?" They said, "They don't
want Indians in there." I said, "Why send me in there?" And they said,
"Because you're the one that looks more like – more like white than any
of us." I said, "Well, they'll know I'm an Indian." But I went in there
anyway and saw that sign. I ordered about ten hot dogs, which were
about one dollar apiece in those days. I ordered them, and they fixed
them for me. They brought them out in a big bag. I said, "Look, I just
now saw your sign. What does that mean?" It said, "No Indians allowed.
No Mexicans or Dogs." I said, "I'm Indian. I'm Indian. I don't want this
if that's the way it is. I don't want to take something – " They said, "No.
No. It's all right. You take this." I knew the kids were hungry, so I took
it. The waitresses were always blaming the managers. They said, "Well,
it isn't our doings, you know." They said that it was the managers that
wanted it done: "It's beyond our control." But the rest of us had to pay
for it.

Long ago, Indian people, when they went to Billings, took their lunches
with them. I remember one proprietor, he came out because I was talking
about why Indian people weren't allowed in there. The waitress went
in back to get him so he could come out and see me. When he came,
he just kind of gasped, like, "Oh, well, come on in." But I said, "No, I
wouldn't feel right." He said, "It's not you. They come in drunk, and
one woman urinated all the way from the booth to the door." I said, "If
one of your own came in drunk and did something like that, would you
classify them, and say 'No whites?' " He said, "Most of them who come in
are drinking." I said, "I don't drink." He said, "You are welcome." But I
didn't go in.

Sometime early in 1944 my Grandma began to give me warnings. She said, "I went after wood, and across the river from the campgrounds I picked up sticks and branches. I was busy. I piled them here and piled them there. I was going to pick them up when I heard a woman scream. I ventured toward where the scream was coming from. Nobody was around."

Then she saw a car, and the back doors were open and "I saw this young man rape a girl, and she was screaming and kicking and crying. I hated to see it. I'm an *old* lady now, and it was way on the other side of the river. I turned my back on it. I felt the weight of my age. I remember a time when I was a young lady, and I was strong. I went to where ladies go for their latrine. This man was stalking a girl. Out of the brush he came, and as soon as she came up from where she was, he grabbed ahold of her. He was going to rape her; he threw her down. I went over there, and I took that man and I twisted his ear almost off. I took the hide off his ear, and he took off running." She said that the girl was crying, "but I saved her that time from being raped. I remembered that when I saw what the girl in the car was going through."

Then she told me, "This same man is, this same man, I see him in my mind's eye, stalking you – *díialichiilik*. He is a dangerous man."

"Oh," I said, "don't worry about me. I'll run, and I'm a fast runner, and I'm strong."

Until she got very old, Grandma relied on her own medicine for sickness, but my sisters Cerise and Mayme might recognize something and say, "This is what it is. Grandma, you better tell the doctor. They have real good stuff for it now." She would say, "I'll be all right. I know what to do." And she did. She always treated herself and doctored herself. I don't know what was wrong with her when she got sick toward the last, but as far as I know, the doctor said, "It's just old age and a broken heart. There's nothing physically wrong with her." My sisters said that she wanted to be with Goes Ahead.

She died of a broken heart – all the changes that had happened to her world, and her own grandchildren so much a part of the other world. She gave up. They had put her on a bed, of all things. Etheline, my brother George's daughter, lay right next to Grandma's legs, under the blanket near her feet. George read the Twenty-third Psalm. Then Grandma said a few words of the psalm, just a few words. George put a crucifix in her hand. Frances, Cerise, Pearl, Mayme – we were all there, and maybe a couple of others. Grandma spoke to each one. She told Mayme, "I will not be here when the paper comes this moon." (She meant Goes Ahead's pension check.) "I'm going one day early, but they will give it to you. Go get it and get some food." She went down the other grandchildren, "You're going to be all right. You're going to be all right, but I'm worried about one. That's Frances. Frances has many little children. There's something ahead of her."

She took my hand, she said, "You will be all right, *díialiitee díimmaachik.* You will go and make it. Whatever you put your efforts in will be so." Her hands were just warm. I was pushing her hair, just pushing it gently. She pointed, and she said, "Four people are coming. I must go." Then she was with Goes Ahead. She went happily.

Everybody started to cry, and I put my hands on her eyelids, and I took her best muffler, and I covered her face. The funeral was at the Baptist church. Pastor Bentley officiated. She was laid to rest with Goes Ahead.[5]

I kept working at the confectionery, but I remembered Grandma's warning. By this time, I had become aware that this man she had told me about *was* dangerous. Sometimes I would be in the grocery store, and he would come in and just look at me. Look at me. The grocer would call me back to wherever he was, as if to get me out of this man's way. Every night when I got off, I asked one of the policemen, usually it was Max Big Man, to follow me in his car when I walked home. We didn't have streetlights in those days. The streets were really dark. Sometimes friends were at the shop, and they would say, "Oh, we'll walk home with you." I knew I didn't want to walk home by myself. I was anxious. I just had this anxious feeling.

One night my niece and her boyfriend said they would walk me home. We walked by this building, this kind of bachelor apartment, where that man stayed sometimes. It didn't belong to him. He was married, but he had separated from his wife, so he was staying in another man's apartment. A lot of drinking and fighting went on there. That night my niece and her boyfriend said, "Let's go in and visit" this guy. I think they thought they were being cute. I didn't want to, but they said, "Oh, we won't stay long. It will be okay." I thought, "Well, they will be with me." So I said, "All right." We were there a little while, and my niece said she had to go to the bathroom. She started out the door. I went to her and said, "There's a bathroom back there." She said, "Oh, those men might hear me." And she left. She was gone a long time. She didn't come back. Her boyfriend said, "I'll go look for her." I got up to follow him out. He left. He closed the door, and it locked. I reached to unlock it, and I felt something hit the back of my head. I knew it was him.

I screamed, and I fought him as hard as I could, and I was strong. I kicked and screamed and hit him with my fists, and he just kept coming after me. He was a big man. I kept fighting him; then I fell and caught my head under the wooden arm of a sofa. I couldn't move. I blacked out. When I came to, I heard somebody knocking on the door. It was some guys that were drunk and carousing around. He wouldn't let them in because the room was wrecked. I was like a rag. He picked me up and put me in this storage place that had a wicker chair in it. I remember he put me there and closed that door. That's when I saw a shadow through the window, and I knew this guy had gone outside. I wished I could disappear. I thought, "There's nothing more to me." I saw his shadow, and I heard him talking to those people. But the damage was done. I didn't know what to do. After those people left, he let me go. I went out that door. I went over toward the railroad tracks. I decided to lie there and wait for the train to come, let everything happen as it will. But I fell. I fell before – then this man picked me up. I asked to go to Pearl's house. I lay on my stomach all night long.[6]

The next day I told Pearl everything. She saw the bruises and cuts on my body, and she was very angry. We went to report it. The judge said, "Well, that happens all the time. There has never been any Crow sentenced for something like that."[7] My brothers wanted to kill the man. No charges were brought against him. I felt as if I had fallen into a trap. I felt defeated. Grandma's dreadful premonition had come true.

I decided to go back to Flandreau. I still hadn't finished my education, so I went back. That's when I found out I was pregnant. Pregnant with the child of the man who raped me. I came home. I was so confused. People said so many different things to me. One of my relatives told me, "I'll take you to Sheridan for an abortion. You cannot have that baby. You will disgrace the family." I was a Christian, and I didn't want to end my pregnancy. My father was brokenhearted, and I felt bad because I loved him very much. Some of my friends said, "Marry him. He has said he wants to marry you. Marry the baby's father."

My dependence on Pretty Shield was always there. I thought, "If you were here, this wouldn't happen. If you're in such a good place, why can't I be there?" This was a bad time in my life. I didn't want to grow up. I wanted to be a child. I wanted to be out there in the wilds with her. I wanted it to be like old times, when I was growing up. I just wanted to be out in the wilderness and do what Pretty Shield did.

I went over to the Baptist missionary then and talked with her like my mother, you might say – Mrs. Bentley. She told me, "Come on up here to the study, and we'll pray." I was with my sister-in-law, my cousin Johnny's wife, Louella. We went up there. We all three knelt down on the floor in that place and we prayed. We prayed for cleansing and for God to show us what to do. When I left there, I felt pretty good. Mrs. Bentley told me not to marry that man. She said, "Don't even give the baby his name. Don't ever see that man again. Don't accept anything from him for this child. *Don't do it.*" And I never did.

I went to work in the hospital. The doctor said, "Put her to work, or she will have a breakdown." I worked as a nurse's aide – a blue girl, we were called in those days. One day an older man came in. He was wearing a ten-gallon hat with feathers on it, and a big scarf tied around the crown. He went to the information window, so I went to the window and said, "Can I help you?" "Yes," he said. "I want to see Sitting Bull's daughter." I said, "I'll have to look and see." I turned around, and I went over to Cordelia Big Man, who was the older one of us. She was standing there fooling with the medication that we were supposed to take out. I said, "Cordelia, that guy at the window wants to talk to Sitting Bull's daughter. Who is she?" She looked at me and laughed, and she said, "That's you. Your father's name is Sitting Bull, *Chíilapawaachish.*" When I heard that, I went over to the window and told him that it was me. He looked at me, and he started to laugh, because I hadn't known it. Then he said, "I want to propose for my son. He wants to marry you."

He said, "I have many cattle over there in North Dakota." (He was Hidatsa.) "You will have all that I have. My land – everything will belong to Francis" (his son). I said, "Oh." I was pretty well surprised about this time, so I said, "Let me think it over, and I will let you know. I can't answer right now." I appreciated him coming. I thanked him for coming, and I told him, "Now I know who Sitting Bull's daughter is." He laughed and left. The son came, and he asked to see me. I talked to him just briefly. I told him that I was not interested in marriage at the time. He was very gracious. He accepted it and left. His brother married my niece, Etheline.

The senior doctor in the hospital was a Christian. He was a good Christian doctor. He didn't like what happened to me, but there was nothing he could do about it. When the baby started to come, I was in labor for four days. Afterward, they told me they should have done a cesarean, but they didn't do that much in those days. Finally, my little boy was born. I said, "I don't know what to call him." The doctor said, "Well, my name is Theodore." So I gave the baby that name.

I'm telling this now not to bring up old hurts or to cause more. But I was hurt. Actually, it was a lifetime of hurt. I have wondered, "Did this happen to me so I could help others?" – which I have done. I have helped girls who were hurt, girls hurt like I had been. Sometimes, I took them to the spiritual realm and brought them slowly back to reality. The past was not their own anymore. They became new in Jesus. He is our righteousness. My stand in Christ is, "I am forgiven, so I forgive others."

After Ted was born, my sister Pearl asked me to come to live in her home. She lived right there in Crow. Finally, I got a place that this cousin of mine said I could rent. I was happy for that because she had a nice place, and I rented it from her.

Things were pretty hard, and I became frightened one day when I was in that house. I became frightened that I was alone with my little baby. Something might happen to either one of us, and no one would ever know. In the middle of the night, that panic – that panic was so heavy on me that instead of going into prayer and meditating on who I could talk with, I took my baby and wrapped him up, and I left my house. I went through the pasture of the Baptist church to go to my sister's place.

Before I was halfway through that pasture and those trees there, the cottonwood trees, I fell to my knees, and in my weakened condition I could not get up. I cried. I cried there in the middle of that field, and I wondered why I was alive. And I looked at the little baby, at Ted. My Uncle Frank Shane's house was not too far away. I thought I would make my way there because my heart was out of rhythm. I could hardly catch my breath. Then I believe somebody saw me from the Shane house, and they came out to help me with my baby. The one they called Philip Shane took me to a cot and told me to lie down. He said, "Lie down and relax, now. You're okay and the baby, too." I lay there and rested. They took care of Ted. After that night I got one of my nieces to live with me. She was there, and when she and the baby were noisy and playing, I was glad. I was glad they were there.

Finally, my sister Mayme took over the care of my baby because I was not well. I was working in the hospital and trying to make a go of it. Mayme thought it would help me if she took him with her to Wyola, where she was living with my sister Frances and her husband, Paul Knows His Gun. Frances was not too well at the time, and she wanted Mayme to be with her to help her. So Mayme decided to take that little baby back to Wyola and care for him. On weekends I could see him. They'd bring him, and then they'd take him back when it was time for me to go to work. I missed that little boy. I missed that little boy as part of me. I just couldn't see him be taken away. Sometimes I'd even go to Wyola in the middle of the week, if I could find a vehicle to take me, or some friends. I went back to live with Pearl. She broke from her husband, and she had a home right there in Crow, so I went to her house. I helped her buy coal and helped with groceries. I was still working, and Mayme still insisted on keeping the baby.[8]

A young Crow man came into the hospital. He was suffering from syphilis. He had been a basketball star, and we always thought he was good-looking. He was about Pearl's age, I guess. His mother had been my mother's best friend. While he was in the hospital, I helped to take care of him. He knew me then, and I talked nice to him because I felt deep, deep hurt within my own self to see one of our boys like that. He wanted to go home to die. He sent his mother to me. She came, and she said, "I'm your mother's best friend, and I came to talk to you." She said, "I want to ask you to come and marry my son." I looked at her and said, "Well, he is – you know what he has." She said, "I know, but he wants to marry you. He doesn't expect anything from you but the care that you have given him in the hospital, that's all." I hated to refuse the woman, but I said, "I'm beginning to think that I don't want to be married to anyone I don't love. I would rather stay alone and not marry at all." So I refused, but I felt sorry for the young man.

Then there was this Crow man who had just come back from the war. He came home. He was wounded, but he was okay. The Crow elders gave him a red feather, and they told him to wear it. They give those to people who are wounded in battle. They can wear a red one – the eagle feather can be painted red. No one else can wear that except those who are wounded. There was quite a lot of talk about it.

He went to my brother Georgie and said, "I'd like to marry your sister. I'll take care of her. I have a horse laden down with gifts. My mother will provide those gifts, and my relatives. A beef, a whole beef will be given to your family. I'll take care of her and her child."

My brother came and told me that he had talked with my sisters. Frances was the only one who didn't want me to do this. The others didn't say anything. They more or less let Georgie say what he wanted. They listened to him, and after he left they consulted among themselves. Frances said, "I wish there was another way out of this." Mayme said, "She doesn't have to take care of her child. I'll take care of it, and she can go on with her life."

I myself thought I had no life left. I was just going to exist on this earth. I'd do what I could to exist, but as for life and plans, "No. I don't care about it. I don't want to even dream about such events or anything else," although I always stuck to prayer. I always stuck to prayer, and then, Mrs. Bentley was the biggest influence in my life at that time. And Johnny's wife Louella was by my side always, it seemed.

My sisters decided I should marry this guy. They told me that Georgie had accepted because he thought that guy was such a hero. I took a bunch of phenobarbital pills and I ran. I left my baby with Mayme, and I went to Hardin. I had some dry cleaning to pick up. I probably went in with Louella, because she was always there. But this dope was working on me, and at times my heart would beat so fast that I could hardly go anyplace. I remember that I had a two-piece pink dress on. I'll always remember that. I had that on when I was picking up my cleaning, and this guy came along and paid for my cleaning. I looked at him for the first time, right in the face for the first time. I said, "I got money. I can pay for it." He said, "Save your money, because I'll be taking care of you from now on."

Somehow they got me to sign the certificate. I was so full of dope, I didn't even know what was going on – that phenobarbital. I thought, "I don't care anymore." I went back to the house, and somebody said that they had already called Bentley. Bentley had talked to this man. I don't want to say his name; I'll just call him Daniel. They said, "Go over to the Bentleys," so I went. Mr. Bentley talked to Daniel, and he talked to me, but do you know, to this day, I don't know what he said. I don't remember what he said. I looked at Daniel, and I thought, "My husband." I don't even remember saying, "I do." (A long time after that day, I think Mr. Bentley told Bill what happened. Mr. Bentley had baptized Bill. He liked Bill very much. He told him, "I have never seen such a reluctance in marriage. She didn't care about him; she didn't hold his hand; she didn't kiss him. Yet her folks thought that she would be taken care of, and the baby.")

I left the Bentleys, and I took off. I don't know what happened to the man. I went over to the house, Grandma's old house, and I went inside. The girls, my sisters, were trying to tease me and make me laugh. He came. Daniel came to the house and asked through the door, "May I talk to Alma?" I said, "I have nothing to say to him." He said, "Can I have some coffee?" This was through the door. The door was locked, and I just sat there like a statue. My sisters told me, "You shouldn't do this, Alma. He fought for our country. He's wearing a red feather. He's noted in the whole community, the whole tribe, as one who came home wounded. He has won the right to wear a red feather." This was something big, I guess. I poured him a cup of coffee, and I stuck it out the door. He sat down on the steps, and he drank it. My sisters said, "You should be happy." I hated it.

I didn't want him to touch me. I didn't want him to. I didn't want to go anyplace with him.

It was Crow Fair time, and he wanted me to parade with him. His family said, "We'll borrow someone's clothes for you to parade in, and after that we'll fix your outfit, and you can have it." I refused. "No. I don't want to parade in anybody else's clothes. I'll just walk with him." That's how it was. I walked with him and his steed with him on it, and his red feather on. I walked with him, and his mother came, too. To the side, staring at me, was Ted's dad.

This walking, as far as the tribe was concerned, did away with all unnecessary shame in my life. It brought me up to the level of the dignitaries of the tribe, you might say. This is one great thing that Daniel did for me. I gained my status, sort of, but I was hardly aware of this because at my age I didn't know some of the old ways that I had never seen happen. I had never seen this happen, so it had never been explained to me.[9]

Later, after I had walked, I was at home in the campsite, and Ted's dad came over to me. I was doing something, holding on to a shade pole or something, and all at once I heard someone lead a horse up. I heard this voice say, "You got it over on me, didn't you?" I heard that voice, and I hated to even look. He said, "So you were all it, and all the eyes were upon you. I was ignored. He became the hero, and you became his." I never said a word. Not even one word to him. I met his eyes only once when he said, "Are you going to say anything?" I turned and looked at him in his eyes, and I looked away. I was just unlearned about what he was saying, actually. Afterward, it was explained to me that a man like him becomes less than a trifle when a woman that he wants marries someone who has done a greater deed than he did. He becomes nothing.

After Crow Fair the man I was supposedly married to threatened to kill me. It wasn't a marriage at all. I didn't stay in camp. I just went because I was called there to do this walking; then I went back to Grandma's house. He came over there. He came over there with a gun that he had borrowed from Isaac Shane. He borrowed that gun – it was a twenty-two – and he asked for some bullets. I think Isaac said that he didn't have any bullets. The man talked like he was going to go after some deer. Finally he came in, and he borrowed two shells from somebody. He came and he showed them to me in his hands. I looked at his hands, and he said, "You see this?" I said, "Yes." He said, "One is for you, and one is for me. I'll kill you before I let you go – or before you divorce me." He was sort of that proud, I guess.

My sisters got all excited. They exclaimed, "He's going to kill her! He's going to do a lot of damage around here!" They wondered if I should go hide someplace. I said, "I'm not going to hide. What if he does kill me, so what?" I didn't care. My sisters would raise my baby anyway. My sisters sent somebody to call the police. The police came and questioned me about it. I said, "I don't care to be married to him any longer. I don't want to have him consider me as his wife. I don't have anything to do with him, and these people saw it all." So the police got a court order that he had to stay a certain distance from me. At least he stayed away from me bodily.

I had the marriage annulled, by doctor's orders.

I was sick then. I used to go to the park area in front of the old hospital. The little birds would come and eat right at my feet. They'd come and eat right at my feet because every morning I had crumbs for them. One of them even landed on my shoulder one time. I went there because it just gave me something to do. It seemed like "I'm important to these little animals. I'm important. They wait for me." But I was in this trauma. There were times when I looked out at those trees, and it was as if they were walking toward me. I was that close to breaking. I was anxious in my mind that they were going to get me. When they got too close, it was frightening. It frightened me, but then I'd think, "That's the park." I was probably less than a hundred pounds.

Looking back, I think that I didn't do away with myself because of my faith, my faith and my love of nature and her little creatures.

9

I Have Crossed
Three Rivers

I came very close to marrying a man who was older than I was, maybe just for security. He was a businessman in Crow Agency, a bachelor type. He had maybe one-fourth Crow in him, but he was more toward the white ways. His mother had a bakery where I'd eat my lunch when I worked at the hospital. She had little booths in there and stools at a counter, and she made the best sandwiches – nice, not greasy. I remember she was watching me eat a hamburger one time, and she said, "You don't eat enough to keep a bird alive. Working like you are, you should eat more than you're eating." She would give me an extra glass of milk or something like that. I would take it because it was from her.

Her son began to talk to me. (This was about a year and a half after my baby had been born.) He was a stranger to me, even though I had known his family for quite a while. He was very kind. "Don't be afraid of me," he said. "I'm trying to help you. I know the upsets you have had. You shouldn't have had to go through those. We feel bad that you want to turn to your lonely side of life. I'd like to cheer you up by taking you to a show or wherever you might want to go." I said that I'd think about it. Then I did. I did go with him to shows and to different occasions that might bring me out of my loneliness. He'd laugh a lot. He would show me something, and I think I asked silly questions, and he just laughed at me and then he would explain things.

One day we were riding on the battlefield hills, and he says, "Look at that." It was pretty at that time, and the stars were just coming out. He says, "Did you ever see something like that before?" I looked up, and the stars were falling out of heaven. A whole bunch of them, it seemed like, just falling out of heaven.

"Oh, my God. I'm scared," I said. Being very religious I thought maybe this was a prelude to Christ coming.

He said, "Well, there's nothing we can do about it if it is."

"I can be home," I replied.

"Just watch it," he urged, "just watch those things fall." Oh, the stars were just falling everywhere.

"Are we going to have any stars left?" I asked. He just laughed.

Finally, he said he'd like to marry me. I said, "Oh, no. I don't want any children. I don't like to be pregnant. I'm afraid."

"You don't have to be," he assured me. "In fact, there's something the doctors are going to adjust in me. Right now, perhaps I couldn't give you a child even if I wanted to. Over there in Sheridan, Wyoming, there's a veterans' hospital, and those doctors believe that they can adjust me to normality." He had gotten hurt in the war.

"I don't want to have sex. No way. I don't want that. That's why I stay by myself," I told him.

"Oh, no. You'll come out of this; you're a young woman," he replied. "We can't go through life like that. I'll go to the hospital in Sheridan. Whatever they do, just pray that I'll be all right. Then we'll get married. When I come back we'll get married." I agreed.

This man was very gentlemanly, very tender. He said to me, "You're young, will you treat me with respect? No doubt young men will be interested in you."

I said, "You don't have to worry about a thing. I'll be the kind of wife that a wife should be. I will help you in your business. I'll be what a good wife should be – loyal. Except if Bill Snell ever comes, then I think it would be goodbye, if he wants me."

He asked where Bill was, and I told him, "As far as I know he's in California, and he's still married." I was sure I would never see Bill again.

This man went on to the hospital in Sheridan, and I was still going to work. He'd call or send me flowers. I was living with my sister Pearl. He ordered a whole bunch of coal for us at Pearl's. When the coal truck came, I said, "We didn't order any coal." The truckers told us, "It was ordered to be put here." So they just filled our little coal shed, and Pearl was glad. I thought, "Well, I don't have to buy it." I used to budget from my paycheck to help her out with the coal. We helped each other a lot, Pearl and I. We didn't have a phone, but I got cards from the man, and I knew that while he was there in Sheridan he was looking very much forward to this thing that we had planned.

In the meantime, Bill came back to Montana, to Fort Belknap. I don't know what happened. I thought that he had a wife somewhere, although he wrote letters to me and admitted, "I have done something wrong. I'm sorry – a terrible thing happened." Good letters, always with love. Still, I didn't really expect to see him anymore. The first letter I wrote him was to tell him about the terrible thing that had happened to me. He answered, "We'll just make the best of it." I wrote back, "You're still married." I assume maybe I didn't want to get married. I didn't want babies. We both were sorry, but it was "Let's go our different ways now."

Then here comes this filling station man. He must have come about four blocks to where we lived. He said, "There's a call for you and you should go right away. If you want to, come with me. It will be quicker." He had a truck. I had to give him fifty cents for coming after me. I must have had a nickel left, because when I got to the filling station, I bought an ice-cream cone; then I went to the telephone.

It was Bill. "What are you doing?" he asked.

"Eating ice cream. Do you want some?" I said, just trying to be funny.

"Are you married?" he wondered. I told him that I wasn't but that I would be in about two weeks.

He then said, "Will you wait until you get a letter from me?"

"Yes," I replied. Then we talked some more. Thirty-five or thirty-six dollars' worth of calling on the pay phone – that's what he finally had to pay after he got through talking with me.

In about two nights or so, I was lying there in bed, propped up. There was this guy, very good-looking Crow guy who came to the house that night and wanted to see me. Pearl said, "She's not feeling too well." He said, "I got to talk to her." So Pearl told me who it was, and I knew that he had gone out with a friend of mine when we were younger, so I thought maybe he wanted to talk to me about her. He came in, and he sat a ways from the bed I was propped in. I asked him, "What did you come for?" "I want to ask you to be my mate," he said. "I have this thought that you should marry me."

I was listening to him when there was a knock on the door. Pearl asked, "Who is it?" I heard her saying in the other room, "Bill." I turned around and this guy was gone out the back door. In the meantime, Pearl says, "Oh, my God. Wait." She came in, and she said, "It's Bill Snell." It was like the blood drained out of my body. I just said, "Well, let him in."

He greeted her first, went on in, and I heard him. He had boots on, of course, and I didn't realize that. His steps made a noise like knock,

knock, knock, hitting the floor. We had linoleum floors in that little place she rented. I thought, "Oh, my God. He's got wooden legs, because of the war. I must not look at his legs." I don't know why that thought flashed through my mind, but he stood there at the end of the bed.

I looked at him, and he said, "It's been a long time, hasn't it?" I'll never forget the words, "It's been a long time, hasn't it?"

I nodded my head yes. I hardly could speak.

"Are you sick?" he asked. "If you are, I'm going to take you home and make you well. I'm going to take you home with me."

He came around the bed, and I couldn't help but look at his feet. They were okay. They were in boots, and I felt much better about it. Bill wanted to know how many kids I had. I told him, "Six," just teasing him. "Well, pack 'em up," he said. "Let's go." I had written him about what had happened to me, so I could tell him, "My little boy is not here. My sister takes care of him."

"I'd like to take you back," he said.

I hesitated. "I'll have to give them two weeks' notice before I leave the hospital."

"Now!" Bill declared. "I have crossed three rivers to get you. I want you to come with me now."[1]

I told Pearl, and she responded, "Well, you can go. Maybe you can come back and get whatever you have to do done." We talked for a little while. We gave Bill some gravy and biscuits; he sat there and he looked at it, and I said, "Eat it." He looked at me, and he ate it. I thought, "Why did I say that – 'eat it' – like a command?" We were all kind of out of sorts. He said he wanted to take me home with him because they were farming at home, and he had no business leaving. He said, "I never stopped once. I came right on through, never slept."

He drove me to the hospital. I went in and told the head nurse that I had to leave. She said, "Alma, you've got to give us time to put somebody in there." So I went out and told Bill again, "I hate to leave because they have been good to me all this time."

He said, "If you don't go tell them that it's an emergency – that you have to leave now – I'm going to go in and tell them myself." I went in and told them.

They reluctantly agreed, "Well, okay. It's not a very good thing to do, but we'll do our best." There was this little sick boy who saw me and asked, "Where are you going?" I went over and told him that I was leaving. He said, "We won't have sunshine no more."

"Oh, yes," I replied. "The one who gives sunshine will give you sunshine." So I left, and that's the last person I saw as I left that hospital.

I went with Bill to Harlem, Montana. On the way, he said that he had to get some sleep, so we stopped to sleep in Great Falls. Then we went on. He didn't say much; I didn't say too much. I could tell he had a lot on his mind, and he wanted to get back to his uncle's ranch. They didn't know where he'd gone, and that was on his mind, too. He checked me into a motel in Harlem when we got there, and he said, "I'll be back, so don't go away. Stay right here." I said, "All right." He left and went down to the family ranch. (He stayed with me that night; then early in the morning, he went down to the ranch.)

When he came back, I thought, "What am I doing here? What am I doing here?" His Aunt Lena, his adopted mom, told me later what had happened when he got back to the ranch. He went in the door. He stopped. That woman was there, his woman. He had told her in the first place not to come with him from California, because, "This is it. This is the end." He didn't love her. She had said, "I'll take my chances." So she had come with him. At that time, I didn't even know that there was a woman there.

Lena told me that when he got to the ranch, he parked the car, and there was a pillow in the car. This woman (Bill's wife) looked in the car, and she said, "Oh, my God. They have a baby." I guess she saw the pillow and thought that. She seemed to know where he had gone. Lena said the woman started weeping, and Grandma Buck (Lena's mother) grabbed ahold of Bill and tried to make him drink a potion of some kind that she'd mixed. She walked right up to him, but he wouldn't take it. He kept away from it. This woman went up to him, and she said, "You came." He took her, and he just threw her to one side. He went in the house, got something, came out the door, got in the car, and left.

He came to where I was at the hotel. He put his arms around me with his head on my shoulder. I was kneeling on the bed. He just grabbed ahold of me, and it's as if he sobbed to me.

I asked, "What's the matter?"

He didn't say anything. I continued, "What did you say?"

He choked out the words, "That woman's still there, and Grandma tried to get ahold of me and make me do this and that."

"Oh, don't worry," I tried to comfort him. "Calm down. There's only one thing we can do, and that is to get me on the bus and send me home.

I'll get home before that job is given to anyone else. I must get back, and you go ahead and try to make it work."

Bill shook his head, "It doesn't make any difference whether you are here or gone; I don't want her. It just won't do any good. I want you to stay."

His mind was in a web, and I thought, "When he leaves, I'll sneak out and go. He won't have too much trouble. He will settle down." We talked it over for a little while, and I told Bill, "Maybe I better go back." He emphatically said, "I *don't* want you to go back."

Then Bill told me that he was going to see his Uncle Albert in some business place down the street, and he left.

He went, and in the meantime I packed up what little belongings I had. I packed up, and I ran down the back stairs, the fire escape stairway. I went down there, and I began asking people which way I should go to catch a bus, to catch a ride out of there to Great Falls.

Bill came back to the room. Somebody told him they saw me going that way, so he ran after me. He came and took hold of my arm. He was kind of rough with me and took me back up to the room.

"Everything's going to be all right," he finally said. "You've got to help me out. I don't want her. I feel sorry for her, but I don't want her. I told her that in the first place, and she said she would take a chance coming here, because you might not want to come with me."

"You didn't tell me all these things," I pointed out, "before."

"If I had, maybe you wouldn't have come with me," Bill replied. "But she has no way of going." The car was in his and her name because she bought it while he was in the marines and she was getting his money. Yet all that time she was living with another marine. But she came back to Bill, and she just made all kinds of excuses.

When his wife learned of our decision – I'd say it was about three days after I had arrived in Harlem – she left with the car.

I shrugged. "Oh, well, let her take the car. We'll get by." I didn't realize how hard it would be to get a car. She had two little dogs, and Bill's uncle had given her, I think, five hundred dollars. I thought, "She ought to be all right." So she left.

Bill took me to the ranch. I thought, "Ooh, what are they going to expect, after they had gotten acquainted with *her*?" I met Lena and her husband, George. He took me to Grandpa and Grandma Buck, and I went over there and just put my arms around them. They were talking Indian to one another, and it was an excitement between them. I didn't understand what they were saying, but their talking and everything was very welcoming.

Lena was the one who had talked the most with Bill's wife, so she turned around, and she talked. She was visiting with me. She said, "It's hard on me to accept one, and then he goes and gets another. She (the wife) talks almost continually about you. I guess Bill must have told her all about you."

Bill got the divorce, and then we went someplace in their car (George's) and came back home married. It wasn't a big affair or anything; we just got married. When I came back to the ranch, my bed was just laden with gifts. And there was a trunk, and it was full of stuff. Bill came in and saw that. He asked, "What's all this?" "I guess Grandma Buck did it," I said, "put all these gifts on the bed." He was amazed at the gifts on the bed and commented, "Oh, that's good. They didn't do that to her," meaning the first wife.

I began to feel accepted by Bill's family, and I wanted to find out more about them. His grandfather, James C. Snell, had been the wagon master for General Nelson Miles. The family had a buckskin shirt that had belonged to James Snell. It had I don't know how many bullet holes in it. Where it was done, I don't know; I think it happened at the time General Miles was hunting down Chief Joseph, chasing him. When they got to the Chinook area, Chief Joseph gave up.

James Snell got acquainted with the Assiniboine Indians. He met and fell in love with a woman named Black Digger. He filled a wagon full of gifts and asked her parents for her hand in marriage. They went over to where Black Digger's land was, and he lived there. He was a farmer. He had huge gardens and would sell to the different places, mostly to the mining communities. Snell and Black Digger had many children. There was an old lady called Maud Bow, and she used to talk to me about Black Digger and Snell. They were Presbyterians. There was a Presbyterian church way out there in the country where these Indians lived. They used to go to that, and he played the fiddle a lot. He'd play for church, and he'd also play for dances. Maud Bow told me that Black Digger would get after James Snell for flirting. He would flirt with women, and she'd get after him for doing that. He said, "No, it doesn't make any difference. I'm not doing anything wrong, just making no difference at all. What's the difference?" Now Black Digger couldn't speak English very well, but one day she began to flirt with men. Snell got after her, and she looked at him and said, "What's she, a dipper?" Maud would laugh when she told me that story, and she always ended by saying that Black Digger really meant to say, "What's the difference?"

The ranchers around that area called white men who married Indian women "squaw men." Some of those ranchers wanted Indian land. I mean they wanted to lease land from the Indians, and they couldn't do it if an Indian woman married a white man; white men married to Indian women wouldn't lease to the ranchers. So the ranchers were trying to find ways to get rid of these people. They would shoot them. They'd shoot them and get them out of the way. Snell, when he'd take his vegetables to different areas across the country, took a shotgun man with him, a man who watched while he drove the wagon. This guy sat with the shotgun and watched all around, but nobody bothered them – or if they did, they didn't succeed. So Snell lived there and he died in his garden.

William Snell, Bill's father, was one of eleven children that James and Black Digger had. People called him "Babe." Babe went into the navy and married Hazel. I believe they met in California. She was not an Indian. They had these two little boys, Curtis and Bill, but things didn't work out. They left California in a touring car. She was pregnant when they left. They came over the desert, and it was extremely hot, and they were having a bad time. When they got to Fort Belknap, Hazel had to go to the hospital because she was having a miscarriage. The little baby was born, the little girl was born almost dead. It was alive for a little while, but it died. That left the two little boys.

Babe was chasing around, and Hazel didn't have a job. She just couldn't take it any longer. She was making her dresses out of flour sacks. She would use the flour up, then use the cloth to make dresses. Relatives of Snell would help her, but he was chasing, dancing, drinking, and finally she left. Hazel knew she couldn't take care of the boys. She had to go to Great Falls to get a job, so Babe's brother George adopted Bill and Curtis.

George was married to Lena Buck. Her parents were the ones I called Grandma and Grandpa Buck. They were Frank Buck, who was part Indian (his Assiniboine name was Plume, which meant eagle plume), and One Woman, who was a full-blood Assiniboine. George and Lena had no children. A friend told me that One Woman had given Lena a contraceptive, a potion, to keep her from having children because she didn't want her to be left with the care of children if the man stepped out, like it was in so many cases. George and Lena had just married, and Grandma Buck had this in her mind, that her daughter wasn't going to go through that heartbreak like so many women did at that time.

That's a change from the old way. Even in One Woman's time she noticed all the behavior changes, in marriages and in young people. I believe that it was liquor that made this drastic change. It seemed to be the trend throughout, drinking every weekend, living for liquor, raising cain.[2] There was nothing else to do. Men, in so doing, would meet some of these women that were also drinking. The good wives who stayed home usually were the ones that caught it. But there *were* some good wives, and not all men were that way. Some of them stayed true to their families. One man, an Assiniboine, told me not long ago, "We love our wives, we love our wives, but I don't know what gets into us. I don't know why we do it, but we do it. We don't want to lose our wives, but we do it. We know full well that this affair is not going to last, but we do it, and we create a lot of misunderstanding and create a lot of problems."

Frank Buck had an interesting family, a romantic family story. His mother was a handsome woman, neat and tall. She was an Assiniboine woman, and the Assiniboines lived toward the Bear Paw Mountains. Captain Frank Buck of the United States Army, who was stationed near what is now Havre, Montana, met this woman at one of his visitations to the Assiniboine camp. They became acquainted with one another, and they fell in love. He told her, "Move your family camp within gunshot distance from where we are at the fort so that I can come to see you." She told her people, "I am going to be Captain Buck's wife. He wants me to be his woman." So she moved away from the regular camp, and he went back and forth. He always brought groceries with him. They were very much in love. They were happy together, and he treated her like his bride, always. She treated him as if there was no other man for her. They had two sons. The oldest was called Belknap Buck and the other one was Frank.

They lived happy until the army received orders to move back to Helena, so Captain Buck asked this woman to come with him. She said, "I cannot come with you. If it breaks my heart, I must stay with my people." He said, "It's going to break mine to leave you and our family. Please let me have the boys, so I can raise them, if you're not coming. I have my orders to leave." She said, "You can have the older boy. I'll be so lonesome without you, as it is. If you take my boys I will surely die from loneliness." So they compromised, and he took the older son, Belknap, with him, and he left Plume – Frank Buck – with his mother. Frank Buck lived and learned the Indian ways – definitely, absolutely traditional. In fact, he was the pipe carrier for the sun dance all his life. Frank Buck named his great-grandson, Bill Snell Jr., "Walks with the Pipe." Grandpa Buck did not know a word of English, but once he went in search of a headstone around Helena to see if his father was buried there.

On the other hand, Belknap went absolutely the white western way. He grew up and became a cowboy. I heard that he was quite a horseman and a good friend of the artist Charlie Russell. They went around together. Very good-looking man, I guess, and so was Grandpa Buck, in his Indian way. They were both raised in Montana, but they never ever saw each. Belknap was raised by Captain Buck's white wife. I feel like this captain had a white wife while he lived with his Assiniboine wife. I was doing a little research on him one time, and I believe that he was married, although he did want to take the boys and their mother back with him.

Before he left, Captain Buck arranged for credit at the trading post. He said, "Whenever this woman and her boy need something, see that they have it. I will pay for it." Frank Buck was raised by his grandfather on his mother's side. Whenever there were needs, this grandfather would saddle up Frank Buck's little horse, and they would ride to the trading post and buy whatever the little boy wanted. Some years ago I got a picture of Belknap Buck. I took it to Lena when she was in the rest home. I asked her, "Did you ever see your uncle?" "No, I never have," she answered. I showed it to her, and she got big tears in her eyes.

Grandma and Grandpa Buck looked after Bill and Curtis quite a bit. They lived right next to their daughter's home, and George and Lena were gone a lot. Finally, Curtis was sent to Mary Sincevere, one of Babe's relatives in Fort Peck. Then Bill was alone. When he was three years old, he began to learn to do chores.

After we got married in 1947, we lived with George and Lena while Bill built a log house for us. It was a nice little log house. We daubed it and daubed it in between the logs. We daubed it with deer hair and mud. Some of the neighboring people came and helped. We just got it nice and cozy for winter. It stayed up well, and it had a porch to it. George and Lena lived in a big log house, and Grandma and Grandpa lived in another log house. Theirs was square, and the roof had four sides, but ours had a two-sided roof. Our stove, our main heating stove, was right in the middle of the house. We had a heating stove, and we had a cookstove. By the time I was there, we were able to get electricity, but Bill had a hard time convincing George and Lena to get electricity. They were kind of

Bill Snell (center) and grandparents – Plume or "Grandpa Buck," One Woman or "Grandma Buck" – at the Snell family ranch in the "north country" (Fort Belknap).

afraid of it; Lena certainly was. My log house even had a flower garden. I put in carnations, of all things, and they came out beautiful even in that country there.

I always think of it as the north country. It was more of a farm area than the Crow reservation. It seemed like crops covered the land, and irrigation ditches were all over the place, and a not-so-clear river, the Milk River. In the distance you could see the Little Rockies and the Bear Paw Mountains, but they tell me that valley is the flattest land in America – no drainage. That's why the mosquitoes were so bad. I wasn't used to mosquitoes like that. People used to look like Arabians out working in the fields; they just covered every part of their bodies that they could.

The weather was extreme. We've seen sixty below more than once. You could hear the cottonwoods pop, hear somebody walking a mile away. The

Alma at the Snell ranch, 1947.

town, Harlem, was about twelve miles away from our place. People used to go there in wagons, tie up the horses by the bars. Toward morning they would come home with those wagons, and they'd be singing – singing those Indian war songs.

When we finished building our house, we came back to Crow to pick up some of my things, and I wanted to take my little boy home with me. We went to Wyola to get Ted. I packed up his toys and blankets. Mayme and Frances and her husband Paul were there.

Paul said, "I don't think you should take Ted with you." Mayme added, "Wait a while. His clothes are coming back from the cleaners." Ted hung to Mayme's neck, and Mayme and Frances cried. They said, "Bill is of another tribe. Why don't you leave Ted with us? We don't know how they will treat him." By this time I was pregnant, and my sisters wondered who would take care of Ted while I was in the hospital having my baby. Ted wouldn't come; I just cried. Bill said, "We better go." So they told Bill to unload the little boy's tricycle and things. I said, "I'll come after him after the baby is born." I cried all the way home. I called, sent letters and little gifts to him. That was bad, being without him, but he was very much loved by Mayme and Frances. He came back to us when he was eleven years old and stayed with us until he went into the army.

I was very much afraid of having another baby. I used to count the days that I had to live because I was so afraid. I thought, "Well, I have two more months to live," and then, "a month to live." To top it off, the doctor who had been caring for me was absent when I came into labor, and the nurses had to take over. If they saw that things were not normal, they were supposed to call another doctor from the next town, which was about twenty-four miles away. It was the fifth of July in 1948 when I went into the delivery room, and I was having such a bad time, the nurses thought they should call the doctor. The nurses were wringing their hands, and I looked up at the wall (I was left alone while they went to another room to consult), and I was praying. I was praying to God. I looked on the wall, and there was a picture of Mary, the Virgin Mary. I said, "You've had babies before. You know how it is. God, your mother has had babies. Help me." When the nurses came back in the room, Faith was born. I was so happy, and Bill was, too. He cried when he saw his baby. He just wept, and he did to every one of his babies. He would dry his eyes.

While we were at Belknap, I began to learn a lot from Lena. She was an influence in my life because of her independence. She knew what to do when George wasn't there. She was a strong, determined woman, and that made her look kind of harsh, but she wasn't. She had a big heart, when I knew her. She always felt sorry for animals that were hurt, and she didn't like people tearing up the ground for no reason at all.

Her cooking was meticulous. It had to be the right kind of pan, that type of thing. And baking bread was weekly, on a certain day. The laundry was done on a certain day: Monday was the laundry day. Sewing was another day, mending clothes, darning socks. I remember all those things had to be done on a certain day. Then she had a time when she would do hobbies. She liked to fool with beading. Grandma Buck did, too, and she tanned hides. I didn't see Lena help her much with the tanning.

They had a different way of tanning hides. They had a blade with scalloped edges looped into a tree; they bent the blade and hammered each end into a tree so that it stuck tight. Then this loop received the hide that was going to be tanned. The hair had already been removed, and

Grandma Buck pulled the hide with her right hand through the loop, then back to the left. She scraped it like that. Now, my own grandma scraped the hide by pegging it to the ground, or tacking it to a wall. She pinned the hide down and scraped it with a scraping blade that she held in her hand. I liked One Woman's blade very well. A lone person could use it to tan a hide, but my grandma had to have us girls circle around and take an edge of the hide and pull it, and send it around, send it around. Move it around for her so that it stretched. Then she took it on her lap, and she scraped it against her leg.

With the Assiniboines, I actually learned how to work in a garden, and to put food in cellars and to can. I learned a lot of canning ways from Lena – what to do and what not to do – and a lot of new ways, like sticking our carrots in dry sand and putting them in the cellar so they would stay fresh all winter long. I learned about different foods, like ducks. They ate ducks a lot, but the Crows didn't. The Crows ate prairie chicken and sage hens, but not ducks that I know of. And very few Crows ate fish. In fact, there's a Crow saying, "You're acting so proud and so silly, why don't you go back home and eat fish?"

Lena taught me about different kinds of teas. My grandmother Pretty Shield always collected mint tea, Crow mountain tea, but the different teas, like yarrow, I learned from them. And I learned about a contraceptive that wasn't used among my tribe. Also, they used cattail much more than the Crows did. They made hide diapers for babies, and lined them with cattail fluff, which was soft and absorbent, and they could throw it away when it was soiled. The Crows used scrapings from buffalo hides.

Wherever I have lived, I've always listened to the old people. I liked to listen to the Assiniboines tell stories. One old lady told me that long ago the people in the north would set the buffalo grass on fire. It would burn up the matted grasses, and new grass would grow. She said she could remember times when all the prairies and the whole sky were ablaze.

Another lady told a story about what happened when people were starving during the early reservation days. Men didn't want to see this done, but sometimes the Indian women would sell themselves to white farmers or ranchers so that their families could have food. The government gave rations but never enough to last for a month. Well, Indian women called all white men John. One day this man took his wife to a field where they saw a white man standing some distance away. Their kids were so hungry, she was going to sell herself to the white man. She stood near the edge of the field and hollered, "Hey, John. Hey, John." John didn't answer. She moved a little closer and waved her skirts in the air: "Hey, John. Hey, John." Still, no answer. She kept moving closer and yelling until she got right up close to the man. Only it wasn't a man at all; it was a scarecrow.

People just laughed when they heard this story, and they told it many times. The laughing was a kind of a bridge. Laughter and teasing about the change from one culture to another was kind of a bridge to take us over. The only way we could handle the new culture that had come on us was either to laugh about misunderstandings or compare it to the old life and get tickled about things we did in the past.

Crow people did it, too. Hank Bull Chief told me a story about when the Crows first received rations. One time they got a whole bunch of watermelons. They boiled the watermelons. One time my dad, with his blue eyes, was talking to John Deernose, and Deernose asked him, "When you look out of your eyes, is everything you see blue?" Dad asked Deernose, "Is everything you see black?" They looked at each other for a minute, then they laughed.

I still laugh about old Warren Early, an Assiniboine man who told a story about a beaver. One time he was out checking his traps, and he saw this beaver working on a tree, gnawing it down. He gnawed and gnawed until there was just a sliver holding the tree up, but the tree didn't fall. So the beaver stepped back just like a man would, looked up at the tree and scratched his head with his paw, trying to figure out what to do. Well, he gnawed some more, but the tree still stood up. So the beaver moved back again, looked at the tree, scratched his head. After Early saw him do this several times, he thought, "That beaver's almost human." He was so impressed with the beaver that scratched his head, he said, "I'll never trap beavers again." And he never did.

We lived on the ranch at Fort Belknap for about a year and a half, and at different times later on, especially if the old people needed our help, we went back. Life wasn't always easy on the ranch. Bill taught me how to shoot muskrats, and we sold their hides for extra money. I even remember one Christmas when Bill got this big beautiful mink. He sold it, and that was the only way we were able to buy Christmas gifts for our kids.

10

Many Roads

After that first year at Fort Belknap, we returned to Crow. Bill worked hauling coal and at the Little Bighorn Battlefield. I was glad to be with my family and friends, although I had made friends in the north country, too. I was also glad to know that the Crow businessman I had planned to marry had found someone else. He married a nice, pretty, red-haired girl that his sister got him acquainted with, and they had several children.

My second little girl, Pearl Jean, was born in 1949 while we lived at Crow, but making a living was hard, so we went to Butte, where Bill worked as an electrician in the mines. Our son, Bill Junior, was born in Butte in 1951. When he was born, he was okay, but he developed an eczema all over his arms and all over his cheeks. He scratched himself so much, I tried to keep little mittens on his hands, and the doctor even put splints on them. Billy went round and round with those splints, trying to get to his face. I patted his skin with a wash cloth, to try to stop the itching. I felt so bad for this little child who had such fair skin.

An Italian woman named Louisa was our landlady. She was an immigrant, from the old country, and she had a little altar in her house, a little Catholic altar where she prayed. I was going to take the kids fishing. I was even going to take Billy because I didn't want him out of my sight. Before I went, Louisa came to me and told me, "Go and look for a place in the river, and when you come to a place where you see rocks in the bottom, that clear, you take the baby's little cap – the one he wears all the time, not a new one – take it and wet it. Then you go over his skin with it. Go over the parts that are affected by this rash. After that, throw the cap in the river. Turn. Put your back to it. Don't look back. You will want to look back. Just keep your back to it." I did as she told me. In a day or so the eczema was gone, gone forever.

My sister Frances died while Bill and I were living in Butte, but before her death she had a kind of miraculous happening. This is what Frances told me. She lived in Wyola, in a nice house. In the center was the living room and the dining room; on each side, a bedroom. She had this tumor. The doctor said it was the size of a grapefruit. She wouldn't do anything about it. She got pregnant, but she didn't know she was, and the doctors didn't either, because of this tumor on the outside of her womb.

She was sick in bed, alone at the Wyola home. It was coming evening time when she saw a light around the window area. She said, "Well, that's Paul coming home" (her husband).

The door opened. She thought, "That's Paul coming." She moved her blanket to see.

Pretty Shield was sitting there. Frances thought, "Well, Grandma's dead, but she's here." Frances told me that then "Grandma got up and went out my bedroom to the kitchen door. I heard her. The light was gone. I looked again for Paul's car. Nobody. I began to pray." In about ten minutes, Paul came home, and she told him. They prayed together. From that moment she *knew* she was going to go.

Before her surgery she dreamed that she heard angels singing, and it was so beautiful she didn't want to come back – such a wonderful place, so beautiful. Before the surgery we were all around her bed. I took my Bible and put it under her pillow. She put her pretty hand on the Bible. The next morning, she said, "Alma, goodbye. I am going. I know I'm going. Don't feel bad. It's beautiful." She died, and the doctor cried. He cried. The tumor was nine pounds. So my sister died that way. Because of that, I always think Pretty Shield is in heaven.

A few years later, in 1952, I had to face surgery also. By that time we had moved to Roseburg, Oregon. Hazel, Bill's mother, became very ill, so we went to be with her. Bill was still working as an electrician. I just got weaker and weaker; I was down to ninety-five pounds. I went to this doctor from China, the Republic of China. He happened to have been Chiang Kai-shek's personal doctor, but he had come to the United States and fallen in love with a lady. He stayed and practiced in Roseburg. He was a Christian doctor. When I went to see him, he had me get down on my knees and pray right in his office. I remember he was at his desk, and we prayed together about this surgery. He said that I was only half there, and "half a horse isn't any good. Half of anything isn't anything." I said, "Well, I have two more weeks until Christmas time. Will you let me go home and spend my Christmas there?" He said, "No, it's got to be done now. I'll get you home for Christmas." I went and told Bill, and Bill told me, "Your sister waited too long for surgery. She didn't make it. So, do it now. You've got to do it now." (My tumor was on my uterus. It turned out to be cancer.)

I kissed my children and went into the hospital. Since we were way over there in Roseburg, I was pretty much alone. I had no relatives close by, only his mother and a couple of friends that we had just got acquainted with. Billy Junior was one year old, and Bill's mother Hazel babysat for me. She couldn't be with me at the hospital, and Bill couldn't afford to quit working because of my hospitalization. Of course, he came after work. He said when he saw me lying there in bed that I looked like a skeleton – I looked like death itself, and he was afraid.

I prayed to God then. I said, "I'm away from my people. They cannot come and sit around me, and at least say funny things so I can laugh and try to get over this terrible thing. So, Lord, you're all I have. You're all I have. Just forgive me of my wrongdoings, my sins, my shortcomings, and cleanse me in your blood, and take me. But I'm going to ask you to find a Christian mother for my children. My husband is young. He will need another woman. Please make it a loving Christian mother who will love my children and bring them up in the fear and admonition of the Lord." So with that, I said my amen. "There it is now. Take me if you want me. Take me now, if it is your will that I be with you."

Suddenly, a light entered the room. It enveloped all of everything in the room, and I was on the bed. I felt its weight, almost. It seemed to move from the top of my head clear through my body. Like mercury, it went through my whole body. And I said, "He has heard me! He has heard me!" I was so happy and elated. I couldn't begin to describe how happy I was. I looked out. People were moving about on the street. As I was looking out the window, it seemed like they all had more energy to them. A lady who had been brought in from surgery was sleeping behind a curtain next to me, and I peeked in. "Hey," I said. "God heard me. The Lord heard me. He's here!" That lady was fast asleep, but I had to tell someone, so I did.

The nurse came in and said, "Now, tomorrow morning, we'll be wheeling you into the operating room. I want you to tell me when you're upset, when you can't sleep. I want you to ring that bell, so I can give you a shot to help you sleep." I told her I didn't need anything, so she went out. She went out, and I must have gone to sleep, but I was so happy all the way through. I didn't dream anything, but when I woke up at times, I was just happy. Then I'd go back to sleep. The nurse came in about eight o'clock in the morning, and she said, "Every time I checked on you, and that was hourly, you were sleeping like a little baby. You had a smile on your face all night long. I just can't believe this. You never were nervous like anybody that's going into surgery." She gave me a shot, and I didn't even feel it. I didn't even know its sensation. They wheeled me into the operating room, and when I was under those tremendous lights, I still had this wonderful feeling within me. The anesthetist put this shot into my arm and said, "Count from twenty backward." So I started counting, and it didn't take long – I was asleep.

I don't know what went on then, but the doctor came to me the next day, and he examined me, and he sat down at my bedside. He asked, "What nationality are you?"

"I'm a Crow Indian from Montana," I said.

"Do you speak your language?"

I said, "Yes."

He wanted to hear my language, so I talked to him in Crow. Then he said, "No. That's not the language I heard." He told me that I had spoken in a different language for three hours straight. "Three hours straight," he said. They had me in there for three and a half hours, and all the way through surgery I was laughing and talking and visiting with someone, and being just happy.

He said he had me open, and he explored my whole system, and "everything is fine." They took the cancer out. They took the uterus, and everything else was just fine. The doctor told me, "I believe with all my heart that that's all there was to it, but it was killing you." He just folded his arms and made a gesture to me. "Everything was fine," he said. Then he told me that the nurses who were assisting him, behind their masks, they sang hymns. The urge to sing hymns was too great for them, so they sang hymns, they hummed hymns.

I went home in three days; I was home for Christmas. When I went to the hospital to get the dressing on the incision changed, that doctor opened the bandages, and he asked the nurse to ask another doctor to come in. When the other one came in, my doctor said, "Look at that." The other one said, "Who did that?" The surgeon said, "Who do you suppose?" I thought to myself, he meant, "Me. Of course." It wasn't until way afterward that I realized my incision was healed and what he meant was that it had been touched by God. Years later, after my children were married, my daughter Faith asked, "Mom, do you remember when you told me that you prayed for a Christian mother for us – for my dad to marry a Christian mother so that she'd be loving and caring for us and would rear us in that faith, the Christian faith?" I said, "Yes." She said, "You know, God did answer your prayer. He gave us you."

I know prayer works, and after my surgery I became more aware of its power and of kind of a healing touch that I have in my hands. I *noticed* that I had a *desire* to pray for people. That was a turning point. Since I had that experience, I have heat – more than warmth – coming out of my hands. I don't feel hot, but I feel an energy. Sometimes I feel it more than other times. Now, when Bill's hurting someplace, he wants me to lay my hand on it, and when I do, he goes to sleep. I always say, "Let's let the Pierced One take this pain away." I say it out loud to Bill, then I lay my hand on him, and I say, in my language, "*Ischawúuannakkaasuua*, take this pain away, so that he can rest." And it's gone, and he goes to sleep.

There was a diabetic at Fort Belknap a few years ago. She was going to have her foot cut off. She was in the hospital, and when I came in, she was very happy to see me. She had told me about her leg, the sore on it. When I went in, she showed it to me: "Here, Alma." I took her foot, and I put my hands all over the sore. I felt compelled to do that. I prayed for her and for her foot to be healed. In a couple of days, the doctor said, "It's healing. Amazing, but you don't have to have your foot taken off." She was able to walk and to work in the senior citizens' center after that.

Another time I was at the hospital, and a young girl came walking up to me real fast. She said, "My little baby is upstairs, sick, and we can't get her to eat anything. She vomits it up all the time. She's really dehydrating from it. She is just so sick. She doesn't even want to be touched by anything."

She looked at me, and I asked her, "Do you want me to go up there?" She said, "Would you?"

I went up in the elevator, and when I got there, sure enough, there was the child, sick with fever. I said, "Hi." A little smile came on her face. I said, "Jesus, baby Jesus, bless this little baby." The little girl let me lay my hand on her, and I said, "You'll be okay. You'll be well. When your mama comes, tell her you're feeling good." Later the mother told me that when she went into the room, her little girl sat up and said, "Mama, I'm hungry."

Some time afterward, that little baby's grandmother called me to come to their country home. When I got there, her husband was sick. His mouth was sucking in, and she was trying to feed him with a teaspoon. The food was coming down the corners of his mouth. He looked ashen, really ashen. The wife said, "Sister Alma, Barney wants you to pray." I felt really helpless, but I said, "Bring me your Bible." So she did, and we read it. We read the last verses of the book of James. I prayed for Barney, and he went off to sleep. I went home, and Bill and our minister, Reverend Cross, were there. I told them about Barney and that the doctor had said there was nothing more he could do for him. They left for Barney's house, but they weren't gone very long. When they came back, I said, "Did you go over there?" Bill said, "Yeah, we did. He was sitting at the kitchen table, eating an egg and asking for another one."

Once I was able to help a little boy with mumps. His name was Charles – Charlie. They would not accept him in the hospital for fear of spreading mumps to other children. His mom, his foster mother, said he was delirious. She didn't think he could get any worse. Bill and I went to his house. I went into the sickroom, and there was this little boy, about eight or ten years old. His face was all jaw, down to his shoulder. His eyes were rolled back, and when I came in, they rolled toward me. I walked over toward this little boy, and I touched him on the head. All I ever said in that room was "Jesus." I felt inadequate. It was too overwhelming. I wanted to get the preacher. In my feeling of helplessness, I walked out of the room.

I felt little footsteps running behind me. I turned around, and here was this little boy, an absolutely, absolutely normal child, no mumps, nothing. The other people in the house just gasped to see him with me. I thought, "Was there another kid in there? Was there another little boy I didn't see or what?" But the other people knew him, and they grabbed ahold of him.

The next morning there was quite a bit of snow on the ground. Snowplows had piled up the snow here and there in front of people's homes. I still had it in my mind, "I got to see that little boy." I went over to his place, and I didn't have to go in the house to see him. He was outside, in great big overshoes, man overshoes, and he was climbing these snow hills. I thought to myself, "My word, that's him." I didn't stop to talk to him. I just watched him for a while, and I just said, "God, you're something else." I couldn't believe it. But that was the touch of God on people who said, "It's up to you, God."

In the middle part of the 1950s, Bill began to make career changes, and in time, so did I. Bill got into law enforcement, working for the Bureau of Indian Affairs, and I began to understand what life was like for a law officer's wife. I was alone much of the time, and because Bill was a federal officer, we went to a lot of different places. Just about this same time, in 1954, we also began to serve God by traveling with missionaries, going out to sing in churches. Bill sang and played his instruments, and I used the Indian sign language to interpret songs. We worked with them locally and traveled on occasion.

I had first started this sign language at the Baptist church in Crow when I was about sixteen. Another girl, Ruby Deernose, usually did it, but one night she slipped off with her boyfriend and didn't come to church. Somebody needed to fill in, so her sister Stella asked me. She said, "Alma, you can do it. Put on her garment and get out there." I had to borrow clothes at first, but then my sisters got me a buckskin dress. I wore that if I was called on. Once, I traveled to thirteen states and Canada doing sign language with the Milwaukee Bible College Choir. Another time I performed at Rex Humbard's Cathedral of Tomorrow in Akron, Ohio.

I remember a disturbing thing that happened while we were traveling with the missionaries. Indians were not allowed to eat in a certain cafe, and the manager of this place came around and took a look at us. After he took a look at us, he said, "Go ahead and let them have what they want." But after that I couldn't eat, so I walked out. I was walking out, and the missionaries said, "That's not a very Christian thing to do." I said, "I just cannot eat it. That's all. I'm sorry." I walked out. I left that place, and I stood before that place, and I commended it to God. Not too long after that we went through there, and it was closed. That was in Beech Lake, Minnesota, in 1958.

I always think, "Whatever happened to make them so bitter toward us all the time?" Another thing I wonder about. They have such a "We don't want you" attitude, but some Indian women go to the same men and, like the Indians say, sell themselves to them, and those men take them. That's what I can't understand. If we're so bad that they can't have us eating in their establishment or anything like that, then why do they take these women and do what they want to with them? It seems like that's a closer encounter than eating off their plates. I know it has happened; I've heard from these women, and they just laughed about it. They laughed about it, but it isn't very funny with me because I *hurt*. That used to make me bitter.

Pretty Shield told me not to discriminate, and not to discriminate is a value I would hold on to. She said, "*Do not discriminate.* Do not make fun of people. Do not make fun of them at all, for you, too, will have children, and you'll want them to be well." "To make fun of people," they used to say long ago, "will come back on your children. You'll be reminded of when you discriminated against another."

In the early 1960s Bill became chief of police in Harlem, Montana. I had a job in a cafe in Harlem, and I was doing well. Ann Churchill, the manager, said, "I don't see how you do it, make these things taste so good, but you are truly a scientific cook." I decided to put in for a job at the hospital, the food department of the Indian Health Service. I had to take a test, and there were other ladies who took that test. They took us to different rooms and gave us our test papers and gave us so much time to finish them. My paper came out the highest; in fact, it was 100 percent. So I got the job. I really appreciate the training I received from the Indian Health Service, the IHS. I worked under some topnotch nutritionists, and I learned how to manage food in a businesslike way. I learned under a nutritionist named Miss Mary Peterson. I appreciate her to this day, because I'm still working with foods, and I have the knowledge she gave me. Also, I went for special courses at Santa Fe, New Mexico, and after a period of learning and experience I was able to become a food service supervisor.

In the early 1970s the FBI asked Bill to go to Pine Ridge, South Dakota, and help with some problems there. At first we thought it would be a temporary move, so I came to Crow Agency and got a job as food and beverage manager of the Sun Lodge, a motel the tribe had built. I worked at the Sun Lodge a short time; then Bill came after me. He said they needed him in Pine Ridge longer, so I should come with him. I worked there in the food service department in the Indian school at Pine Ridge. I had thirteen cooks and four maintenance men under me. Most of them were "politically in" as far as jobs were concerned, so they were of the "goon" faction, Wilson's Goons. Wilson was the chairman of his tribe. Some of them, Wilson's people, even got on me for hiring people from the American Indian Movement side.[1]

When I first came to Pine Ridge, I felt there was some truth to what the AIM people were saying. I felt bad. I pondered a long time before I found out that it was error. This is how I described it: it was error riding on the back of truth. There was truth in it, but then, all this error of violence and killing. I just don't go for that – taking beef from ranchers without asking, tearing down churches (that was a soft spot for me), and the stories that came out of there about how Indians abused one another.[2] You had to be careful that you weren't shot at, just because you were married to a police officer. When the fear of violence was pretty high, Bill would call me and say, "You go down in the basement until I get home." Sometimes the violent ones went around shooting at buildings right at the window line, but they never touched my house.

In fact, AIM people came to my house, just to have coffee and visit – not the leaders but the ordinary supporters. They'd come and eat with us. They liked my home. When I moved to Pine Ridge I had these red curtains. They had been custom-made for my house at Fort Belknap, but they fit the windows in Pine Ridge. I put them up, and I put out all my Indian artifacts, like my beaded pouch, my stone food pounder, things like that. The AIM people saw my curtains and Indian things, and they liked to come to my house. They might have thought that I was one of them, but I was in the middle. There were three divisions at that time, the goons, the AIM, and the people in the middle who just wanted peace.

There was a Wesleyan minister there (he had been there a long time) who decided to be a representative for those who were not AIMs or goons either one. This minister agreed to go and represent the Pine Ridge Indians, the ones in the middle, and negotiate with the others to see if he could be of any help at all. He sat around in council with the AIM group. He was the only one who would go. No one else would go. They were afraid. (I always wonder what would have happened if there had been an Indian person sent as a representative.) He went there, and I guess he spoke peace to them. They said they didn't want any of that. Some of the warriors that were there, the younger ones who were standing guard, were ordered by their leaders to take him out in the hills, and I suppose they were told what to do with him. They took him out there; they shoved about a dozen eggs down his throat, shells and all. He swallowed as fast as he could, as much as he could, because he didn't want to breathe any of the egg shells into his lungs. He didn't. This is what I was told. They broke some of his bones and left him for dead after they beat him up. I think it was marshals that found him out in the hills. They took him into the IHS hospital, and he lived to tell about it.[3]

There was a young German girl there who sympathized with the movement; she thought it was the whole people that was involved. She came to work in the IHS hospital at Pine Ridge. From there she went around and visited us Indian people. She visited me a lot. She believed in God and was very sympathetic toward the people. Then one day policemen picked her up, coming back from the Porcupine area where she had gone to visit the AIM radicals; she had been sent back with just her shawl and her shoes. The police took her to the hospital. They examined her. She had been abused.

Other women were mistreated, too. I was told when the AIM people went off to demonstrate, leaders lived in Holiday Inns and told their followers, "Go to the Salvation Army and find a place to stay." In Rapid City, South Dakota, the Salvation Army gave them this big building to sleep in. There was nothing in there but mattresses, but it was a place to sleep. The man that told me this story said that he was in there, and he heard a girl in the bathroom, asking for help. He went over there and told the guy who was bothering her to leave her alone. That's what he said. That always happened to the women.

I hired two boys to work at the school. Later I found out they were AIM. I'm not going to give their names; I'll call them James and John. They were brothers. Some of the people that were against AIM objected because I had hired those two brothers. I told those people at the school, "To me, these are two Indian people who need a job." They worked as janitors, and they did a good job. I told these ladies who complained, "If anything happens – if these two boys do anything that's not allowed – something will be done. But they deserve a chance." They were good at their work. They came to my house and visited, and they called me "Mom" after a little bit. One day they came and asked me at work, at my desk, "How come you are so nice? What makes you so nice?" I pointed to my little Testament that I had on my desk. I said, "Maybe it's that." They looked at it and said, "Is that a Bible?" I said, "Well, that's the New Testament of the Bible." They talked for a while and they left.

Later, there was a revival meeting going on in the Southern Baptist church. Bill and I attended it. One evening, these brothers said, "May we go with you?" Now the boy James had a jacket on. (I think I still have that jacket. I hope I do.) He had the flag upside down, and he had different patches that said sayings I didn't like, had them all over the jacket. The other one, John, said James had been very violent at one time. He thought he had killed a man, stabbed him thirty-six times. The man lived to tell who had done it, so this boy lived in fear of what might happen. I said, "You need not live in fear. If you pray and accept the ways of Jesus Christ, who died for you, you need not live in fear."

While this church meeting was going on, these two boys wanted to go. They came. They attended church. I don't remember what night it happened. The meeting lasted about a week, and within that time, James went up first to accept the Lord as his personal savior. And he cried. He had long braids, very pretty braids, and John was sitting behind me in the next row. He tapped me on the shoulder and said, "Mom, Sioux men don't cry. Look at my brother. He's shaming me out. We just don't cry." He was really disturbed about that. I turned around and looked at him and said, "John, you're next." He said, "No way." James came back from the altar, and as he went on back, he took his jacket off and gave it to me.

The next night or so John went up. James had been speaking to him about how he felt so good and so free. So John went up, and he accepted the Lord. I could see his body flex tight as he was standing there. He became very rigid. When they got through praying for him, he came down the aisle, and he had tears coming down his face. I looked at him and I smiled, and he said, "Don't you tell anybody." That boy, I understand, is involved with missionary work in Oregon. James, as far as I know, is in Pine Ridge, running a successful business.

After we left Pine Ridge, we moved to Ashland, Wisconsin, because Bill had an assignment as a criminal investigator with the BIA there. Just as we were getting ready to move, my family experienced a time when the Lord was immediately with us. It had to do with my son Bill Junior, his wife Karen, and their little baby boy, Billy. We called him Billy Three. Bill and I knew we had been transferred to Wisconsin, and I hated to leave Bill Junior and his family. I prayed. I prayed hard, almost continually.

Then I saw a vision. There were angels in my son's little trailer home. Some were gliding over and playing string games, some kind of string games with their hands, like we used to play when we were kids; they were just casually around. Others were leading this little child into the kitchen where his mother was standing near the stove. I was made to see that. I saw Bill Junior in a rocking chair in the living room, and the angels were in there, and on the outside of the trailer, too. Inside and out, as if there was no wall.

My vision turned to the trailer and to a white car they had at that time. Bill Junior had put in for an Arizona position, and he didn't know whether he was going to get it or not. In that transfer of my vision from his home to his white car with a U-Haul behind it, I saw that they were moving to this new job. And the angels, again, were around, and they were going to guide them to that place. But I saw a different angel come from above. He had a little golden something, like something to light a candle with.

He went and touched the mouth of Bill Junior. I saw Bill Junior walking hand in hand with his little boy, and his wife was ahead of them going toward the car. I knew he was going to travel, and it would be toward this new job he wanted.

Within a week after we got to Wisconsin, Bill Junior got word that he had the job and they were moving to Arizona. I said, "The angels be with you." In their travel they got to a town in Colorado that had a long descent into the town. His brakes gave out. They were going downhill with a trailer behind them. His wife started to cry and hung on to the baby because she knew that was all there was. Bill Junior said, "Help us God." He prayed in that quick manner. As he was going down, he thought, "Oh, my family, Lord."

He said that it was as if someone took hold of the wheel, the steering wheel: "I didn't operate it at all. It was operated by a different force, and we got to the bottom of the hill safely." If I remember correctly, someone who was nearby, observing, said, "It is a miracle you got down here with that load behind you, without anything happening." Bill Junior said, "It *is* a miracle. *Someone* was at the wheel." In that vision I saw it. The angel touched him along his mouth and blessed him, and he had the hand of Billy Three. The angels were white. They were dressed in white. I didn't see any wings on them, but they were drifting around in the room of that house and out. In the house and out, just like there were no walls.

I worked for the Crow tribe for a moment in my life. In the year 1976 the tribal chairman asked Bill to come to Crow and head up the police department. When Bill told me about it, I really didn't want to come back for some reason, but we came. I began working in the tribal social services. The chairman hired me to take the place of this social worker–administrator. She oversaw all the programs, the social-type programs, on the reservation. We had all kinds of *needed* social activities. Somebody brought up the idea of organizing a women's club, and I thought back to the one that had been here before, in Pretty Shield's time. They had done a lot of things for the tribe. We wrote to the state, and the national General Federation of Women's Clubs instated us. One thing we did was to distribute clothes and things that Target, that store, donated to the reservation. They gave so much, everything from skates to jogging shoes and jeans, all kinds of jeans. Target had been donating before the Women's Club got started, but it was sort of abused in the dispersing of what they gave. It seemed like the ones that had political jobs went through the things and took what they wanted, and the rest went to people they chose.

We set up in some empty rooms in the Sun Lodge – the old motel had been abandoned – and when the Target truck would come, we would take the clothes in, stack them, hang them up, and put them in categories. When people came in, either political faction, the workers in the rooms would say, "So and so came in. What shall we do? He votes on the other side." I'd say, "Give it to him. Give it to them. They're Crows. Just sign their names. Get their sizes. Let them have what we think they should have. One of each thing for their kids and themselves. Put their names down." We had lots and lots and lots of names of people that came in there, took from our little storage, you might say, and they were very happy to do so. There were blankets, blouses, dresses, underclothes, baby clothes. Oh, people made use of that. I thank Target to this day for making those hearts happy.

The Women's Club also helped to distribute commodities. The state had gotten to the place where it wouldn't fool around with the tribe any longer because we had failed to meet some of their specifications. Money that the state had provided for building a distribution center was spent on something else. We had no money to build a commodities building, so the state closed us out. I looked for a building so we could bring the commodities back. I found one in Lodge Grass. It had been a clothing factory, but it was vacant. I asked for that building. Our chairman at that time asked, "Why in Lodge Grass?" I said, "It's the only building that's good enough. We have to get a building that the state will accept. They'll take that building. They have looked at it and said that we could fix it up for a commodities building." There was an argument, but the tribe finally said, "Okay. You can have the garment building." The state came and fixed it all up. It had brand-new walk-in coolers, and they made kind of a little store out of it. We had little carts so that people could go around and get what they liked, then they brought it over and had it checked out. It was very good. It was very good, and the workers did fine. And lo and behold, a few years later, it went down the drain. Now the state has commodities distribution in Hardin.

In the meantime, Hardin didn't want drunks on the streets. They were an eyesore as well as a responsibility. They didn't want them there. They had a patrol that would pick them up, the Crows that were drunk, and haul them to Crow Agency and let them off on the streets there. They would tell them, "Go home. Go on home. Get off the streets.

Go on home." When they got out on the streets at Crow, they went knocking on doors. Some people were asleep. They didn't want to be bothered; they were working people and had to have their rest, and this was a nuisance to them. I know they loved them if they were their own family, and some were taken in and put to bed. But where would the rest go? They had no place to go. So the Women's Club thought perhaps we could get together, and the patrol could bring them to a halfway house.

The Sun Lodge, of course, was closed up, so I asked, "Where's the furniture from the Sun Lodge?" One of the ladies told me, "Well, they've been stealing the drapes, stealing the TVs, stealing the furniture, stealing from themselves." The Crows who were stealing more or less wanted to take something before so-and-so did: "If they're going to take it, I'm going take it." Most of the beds were gone, but there were some queen-sized beds left, so I decided that we could use two or three of them in our halfway house. Some ladies could lie across those queen-sized beds, and maybe one bed could sleep about four. I was hoping that there would not be that many each time. So we got some for men's beds, too. We put plastic on the mattresses in case anyone got sick. We posted a lady in that halfway house to manage it. She had worked in them before. She knew what a drunk was. She knew their sicknesses. She knew when they needed medical attention and she should call the hospital. All these things. She was a paid worker.

We needed someone to watch the men. The jailer had said, "I'll get my trusties to help you, a couple of them." So he brought them, and they helped us put up the beds. They helped us with everything there, in a little brick building by the jailhouse. Then the jailer asked, "Who's going to watch the men when they come in tonight?"

"These two here," I told him, "these two (meaning the trusties); we'll hire them. They'll work."

The jailer was doubtful, "These two? Alma, you're going to hire these – ? They'll just go out and drink again."

I answered, "No, I think they'll be responsible. They know what they need. They know what these men go through, and this lady in there will oversee them all."

Well, those boys were kind of shocked, too, when I said that. But they agreed to do it, and they came out of it real good. Later, one of them asked if he could take over my position as the director of the detoxification center. I didn't care. I didn't want any power; I wanted to see things go.

The Women's Club was right there all the time – everywhere. I think there were about thirty-six of us. We were going to build different business places in the Fort Smith area, near the marina at Bighorn Lake, for Crows to own and run themselves. It wasn't going to be a mall but a marketplace, with different crafts like beadwork, and sewing, and foods. We also wanted to take over the marina and put a guide business there, get people who knew the country real well to take visitors up into those hills and tell about them.

Our plans just got beat down, beat down by factionalism. The Crows were fighting back and forth, and we were believing lies. That's our downfall. We're easily fooled. In the Women's Club we went to council meetings, then we gathered together and said, "Was this right? Why are you for this, or, for the opposite side, why are you against it?" We hashed things out, no matter which side. If we thought something was for the betterment of the Crows, we tried to vote for that and get something going.

In the end, even the Women's Club got fooled. We planned on putting someone in charge of different entities concerning tribal business to check and see what we could do to help in each area. We didn't get to that place. Some of the workers volunteered: they were volunteers. I got money; the tribe paid me. I think some politician got ahold of some of the volunteers and said, "You should be paid. You need to get paid. You're voluntary work. Go to the comptroller." So they went to him, and he said, "No. I can't pay you." There are some people who know (Bill knows, too) that when I got my check, it was dispersed to those who helped. I only had a little to pay my rent, pay for my food, and gas money. It wasn't anything that I kept for myself. Bill said, "My bank account is dwindling. You better quit this job." I was using our money, too. "We're going to go broke," he said. I didn't mind quitting because they were pretty much pushing me out of the way because of jealousy. The club dissipated. Two or three women and I continued to send reports, trying to hang on to this thing, but we were unable to do so.

Sometimes the Crows are their own worst enemies. Greed, that's what I'm trying to say. Greedy. They trained each other to do it. They trained one another to do that. They fatten one another up, too, for the kill. Boy, they can put it on, too. Straight on. Their faces are hard as rock anymore. They're destroying themselves by trying to outdo one another in status.

11

Old Songs,
New Fruit

Bill and I left Crow and went back to Belknap in 1979. I worked in the IHS food service at first. Then I began to develop a program for senior citizens on the reservation. It was during this time that I started to give presentations on Indian culture. We hadn't been there too long when the schools in Harlem asked me to speak.

I always did use earth things because of my upbringing, and I was proud of it. I was proud that I knew what I was doing, and we could survive. At first, I had fun just going and picking the wild stuff, digging roots and things like that. There were people who understood me in the family, and that made me want to go ahead and have fun doing this. I know there's a lot of food in the stores, but somehow nature's giving seems to be more healing because it is so natural. We didn't put the seed in. It was *Akbaatatdía* who put the seed in, and it flourished.

It came about that the schools were wanting to teach Indian children to know themselves – to know who they were and to be proud of their past, to not condemn themselves so much. Harlem School District Twelve called on me to come and tell stories and show some of the foods and even some of the relics Indian people used long ago. That's where the beginning was. I had meager things then. I had some berries, some roots, some relics, but this became a motivation in my life. I wanted the children to know absolutely that this plant is different from this one. "Now, you can use this plant, but you can't use this. This is food. You use this for food; use this one for medicine." Although to my way of belief, what we eat *is* medicine – balancing the human being inside. When you do that, when you're in balance, you're happy, and you don't have too much trouble with your health. Your immunities build up so that you can fight diseases.

I didn't want the children to lose this precious knowledge of how their people did things – and spirituality, too. They not only used natural plants and roots, but they also had their own way of thanking the Creator for these things (as I never see others do while they're picking up their groceries in the grocery store). The lodges that they used to make, the weapons, the storing, preparing – all these things had an art to them, and I wanted the children to learn it. I wanted them to be what they are, to know what their ancestors used to thrive on. I'm trying to balance it all out and teach these things.

The kids do want to learn, and it's not only Indians. It's white kids that want to learn all about this. It gives me great pride to show them what we know and what we understood and used. I want them, the Indian kids, to keep their traditions and to know, "We had our place, and we have our place."

In 1983, Bill had a heart attack, and that caused me to do even more thinking about looking for a healthier way to live. When Bill got sick, he was tending his garden at Fort Belknap. I was over at the reservation agency, about six miles away, and Lena was with me. I said, "Lena, I think I better go check on Bill, because I feel strongly that something's wrong." She said, "Oh, you better go." So we jumped in the car and went down there. He was leaning on his shovel, and I thought, "Oh, he's just resting on his shovel, like he always does." But I came on up, and he turned very slowly, came over to me slowly, and got in his pickup.

He said, "I got very bad pain."

"Well, let me drive you," I urged. "I'll come back after the car. Let me drive you."

"No," he said. "I believe I can make it. You drive behind me."

So we drove off. I drove behind him, and we got to the house. He made an appointment with the veterans' hospital in Miles City, but before we got there, he had another pain. Bill Junior rushed him to the hospital in Billings. They found out it was a heart attack.

They took him right away, and they said he needed surgery. The doctors told him, "It's about a 50 percent or 60 percent chance of recovery." Bill says, "Well, go for it. Don't put it off. Do it now. It has to be done." There were two things they had to bypass, and we were all waiting, and the doctor came out and said, "Mrs. Snell, he's my star patient. Everything has gone well. He has a small strong heart. I held his heart in my hand. It fit right in there. He has a small heart." Ted spoke up and said, "I always knew my dad didn't have a very big heart." Everybody laughed. But the doctor told us there was no reason why he couldn't recover and lead a normal life. We thanked God. We were so relieved. He came out of it good, and since then he's been working – working harder than some men that are much younger than he is.

At the time, I thought, "Gosh, if I practice my grandmother's teachings, maybe it will help him." I really put an effort into it after that. I guess it was that happening that made me do it. I thought, "We've got to." That's what I trusted in my own mind; I trusted the old-time ways that we used to have and that are still out there. I thought, "It's bound to help." We changed so that we weren't so elaborate about our feeds.[1] We used to go out almost every weekend and have a great big platter of steak or a pile of fried fish. We just quit that. We just quit that, and we started going to plain, plain without grease, without salt, and we eat a lot more fruit than before. We ate good on the farm. I don't think there's a place where we could have had better meals than the farm, but the stress he had was one of those things, too. I began to look for things he could take for stress, too.

Now, because I work with plants, some people choose to call me a medicine woman. There's no mystery about me. Nothing mystic. It's all fact. Everything I used for treating people is fact. My prayers are to a God of mystery. He said, "You have dominion over these plants." There are no mystical or strange things about what I use. Everything I use is blessed by the one mystery, God Almighty.

I had a real blessing in my life when Billy Graham came to Billings in 1987. I had gone to a church in Billings, and this young man came up to me and said, "Will you do your sign language for the Billy Graham Crusade?" I thought, "Wow!" I just about fell over. They had to do a research study on me, a background study, and it was about two weeks before they wrote me and said, "Yes, we will have you." I was very happy about that. Billy Graham was sitting right on the platform, and he spoke a little bit. Right next to me was one of his singers. I think it was Myrtle Hall. She talked to me quite a bit. The soloist I interpreted for was Walter Arties. He sang, "The Lord's Prayer," and his voice was so soft and melodious, it took my emotions to high heaven.[2]

It took me back to a time when certain songs came to me. The songs just came, kind of like when songs came to Grandma. One time I was at Crow Fair, and they were judging the parade. The parade had circled into the place where it ends, and the judges were going around, I guess. I was kind of on the outskirts of the crowd, and I looked up. I looked up, and I saw a swarm of eagles. I seemed to be the only one who noticed them. But there was a bunch of eagles, just circling around. The leader was going way up, way up. This one that was way on top circled and looked down. The others were still swarming around, going up toward where this lead eagle was. The eagle seemed to turn around and look, and I thought, "Among all these people, do you see me? Why aren't the people looking up?"

I mentioned this to a few people around. I said, "Look up." They exclaimed, "Ahhh!" But they were so enthralled in the judging of the parade, they didn't notice, except those on the outskirts. I felt, "Ah, the eagles are gathering together, and they are circling about, following the leader of the eagles." And a song came to me. It went like this

Déaxkaashe íiwatxuak
Isbassóo biiwiiíkaak
Biiwiiíkaak húuk
Apsáalooke ashé iikóowaatiiok
Baakoochihleeté dáukoosh
Baakoochihté déesh bíik
Déaxkaashe Isbassóo
Biiwiiíkaak húuk
Baawaaláat Baaxpáam
Báaschiiwuun dúusaauk
Baakoochihté dáukook
Ahkálathak

The eagles are gathering
The leader sees me
He sees me and is coming
The Crows are assembled
Nothing is everlasting
"I am everlasting" (says the eagle)
The leader of the eagles
Sees me and is coming
They put the Bible in my hand
It is everlasting I believe

Another time, when I was in Fort Belknap, I woke up and I heard this song. I woke up one morning early, and a woman was singing this song. I've always remembered it.

Baláashe báxxiia
Baláashe Jesus húuk
Awáke bawáatchishkaate ahosh
Ikuuluuk biikóoiiwuuluuk
Biikóohiiwiiluuk
Baakóoshiiwiik
Baláashish báxxiiluuluuk

Lift up my name
My name is Jesus
All those who are in need shall see my name
They will come to me
They will come close to me
I will help them
If they lift up my name. Lift up my name

This is my song. It stays with me. It was given to me.

We left Belknap for the last time in 1988. During our last years there, Bill became Appeals Judge for the reservation. I took care of Lena, who had become very ill, and at the same time I enrolled in a course to learn about writing children's stories. I wrote stories about growing up with Grandma, about Bill's boyhood on the ranch, and about nature. I received a certificate when I completed the class, and I still think about getting some stories published, especially the ones I tell about little animals and nature.

Even as a child, when I heard a bird call, I'd quit playing and I would listen and say "*Aho.*" My girlfriends never did that. And now, when I go about my daily life trying to be a mother of today or a grandmother today and trying to understand the younger generation, I find myself doing like Pretty Shield did. I hear a bird during the course of a day or even in the city, sometimes. I hear a bird, and I know what it means: "That means rain." Then my mind quickly returns to the places where we used to go pick up kindling and dry wood and pile it up. Grandma said, "When the bird says 'rain,' gather up the kindling. Get some dry wood for the fire." My mind flickers through that. If I hear a little chickadee say a little call, "Summer's near – *iisoopiilich*," I say, "*Iisoopiilich, aho!*" I don't care whether I'm in the city or out in the country, if I hear that little call, I thank her for the message that we have made another season and we're here. *"Tisoopiilich*, change of season," and I say, "Thank you, little chickadee, you're so pretty."

I talk to creeks. Creeks are so playful; some creeks are so playful and so happy, but others are so calm and collected. They move on, like they're just content to be that way. Others rush around so much they seem furious. I always say, "Why are you so furious? What is that you're after? Where are you going?" And they – I feel a sort of vibes from them that say, "Well, follow me and find out." Or if it's a laughing creek, I tell it, "You're very happy. Shall we play some more? Do you play all day long? Do you frolic all the time?" It's just as if it says to me, "Come play with me until you're tired. We love to play with you." I go in there and look for rocks, and if I find a pretty one, it's just like they wash it off for me. Ripples come and wash it off, and I look at the creek and say, "Well, thank you. That's real clean." They smile and laugh. That's my way of looking at water.

Today, if people ask me what I do, I say, "I'm a rootdigger." Bill and I go into the foothills of the Big Horn Mountains and gather what I need for my presentations. Bill takes care of our place, but he helps me in the things I do. He says that I stuck with him through all his police years; he is going to support me in what I'm doing now. Sometimes we get tired or anxious about all that goes on. A day never goes by when somebody doesn't come to our place – two or three at the least. Sometimes I get a dozen. They come from Australia, Africa, Germany, and everywhere in America. They come for prayers, for medicinal herbs, for food, for information, or just because they want to come. I don't always know how they find me, but they do.

I have a push in my heart to keep up Indian cultural values. I'm sure that Pretty Shield is the source of that push. In the winter of 1995, I was – I don't know whether I felt like I was letting everything else go, everything but my roots and my plants, but I felt that I should give it up. I thought, "I should give it up because I don't see where it's getting me. It's taking a lot of time, and we have a lot of other food and medicines. Why am I doing this? Am I trying to prove a point, that my people knew about these things before, or am I trying to relive my life? What am I doing? I think I'll just quit. I'll drop it." Both Bill and I decided, "Yeah, that's enough. It's enough. We'll do other things."

That night I went to bed, kind of content that I had made up my mind that I wasn't going to do this anymore. And I dreamed. Just before I woke up, I had a dream; I woke up to it in fact. In the dream – right behind

The "rootdigger" at work, Windblowing Place, 1996.

Alma and Bill, Windblowing Place, 1996.

my house here, above the horizon just behind my house – a light came. A light came as I was standing there holding something in my left hand which I didn't see when the light came. The light didn't have a form of a man or anything like that, but it had a billowy look about it. It came and just saturated me with light. All over me, all around me was light. I had my – I was grasping this thing in my left hand. When the light came on, I was awed by it. Yet I wanted to see what I had in my hand, and I couldn't see it because of this light. It enveloped everything. I couldn't see what was in my hand, but my attention went to the right. As I had my hand out to this great light, there stood Pretty Shield. Not really standing on the ground but kind of on the cloud in the light, in the light, and she had a white gown, a white garment on, and her hair was down. It was long, to her waist almost. She was a young girl. I thought, "Pretty Shield." In my mind, I thought, "Pretty Shield." She said, "It's okay. It's all right." As I observed her saying, "It's all right," I knew she meant not to give it up. "It's all right. It's good. Don't be afraid." I looked up to the light again, and this huge being-like, way up there in cloud form – which was

The three surviving Hogan sisters, Pearl, Alma, and Cerise, in 1995 at the Healing of the Nations ceremony, Scouts' Day, Little Bighorn Battlefield National Monument.

the light – started to kind of draw itself in. I looked in my left hand, and I had a turnip in my hand, and that turnip had its foliage hanging on it yet, and its root in my hand. I woke up to that, so I felt I must go on.

The demand, the need, keeps coming, and I keep going. It is as if I need to help people. I think I am to continue to help my people – all people. But for my people, I want them to know themselves, to be a cultured people. My main concern is that we hold on to the cultural values of the past. These values strengthen this royal blood that I have in me. These are royal people of the Western Hemisphere, that were on the Western Hemisphere. I believe the clanship is good. That kept our blood strong. I believe in the value of treating your elders with respect. *The value of loving your children, loving your children to where they are responsible for their children. We must put the heart back in the child.*

Do not abuse nature, for to do so is abusing yourself, actually. Every morning, *every* morning when you wake up to the day – you give thanks. Give thanks. "This day you have given me to walk on the face of this earth. Guide me through it and protect me as I go along."

And pray.

The culture that we are now in is confused. The discipline that follows in normal life today is entirely different from long ago. Alcohol was not our heritage; neither were all this overdoing of dope and all this relying on someone in the family to keep getting them out of trouble these days. I am tired of Indian people being viewed as a fester on society, "just another drunken Indian." They refused alcohol in the beginning because they knew it wasn't good. I want Crow children to know they have a place under the sun. That place is that they are a Crow tribe of Indians. The material in their roots is as good or better than what's happening today.

I think we are beginning to blossom from our roots. A blossom is growing, and I am glad.

And by the river upon the bank thereof, on this side and on that side, shall grow all trees for meat, whose leaf shall not fade, neither shall the fruit thereof be consumed: it shall bring forth new fruit according to his months, because their waters they issued out of the sanctuary: and the fruit thereof shall be for meat, and the leaf thereof for medicine.

Ezekiel 47:12

APPENDIX
ONE

TIME LINE OF THE LIFE OF ALMA SNELL

1923 Alma's birth.

1924 Death of her mother. Maternal grandmother, Pretty Shield, took over care of Alma and her siblings at her home in Benteen, rural area of the reservation.

1931 Family moved to community of Crow Agency. Alma started school.

1937 Alma enrolled in seventh grade at boarding school for Indian students in Pierre, South Dakota.

1940 Alma entered boarding school in Flandreau, South Dakota; met Bill Snell, her future husband.

1941 Summer: romance with Bill Snell.
    Winter: Bill enlisted in U.S. Marines; Alma remained at Flandreau.

1942 Alma returned to Crow Agency, then worked in farming community of Toppenish, Washington, and as babysitter for her sister in Tacoma.

1944 Death of Pretty Shield.

1945 Birth of Alma's first son, Ted.
    Alma's first marriage (annulled).

1947 Alma married Bill Snell. Couple moved to Bill's home community at Fort Belknap Reservation in northern Montana.

1948 Birth of their daughter Faith.

1949 Birth of daughter Pearl Jean, at Crow Agency. Family went to Butte, Montana, where Bill Snell worked as electrician in copper mines.

1951 Birth of Bill Junior in Butte.

1952 Family moved to Roseburg, Oregon, because of illness of Bill's mother there. Alma had surgery for cancer.

1954 Family returned to Fort Belknap. Bill ranched and became Chief Judge of Tribal Courts. Alma and Bill traveled with evangelical missionaries, singing and translating songs in Indian sign language.

1957 Bill and Alma went to Rocky Boy Reservation, MI, where he administered law enforcement agency.

1958 Death of Alma's father, George Hogan. The Snells moved to Fort Yates, North Dakota, where Bill became captain of police.

1962 Back in Fort Belknap. Alma began to work in food services for Indian Health Service.

1972 Pine Ridge Reservation, South Dakota. Alma supervised reservation school's food services. Bill was involved in criminal justice work centering on the issues that culminated at Wounded Knee.

1975 Transfer to Ashland, Wisconsin, where Bill was a criminal investigator.

1976 Return to Crow Agency. Alma worked in the tribe's social service agency.

1978 Bill worked for BIA in Michigan. Alma worked for a state senior citizens' program and received an award from the governor of Michigan for her service.

1979 In Fort Belknap again to care for Bill's adopted mother, Lena. Alma worked for senior citizens, began presentations on Native American culture in area schools, completed course in writing children's literature. Bill served as Appeals Judge at Belknap.

1983 Bill suffered serious heart attack.

1988 Alma and Bill "retired" to their Windblowing Place on the Crow Reservation.

APPENDIX
TWO

ANCESTORS OF ALMA STUART HOGAN

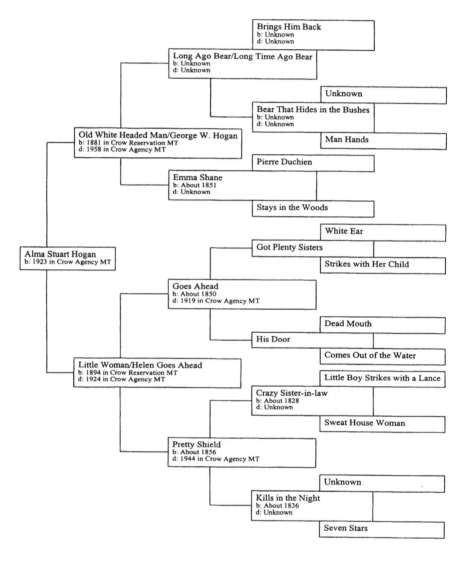

ALMA SNELL'S YELLOWTAIL CONNECTIONS

Records identify Pierre Duchien in a variety of spellings, including Chienne, Du Chien, de Chien, and Peter Shane. A fur trader, he had wives in a number of tribes across the northern plains; hence, the individuals listed here represent a fraction of his descendants. Magdalene Moccasin, Little Big Horn College archivist, is one of them. She is currently researching the Duchien family history, using the tentative title "The Many Wives of Pierre Duchien."

Joseph Medicine Crow, author and tribal historian, is the son of Amy Yellowtail.

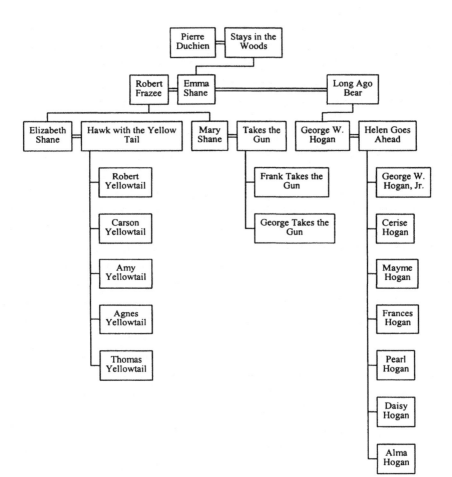

Notes

INTRODUCTION

1. In 1866 timber from the foothills of the Big Horn Mountains moved along the Wood Road to become part of the construction of Fort C. F. Smith, one of three outposts established to guard the Bozeman Trail. Fort Smith, located on the Bighorn River approximately seven miles from Windblowing Place, was the scene of the so-called Hayfield Battle, an attack (probably by Cheyenne warriors) on contract farm workers and a few U.S. soldiers in 1867. The army withdrew from Fort Smith the following year. I am indebted to the late Paul Gordon, National Park Service historian, for this information. His beautifully illustrated book, *Bighorn Canyon National Recreation Area* (Helena MT: Falcon Press, 1990), provides valuable insights on the geology, geography, ecology, prehistory, and history of the Bighorn region. Another example of the intersection of past and present in Alma Snell's life is an event that took place on the first weekend in July 1996. The Bullinsight pasture became the scene of a Pentecostal camp meeting, complete with a large tent, a Canadian Indian evangelist, electronically amplified music, and sumptuous meals to which Alma contributed generous amounts of food and service.

2. Frank B. Linderman, *Red Mother* (New York: John Day, 1932); reprinted as *Pretty-shield: Medicine Woman of the Crows* (Lincoln: University of Nebraska Press, 1972), 10 (page citations are to the reprint edition).

3. Frank B. Linderman, *American: The Life Story of a Great Indian, Plenty-coups, Chief of the Crows* (New York: John Day, 1930); reprinted as *Plenty-coups: Chief of the Crows* (Lincoln: University of Nebraska Press, 1962), 310 (page citations are to the reprint edition).

4. The tribal segment that remained as farmers in the Missouri River valley became known as the Hidatsas.

5. John C. Ewers, *Plains Indian History and Culture: Essays on Continuity and Change* (Norman: University of Oklahoma Press, 1997), 12.

6. Peter Nabokov, "Cultivating Themselves: The Inter-play of Crow Indian Religion and History" (Ph.D. diss., University of California, Berkeley, 1988), 11-12, 87-112. My overview of early Crow history is based on Nabokov's excellent discussion of how the Crows have created their cultural identity; on Joseph Medicine Crow, *From the Heart of Crow Country* (New York: Orion Books, 1992); and on Frederick Hoxie, *Parading through History: The Making of the Crow Nation in America, 1805-1935* (Cambridge: Cambridge University Press, 1995). It is Nabokov's thesis that because of its concern with regeneration, the ritual complex associated with the Tobacco Society "is the tribe's prime symbol bank and historical digest" (8). Ceremonies involve the planting and harvesting of a unique and sacred variety of tobacco, as a representation of regeneration, by chapters or subgroups of the society. Group regeneration is assured by a process through which longtime chapter members adopt new initiates and instruct them in the sacred rites. There is a Crow prophecy that when the sacred tobacco ceases to exist, so will the Crow people. The last time Crows attempted to harvest the sacred tobacco was in 1974. Their efforts failed.

7. Ewers, *Plains Indian History*, 13. Margot Liberty and Raymond Wood, editors of *Anthropology on the Great Plains* (Lincoln: University of Nebraska Press, 1980), 5, point out that despite certain strong similarities, Plains tribes developed a variety of religious practices, languages (thirty-three different languages were spoken in the area), and family systems; this "internal diversity" precludes delineation of a "standard average" culture on the Great Plains.

8. For an account of a myth in which Old Man Coyote's wife and Red Woman, both of whom had supernatural power, engaged in a lengthy conversation that resulted in numerous decisions about such important issues as the use of fire, the cycle of the seasons, the presence of air, differences between men and women, and the geographical location of the Crow people, see Robert Lowie, *Myths and Traditions of the Crow Indians* (Lincoln: University of Nebraska Press, 1993), 27-30.

9. Martha Harroun Foster, "Of Baggage and Bondage: Gender and Status among Hidatsa and Crow Women," *American Indian Culture and Research Journal* 17, no. 2 (1993): 121-52.

10. Additional information on Crow women may be found in Robert Lowie, *The Crow Indians* (New York: Rinehart, 1935; reprint, Lincoln: University of Nebraska Press, 1983), 60-61, 74-81 (page citations are to the reprint edition); Joseph Medicine Crow, "The Effects of European Culture Contacts upon the Economic, Social, and Religious Life of the Crow Indians" (master's thesis, University of Southern California, 1939), 37-38; Peter Nabokov, "Vision Quests of Crow Women," *Indian Notes* (Museum of the American Indian, New York City: Heye Foundation) 10 (summer 1974): 66-83. On plains women in general, see

Patricia Albers and Beatrice Medicine, eds., *The Hidden Half: Studies in Plains Indian Women* (Washington DC: University Press of America, 1983).

11. Rebecca Tsosie, "Changing Women: The Crosscurrents of American Indian Feminine Identity," in *Unequal Sisters: A Multicultural Reader in U.S. Women's History,* 2d ed., ed. Ellen Carol Dubois and Vicki L. Ruiz (New York: Routledge, 1994), 510–11. Albers and Medicine, *The Hidden Half,* 13–14; and Lillian Ackerman and Laura F. Klein, eds., *Women and Power in Native North America* (Norman: University of Oklahoma Press, 1995), provide other analyses of these themes.

12. Keith Algier, *The Crow and the Eagle: A Tribal History from Lewis and Clark to Custer* (Caldwell ID: Caxton Press, 1993), 52–81; Edward Denig, *Five Indian Tribes of the Upper Missouri,* ed. John C. Ewers (Norman: University of Oklahoma Press, 1961), 155–57.

13. Charles J. Kappler, ed., *Indian Affairs Laws and Treaties,* 4 vols. (Washington DC: U.S. Government Printing Office, 1938), 2:594–95.

14. Kappler, *Indian Affairs,* 2:1008–11; Hoxie, *Parading through History,* 131–33.

15. Frederick Hoxie, *A Final Promise: The Campaign to Assimilate the Indians, 1880–1920* (Lincoln: University of Nebraska Press, 1984), 70–81.

16. U.S. Senate Committee on Indian Affairs, *Opening of the Crow Reservation: Hearing before the Committee on Indian Affairs,* 64th Cong., 1st sess., 1 June 1916, 64. The Indian Rights Association pamphlet, *A Threatened Raid on Crow Indian Lands* (Philadelphia, 1916), is cited in Hoxie, *Parading through History,* 259.

17. Robert S. Yellowtail, *Robert Summers Yellowtail* (Albuquerque NM: Cold Type Services, 1973), 1–6.

18. Hoxie, *Parading through History,* 263–65.

19. Kappler, *Indian Affairs,* 3:271–77.

20. Medicine Crow, "The Effects," 14–16.

21. Medicine Crow, "The Effects," 4–5; "Report on Hygienic Conditions of Indian Homes, 1923," item 15, box 88, Records of the Crow Indian Agency, Federal Records Center, Seattle WA, cited in Hoxie, *Parading through History,* 299–300.

22. Agnes Deernose and Fred Voget, *They Call Me Agnes: A Crow Narrative Based on the Life of Agnes Yellowtail Deernose* (Norman: University of Oklahoma Press, 1995), xviii; Fred Voget, *The Shoshoni-Crow Sun Dance* (Norman: University of Oklahoma Press, 1984), 16–23.

23. Hoxie, *Parading through History,* 170, 299–300.

24. Hoxie, *Parading through History,* 296.

25. Rodney Frey, *The World of the Crow Indians: As Driftwood Lodges* (Norman: University of Oklahoma Press, 1987), 4–5.

26. Medicine Crow, "The Effects," 74.

27. Medicine Crow, "The Effects," 78–79.

28. Medicine Crow, "The Effects," 89; Nabokov, "Cultivating Themselves," 260–65. Frey, *Crow Indians*, 155–58, records an incident in which a Crow man showed him a cactus peyote button and said, "This is who I pray to when someone in my family is sick or in need of something." A picture of Jesus was glued to the reverse side of the button. Frey also points out that most Crows who follow more than one sacred tradition carefully avoid mixing rituals of one form of faith with another. A Catholic would be reluctant to include Christian prayers in a sun-dance ceremony or Native American Church practices in a Catholic celebration.

29. Hoxie, *Parading through History*, 201–29.

30. Charles C. Bradley, "Early Reservation Days," 1975, Little Big Horn College Archives, Crow Agency MT (typescript), 56–60.

31. Charles C. Bradley and Susanna R. Bradley, "From Individualism to Bureaucracy: Documents on the Crow Indians, 1920–1945," 1974, Little Big Horn College Archives (typescript), 311–14.

32. U.S. Department of the Interior, Office of Indian Affairs, *Annual Report of the Commissioner of Indian Affairs to the Secretary of the Department of the Interior, 1906* (Washington DC: U.S. Government Printing Office, 1906), 17–23. As Crows gained more control of Crow Fair, they decided to hold it in August. It continues today as the reservation's central social occasion. The festivities include family reunions, feasting, powwow dancing, rodeo competition, and a daily parade that harks back to the time when the Crow people moved their camps in search of buffalo.

33. Deernose and Voget, *They Call Me Agnes*, 174, 180–97. Clearly, the Armistice Day observance is a carryover from the buffalo days when Crow camps celebrated the return of victorious warriors with dances, songs, and feasting.

34. Quoted in Hoxie, *Parading through History*, 303. Hoxie links the social separation to the economic situation wherein whites gained advantage by purchasing or leasing desirable acreage from individual Crows, who became increasingly dependent on lease revenues as a source of income.

35. Shortly after the death of Congregationalist minister James Burgess in 1917, the Crows organized a new Reno district church, naming it the Burgess Memorial Congregational Church. Goes Ahead became its first deacon, and George Hogan was its first secretary. The Baptists who assumed responsibility for the church in 1921 sent Chester and Laura Bentley as missionaries in 1923. The Bentleys worked at Burgess Memorial Baptist until 1960. They and that church deeply affected Alma's life.

36. Gretchen M. Bataille and Kathleen Mullen Sands, *American Indian Women Telling Their Lives* (Lincoln: University of Nebraska Press, 1984), 21–24.

37. Rayna Green, "The Pocahontas Perplex," in *Unequal Sisters: A Multicultural Reader in U.S. Women's History*, ed. Ellen C. Dubois and Vicki L. Ruiz (New York: Routledge, Chapman & Hall, 1990), 20. Green also discusses the issue of Indian women and myths in her *Women in American Indian Society* (New York: Chelsea House, 1992), which is an excellent introduction for nonspecialists. Donna J. Kessler, *The Making of Sacagawea: A Euro-American Legend* (Tuscaloosa: University of Alabama Press, 1996), analyzes the reasons for and impact of legends associated with the Shoshoni woman who journeyed with the Lewis and Clark expedition.

38. Linderman, *Pretty-shield*, 9. In referring to *Pretty-shield* as an autobiography, I am following the practice of Bataille and Sands (*American Indian Woman*), who put it in that category. An earlier collaboration, similar to that of Linderman and Pretty Shield, occurred between Gilbert L. Wilson and a Hidatsa woman named Maxidiwiac or Buffalo Bird Woman. Wilson used their work in his University of Minnesota doctoral thesis, *Agriculture of the Hidatsa Indians: An Indian Interpretation*, Studies in the Social Sciences, no. 9 (Minneapolis: University of Minnesota, 1917); reprinted as *Buffalo Bird Woman's Garden* (St. Paul: Minnesota Historical Society, 1987). See also Wilson's *Waheenee: An Indian Girl's Story, Told by Herself* (St. Paul: Webb, 1921).

39. Frank B. Linderman, "My Camp Kettle Career," *Frontier and Midland* 19, quoted in Harold G. Merriam, "Sign-Talker with Straight Tongue: Frank Bird Linderman," *Montana: The Magazine of Western History* 12 (Summer 1962): 4. My information on Linderman's early experiences in Montana comes from this article. Merriam also edited Linderman's memoirs, *Montana Adventure* (Lincoln: University of Nebraska Press, 1967).

40. Linderman, "Camp Kettle," quoted in Merriam, "Sign-Talker," 6.

41. Norma Linderman Waller, "Introducing Frank Linderman and His Books," n.d., Frank Bird Linderman Biographical Papers, Parmley Library, Billings MT (typescript), 2.

42. Day Child, Rocky Boy Reservation MT, to Linderman, quoted in William Bevis, "Frank Linderman's Work," an article that accompanies the description of the Frank Bird Linderman Collection, K. Ross Toole Archives, University of Montana, Missoula.

43. Merriam, "Sign-Talker," 10.

44. John Frost to Linderman, Pryor MT, 29 July 1926, box 1, folder 5, Frank B. Linderman Papers, Special Collections, Montana Historical Society, Helena (on loan to the Museum of Plains Indians, Browning MT, for microfilming). I follow Frost's capitalization and syntax.

45. Frost to Linderman, Pryor MT, 16 May 1930, box 1, folder 5, Linderman Papers.

46. Linderman to "Mrs. Draper," Goose Bay MT, 31 March 1931, Linderman Letters (courtesy of the Frank Bird Linderman heirs).

47. Frank Bird Linderman to "Daughters," Goose Bay MT, 8 April 1931, Linderman Letters (courtesy of the Linderman heirs). The daughters were Verne and Wilda Linderman and Norma Waller. Linderman communicated with Pretty Shield through an interpreter, Goes Together (Kitty) Deernose, and by means of sign language, at which they both were adept.

48. Frederic Van de Water to Linderman, 22 November 1932, Linderman Collection.

49. *Christian Science Monitor*, 26 November 1932.

50. Richard Walsh to Linderman, New York, 3 February 1933, Linderman Collection.

51. Hermann Hagedorn to Linderman, 15 August 1935, Linderman Collection.

52. Peter Nabokov, ed., *Two Leggings: The Making of a Crow Warrior* (Lincoln: University of Nebraska Press, 1967).

53. Thomas Yellowtail and Michael O. Fitzgerald, *Yellowtail: Crow Medicine Man and Sun Dance Chief* (Norman: University of Oklahoma Press, 1992).

54. Deernose and Voget, *They Call Me Agnes*, xi.

55. Tsosie, "Changing Women," 515, 528.

56. Anthologies such as Ackerman and Klein, *Women and Power in Native North America*; Albers and Medicine, *The Hidden Half*; and Nancy Shoemaker, ed., *Negotiators of Change: Historical Perspectives on Native American Women* (New York: Routledge, 1995), discuss these topics. *The Woman's Way* (Alexandria VA: Time-Life Books, 1995), and Green, *Women in American Indian Society*, give good overviews of women's cultures. Kathryn Braund, *Deerskins and Duffels* (Lincoln: University of Nebraska Press, 1993), examines specific issues relating to Creek women; Theda Perdue, *Cherokee Women: Gender and Culture Change, 1700–1835* (Lincoln: University of Nebraska Press, 1998), is a perceptive study of Cherokee women.

57. Frank B. Linderman, *Lige Mounts: Free Trapper* (New York: Scribner, 1922); reprinted as *Morning Light* (New York: John Day, 1930) and *Free Trapper* (London: Faber & Faber, 1931, 1933).

58. Tim McCleary, *The Stars We Know* (Prospect Heights IL: Waveland Press, 1997), 8.

59. This suggestion follows that of Rodney Frey, ed., *Stories That Make the World* (Norman: University of Oklahoma Press, 1995).

1. GRANDMOTHER'S GRANDCHILD

1. Little Woman's older children were George Jr., born in 1911; Cerise, 1913; Mayme, 1915; Frances, 1917; Pearl, 1919; and Daisy, 1921 (died in infancy). Alma was born January 10, 1923. She was named for Alma Stuart, a friend of Little Woman. The individual who registered her birth understood her name to be Elma and indicated on her birth certificate that she was a male. Alma did not correct the error until 1994.

2. Little Woman died in 1924. Pretty Shield told Linderman, "My daughter stepped into a horse's track that was deep in the dried clay and hurt her ankle. I could not heal her; nobody could. The white doctor told me that the same sickness that makes people cough themselves to death was in my daughter's ankle" (Linderman, *Pretty-shield*, 249). Johnny Wilson was the son of Pretty Shield's other daughter, Pine Fire, who died shortly after Little Woman did. According to the Crow kinship system, which is matrilineal, the son of one's maternal aunt is a brother. For a thorough discussion of Crow family and clan relationships, see Lowie, *The Crow Indians*, 19–32.

3. A note on style: all Crow words are italicized. Comments in parentheses are part of Alma's narration. Rather than interrupt the story with editorial brackets for dates and a few explanatory details, we agreed simply to insert them in the text.

4. This is the same Robert Yellowtail who spoke before Congress in 1917. In 1934 he became the first Crow to serve as reservation superintendent. Thomas Yellowtail, whose autobiography is discussed in the introduction to this volume, became a well-known sun-dance leader and traditional healer.

5. Amy White Man was a daughter of Lizzie Yellowtail, as is Agnes Yellowtail Deernose, who told her life story to Fred Voget. Amy was adopted by her grandmother, Emma Shane. Joseph Medicine Crow is Amy's son.

6. Alma does not know the exact date of this incident, but it must have occurred in the mid-1880s. George Hogan was born in 1881.

7. Hogan's daughter Mary Elizabeth says her father told her that the children leaving Crow Agency by train were doing "okay" until Julia High Hawk screamed, "We'll never see our Crow country again!" Then everyone started to cry.

Several years ago Mary Elizabeth's son, Barry Rawn, was working in Arizona with a man named Jack Hogan, who owned a construction company. Barry told his employer that his family name was also Hogan and that his grandfather had received the name from an army officer at Carlisle. Jack Hogan then replied that his uncle, also named Hogan, had taught at Carlisle about the time of George Hogan's arrival there. The unanswered question: Was that the same Hogan who gave Barry's grandfather his name?

Hogan's widow, Lillian, says that young George could not afford to return to Montana during vacations, so he spent his summers working for farmers near the school.

8. Hogan married twice after Little Woman's death. He had two daughters, Ataloa and Ferole Mae, by his second wife, Marjorie White Hip, who died while she was still a young woman. He and his third wife, Lillian, also had two daughters, Mardell and Mary Elizabeth. Lillian, who survives him, celebrated her ninety-second birthday at Crow Fair in August 1996. She and Mary Elizabeth were generous in sharing their memories of George Hogan.

9. When Goes Ahead converted to Christianity, he abandoned the use of traditional Crow spiritual or medicine powers and wanted Pretty Shield to do the same (see chapter 2). She became a church member too but still occasionally relied on Crow medicine.

10. Alma closed her eyes while she recalled her grandmother's words. She would say a phrase in Crow, then translate it into English.

2. PRETTY SHIELD AND GOES AHEAD

1. Pretty Shield was born about 1856, so she would have been nine in 1865.

2. The term "fat hanging on the racks" refers to fresh meat placed on racks to dry.

Lowie, *The Crow Indians*, 49–56, describes Crow courtship and wedding customs. Pretty Shield's arranged marriage to Goes Ahead followed a typical pattern, although some Crow women selected their own mates. It is probable that Goes Ahead or his male relatives had given horses to Pretty Shield's father earlier. Joe Medicine Crow, "The Effects," 37–38, states that women sometimes bragged about the number of horses their fathers received at the time their marriage agreements were made.

3. Pretty Shield told Frank Linderman (*Pretty-shield*, 131), "Standing-medicine-rock, my oldest sister, was not a good woman. I mean that she liked other men, and that she sometimes forgot that she belonged to Goes-ahead. I knew about this, and talked to her. But I did not tell on her. It was my brother's duty to do this, according to our tribal custom, and not mine, so that I only talked to her." According to Lowie (*The Crow Indians*, 55), Crow men responded to infidelity in a variety of ways, although adultery was often a reason for divorce. When Alma was a teenager, she saw a woman throw away her husband. She had an announcement made at Crow Fair: "I'm throwing him away. Anybody can have him." The husband persuaded his wife to take him back; the next year, at Crow Fair, he threw *her* away.

4. According to Tim McCleary, who teaches at Little Big Horn College, the Crow people recognize an impersonal, nongendered creator called *Iichíihkbaalia*, which is commonly translated as First Maker or First Worker. This omnipotent being placed power known as *baaxpée* in all things. *Baaxpée* is most often translated as "medicine" but is better understood as supernatural power. Through *baaxpée*, *Iichíihkbaalia* is omnipresent.

The teachings of Christian missionaries at the turn of the century led the Crows to create two new terms to identify or describe the Christian concept of God. These are *Akbaatatdía*, One Who Made Everything, and *Báakkaaawaaishtashiile*, White Man Above. McCleary explores Crow religious interpretations and experiences in great depth in *"Akbaatashee*: The Oilers Pentecostalism among the Crow Indians" (master's thesis, University of Montana, 1993). The Crows call Four Square Pentecostalists "oilers" because of the olive oil used to anoint the foreheads of persons seeking to be healed.

5. For Crow beliefs about vision quests, see Lowie, *The Crow Indians*, 238–55, and Frey, *Crow Indians*, 59–76. Crows receive spiritual powers or "medicine" through the intervention of a medicine helper or "medicine father," often referred to as a *person*, who serves as a mediator between the natural and supernatural worlds. Crow men sought (and seek) such mediators through the vision quest process of fasting for four days and nights, as Goes Ahead did. The medicine helper often, though not always, appeared in the form of an animal or a plant. Traditionally, women did not seek medicine power through fasting, but sometimes they asked for and received assistance when they were away from camp, grieving over the death of a loved one or mourning a similar crisis in their lives. This happened to Pretty Shield. See Nabokov, "Vision Quests," 66–83.

6. Breath feathers are the short, downy feathers from the eagle's chest. Pretty Shield explained to Linderman that "Son-of-the-morning-star [Custer] was going to his death and did not know it. He was like a feather blown by the wind, and *had* to go. . . . He *had* to fight because he *had* to die, and this made others die with him." Goes Ahead told Pretty Shield that Custer died in the Little Bighorn River. See Linderman, *Pretty-shield*, 233–37.

7. Boyes gave Alma Snell a photograph of the blaze in 1973. In a letter of July 1996 he drew a map of the tree's location and a sketch of the blaze, which he called the "winged serpent." Subsequently, Alma, her sister Pearl Hogan, her grandson Billy Snell and his wife Christine, and I tried without success to locate the tree; prairie fires have damaged many trees in the area since 1973.

8. Joseph Medicine Crow, in *From the Heart of Crow Country*, 44, describes a similar vision that appeared to his grandfather, Chief Medicine Crow.

3. MY CAMP IS IN A DIFFERENT PLACE

1. Crows have maintained the tradition of having multiple names, a non-Indian name and at least one tribal name. Shortly after birth a baby receives a Crow name from a respected elder or wise one (medicine man or woman). Certain circumstances, such as illness, may lead to that name's being changed.

2. "Crow" is a shortened and widely used reference to the town of Crow Agency.

3. Lakotas had killed the aunt's husband and two daughters. When Pretty Shield married Goes Ahead, they invited the aunt to live with them (Linderman, *Pretty-shield*, 20–21).

4. Pretty Shield gave the name Sits with a Bear to Beverly Wilson, one of her great-granddaughters.

5. When Pretty Shield told this story to Linderman, she recalled that she was a young married woman when she had the buffalo calf. She said that she liked to put a saddle on it and ride her daughter Pine Fire around camp on its back (*Pretty-shield*, 143–44).

6. Johnny Wilson, who married Louella Charges Strong, became tribal chairman in his later life. Alma recalls that an older friend, Agnes Schaffer, told her about a time when a group of Crows from the Reno District were camping along the Little Bighorn, and Johnny, then a small boy, jumped on Goes Ahead's shoulders and pulled his grandfather to the ground. The old man straightened up, looked at his grandson, and said, "You will be a chief, someday."

7. Alma describes bear root (biscuit root, *lomatium macrocarpum*) as an important medicinal herb for the Crows. She says, "They guarded this plant well. They placed it in their lodges, and they treated it with utmost care and protection. The root of this plant was used for almost every ailment. Midwives kept it in tote bags that went along with them wherever they went. Brewed into a tea, it was given to laboring women to ease childbirth pains. Bear root tea also reduced pain from toothaches and arthritis, and it was used for colds and bronchial disorders. Only certain individuals had the authority to gather it. They usually said prayers and did much talking before proceeding to remove the root."

8. As Alma talked, she moved her hands and pulled an imaginary sinew through her mouth just as she had seen Pretty Shield do. The repetition of her words and the repetitious process of repairing the moccasin seemed to create a tangible link to the past.

9. When Alma told anthropologist Peter Nabokov of this incident, he said the pouch probably contained sacred tobacco seeds that Pretty Shield would have owned as a member of the Crow Tobacco Society. Alma recalls that Pretty Shield adopted fourteen people into the Tobacco Society. She made buckskin garments and moccasins for them. They reciprocated with gifts of meat, hides, or clothing.

10. During his lifetime, George Hogan earned a living in various ways. He worked for the Bureau of Indian Affairs; he ranched or occasionally worked for other ranchers; and in 1940–41 he collected oral history from Crow elders as part of the Federal Writers' Project of the New Deal's Works Progress Administration.

11. Alma enjoyed a similarly exhilarating experience in September 1996 when she received a buffalo from the tribal herd so that she could use its parts in her demonstrations. (Tribal authorities were culling the herd that the Crows keep for symbolic and ceremonial purposes.) After the buffalo had been taken into the Little Bighorn River and shot, Alma went into the water and butchered it. She emerged blood-spattered and triumphant, with shining eyes and another vivid story to tell her family and friends.

12. Apparently, Pretty Shield had received a book before Linderman brought her a copy. A letter to Linderman from Anna Sloan, the wife of an agency clerk named James Sloan, noted, "When Pretty Shield understood what it was she was getting, she held the book tight to her and tears came into her eyes, she said, 'tanks, tanks, tell him tanks.' " Anna Sloan to Linderman, Crow Agency MT, 10 November 1932, box 1, folder 5, Linderman Papers.

13. Cerise also recalls that when Linderman visited Pretty Shield's small home at Crow Agency, he would ask for and get "his special chair" and would complain, in a joking way, about the coffee being too strong.

4. TURNING THE STORM

1. Cerise went to Chemawa in 1929 and remained one year in that school, which had been built following a fire that destroyed its precursor – the Training School for Indian Youth – in 1885. Like most Indian boarding schools, its original goal was the assimilation of Indian youth into the dominant culture of the United States. By the time Cerise was a student there, Chemawa was a four-year high school that emphasized vocational education. It continues to serve Native American students today, primarily from tribes of the Northwest.

2. Saint Xavier MT.

3. Pretty Shield identified the Creator as *Magah-hawathus (Bachaáhawatash)*, which Linderman translated as Man-alone or Lone-man (*Pretty-shield*, 25). Mandan/Hidatsa tradition views *Bachaáhawatash* as cocreator with *Íichúhkbaalia*. The fact that Pretty Shield and Goes Ahead prayed to *Bachaáhawatash* reflects their membership in the River Crow band. River Crows were closer to the Mandan and Hidatsa than the other two Crow bands, the Mountain Crow and the Kicked in the Bellies.

4. When she refers to "missionaries," Alma is speaking of the Baptist denomination, which established a stronghold on the eastern side of the reservation, where she lived.

5. Laura Bentley named the Philathea class by combining the Greek words *philia* (love or friendship) and *alethea* (truth). Groups usually called Philalethea Societies were common in colleges in those days; they were organized (according to a former member of one) by "earnest persons in search of truth."

6. Alma estimates that she was fifteen or sixteen when these incidents happened. She states emphatically that she was not one of the girls who were smoking.

5. WOMANHOOD

1. Each of Alma's siblings who was born before the 1920 passage of the Crow Act (see the Introduction) had received title to 1,000 acres. They also inherited portions of their mother's allotment, as did Alma.

2. Agnes was the daughter of George Hogan's half-sister Elizabeth Shane. Because of Crow kinship patterns, Alma referred to her as an aunt. Because of Agnes's age, Pretty Shield viewed her as a "mother" to Alma.

3. Lowie, *The Crow Indians*, 44–45, points to disagreement among his informants on whether women, during the buffalo days, were required to live in separate lodges at the time of their menstrual periods. He describes a cleansing process similar to the one Alma recalls. Thomas Buckley and Alma Gottlieb, eds., *Blood Magic: The Anthropology of Menstruation* (Berkeley: University of California Press, 1988), analyze differing beliefs and behaviors related to the menstrual cycle. Alma remembers that among traditional Assiniboines, young men served meals, perhaps because of cultural concerns about menstruating women.

4. Typically, Crows do not discipline their children by hitting them, so the teacher who slapped Alma was the first adult to strike her.

5. "Girls' rules" called for a court that was divided into two equal sections. Each team had three forwards, who were required to remain in their offensive half of the court and attempt to score baskets, and three guards, who defended against the opponent's forwards. No player could cross the dividing line at center court; defensive players who gained possession of the ball had to pass it to their forwards.

6. Alma does not recall whether either team had a substitute when she and the girl who scratched her were removed from the game.

7. Alma's comment "we hit them without killing them" refers to one of the four exploits by which Crow men acquired honors in battle. A warrior could "count coup" if he was the first to strike – but not kill – an enemy in combat. The three other actions that earned coup were leading a successful war party, taking

an enemy's weapon from him, and stealing a tethered horse from an enemy's camp.

Pretty Shield told Linderman several stories of women who went to battle, but she also commented that men did not like to talk about women who fought (*Pretty-shield*, 202–3, 227–30). On the role of Crow women, see Lowie, *The Crow Indians*, 60–61, 74–81; Medicine Crow, "The Effects," 42–46; and Nabokov, "Vision Quests." On plains women in general, see Albers and Medicine, *The Hidden Half*.

8. Alma first told me this story over a cup of tea at Polly's Cafe in Fort Smith. When we decided to record it, she wanted to be sure that all the details were accurate, so she listened to the Hank Bull Chief tape and translated it from Crow to English. The version that she had told at Polly's ended with Comes along the Shore's return to the Crows and her marriage to Knife. Lowie, *Myths and Traditions of the Crow Indians*, 268–69, includes a similar account – some details differ, but its theme is the same – and it too ends with the marriage of Knife and the heroine, who is identified as "Comes-from-across." It is not unusual for American Indian stories to have several versions, possibly for teaching purposes.

6. LONELINESS AND THE NIGHT SKY

1. Flandreau Indian School, which continues to serve approximately five hundred students today, began as a BIA boarding school in 1893. As in the past, it draws students from a large number of western plains tribes.

2. Pretty Shield told Linderman (*Pretty-shield*, 24) that she took a strap to one of the grandchildren but later felt ashamed of hitting her.

7. ASSINIBOINES HAVE STRONG MEDICINE

1. Many young Indian men of Alma's time followed the custom of asking a female relative, a sister or cousin, to act as a go-between when they wanted to meet a particular girl.

2. The fact that Pretty Shield had a campsite at Crow Fair was typical. Even now, many Crows who live within walking distance of the fairgrounds, which are situated across the Little Bighorn from Crow Agency, put up tipis and erect "shades" to shelter their outdoor living arrangements there.

3. The last authentically Crow sun dance had occurred in 1875. The revived version, held twice in 1941, reflected Shoshoni traditions. Truhujo was Shoshoni. Voget, *The Shoshoni-Crow Sun Dance*, and Michael O. Fitzgerald, *Yellowtail: Crow Medicine Man and Sun Dance Chief* (Norman: University of Oklahoma Press, 1991), are good sources on the sun dance and its return to the Crow reservation.

4. Alma was working in a campus bakery and tea room at the time Bill left.

8. A BAD TIME IN MY LIFE

1. Alma says that a large number of Crow people left the reservation to do farm labor during the war years: one person would receive a contract to supply an agricultural business with workers, and this individual would (as Deernose did) recruit relatives and friends to join the enterprise.

2. Bill Snell served in the Eighteenth Combat Engineers of the Second Marine Division. He fought at Guadalcanal and was part of the first unit to attack the beaches of Tarawa. He participated in the invasion of Saipan, where he suffered a shrapnel wound, but he removed the metal from his hand and arm and continued to fight. He was hospitalized for malaria in 1944. Discharged in December 1945, he received the Assiniboine name "Day Chief" when he returned from the Pacific. His older brother, Curtis, who had been a prisoner of war in Europe, received the name "White Boy."

3. The push dance is a Crow version of the fox trot, modified so that women ask men to dance, and the men "push" the women backward while dancing.

4. The National Youth Administration was a New Deal agency that trained young people for jobs.

5. Pretty Shield died 30 April 1944 and was buried in the Custer National Cemetery. Her coffin was placed on top of Goes Ahead's. Alma's family recalls that a bizarre incident occurred just before Pretty Shield's burial. As the ground was being prepared for her grave, an army officer who was visiting the cemetery decided that he wanted to see Goes Ahead's remains. At his request, the old scout's grave and casket were opened.

6. Years later a neighbor told Alma that he had heard a commotion in the apartment that night, but because it was so frequently a scene of drunken brawls, he didn't think much about it.

7. Alma reported her rape to a judge in the Crow Tribal Court system.

8. Mayme Hogan's decision to care for Alma's son was in accord with Crow traditions of family relationships. Frequently, grandparents or aunts and uncles adopted a Crow baby, particularly a firstborn child. This practice, which still occurs occasionally, derives from the buffalo-hunting days when life was fraught with danger and when elders needed youngsters to help with everyday tasks. The time that Pretty Shield, as a child, spent with her aunt to "heal her heart" reflects a similar situation.

9. The custom of a wife receiving honor because she rides or walks beside the horse of a warrior husband is another tradition from the buffalo days. Pretty Shield liked to speak of the fact that Goes Ahead always selected her to ride his war pony.

9. I HAVE CROSSED THREE RIVERS

1. The three rivers were the Missouri, the Musselshell, and the Yellowstone. The journey had taken two days because of bad road conditions.

2. Alma's use of the term "throughout" implies that this situation was not confined to Assiniboine men.

10. MANY ROADS

1. In 1972, Bill Snell accepted a BIA transfer to Pine Ridge, the scene of confrontation between the Oglala tribal administration and activists within the tribe who received support from the American Indian Movement (AIM). Those who backed tribal chairman Dick Wilson were known as "Wilson's Goon Squad." Bill's task was to alleviate factionalism within the tribal police force in order to provide unbiased law enforcement. He says that his job was to get neutral people into the law enforcement agency, neither "goons" nor AIM advocates. In his words, "We had to weed out a few officers, but our job was to protect the people. If somebody broke the law, I arrested him. I even arrested Wilson one time."

In 1973 the tension at Pine Ridge escalated when Indian activists captured and occupied major portions of the reservation community of Wounded Knee for seventy-one days.

2. Alma explains that the phrase "the stories that came out of there" refers to conversations she had with people involved in the conflict at Pine Ridge and to information acquired from Bill, who interviewed ranchers, law officers, and others in the course of investigating various incidents.

3. This incident occurred in 1972.

11. OLD SONGS, NEW FRUIT

1. "Feeds" is a Crow way of saying "feasts."

2. Alma recalls that Laura Bentley and her daughter Myrtle Hubley came backstage after the service, and Mrs. Bentley said, "Your father would be so proud of you." Subsequently, Alma translated songs into sign language at Mrs. Bentley's funeral.

Index

Singing an Indian Song
A Biography of D'Arcy McNickle
By Dorothy R. Parker

Crashing Thunder
The Autobiography of an American Indian
Edited by Paul Radin

Turtle Lung Woman's Granddaughter
By Delphine Red Shirt and
Lone Woman

Telling a Good One
The Process of a Native American
Collaborative Biography
By Theodore Rios and
Kathleen Mullen Sands

William W. Warren
The Life, Letters, and Times of an
Ojibwe Leader
By Theresa M. Schenck

Sacred Feathers
The Reverend Peter Jones
(Kahkewaquonaby) and the
Mississauga Indians
By Donald B. Smith

Grandmother's Grandchild
My Crow Indian Life
By Alma Hogan Snell
Edited by Becky Matthews
Foreword by Peter Nabokov

No One Ever Asked Me
The World War II Memoirs of an
Omaha Indian Soldier
By Hollis D. Stabler
Edited by Victoria Smith

Blue Jacket
Warrior of the Shawnees
By John Sugden

I Tell You Now
Autobiographical Essays by Native
American Writers
Edited by Brian Swann and
Arnold Krupat

Postindian Conversations
By Gerald Vizenor and A. Robert Lee

Chainbreaker
The Revolutionary War Memoirs of
Governor Blacksnake
As told to Benjamin Williams
Edited by Thomas S. Abler

Standing in the Light
A Lakota Way of Seeing
By Severt Young Bear and R. D. Theisz

Sarah Winnemucca
By Sally Zanjani

CPSIA information can be obtained
at www.ICGtesting.com
Printed in the USA
LVOW03s1039281216
518962LV00016B/154/P